D1105906

THE NATIONAL SECURITY COURT SYSTEM

MR. Patrick Henneberry, JR. —

With gratitude and thanks for your service in the submarine fleet. You served us well and I am thankful for your support, service and sacrifice.

With all the best,

[signature]

GLENN SULMASY

THE NATIONAL SECURITY COURT SYSTEM

A Natural Evolution of Justice in an Age of Terror

OXFORD
UNIVERSITY PRESS

2009

OXFORD
UNIVERSITY PRESS

Oxford University Press, Inc., publishes works that further
Oxford University's objective of excellence
in research, scholarship, and education.

Oxford New York
Auckland Cape Town Dar es Salaam Hong Kong Karachi
Kuala Lumpur Madrid Melbourne Mexico City Nairobi
New Delhi Shanghai Taipei Toronto

With offices in
Argentina Austria Brazil Chile Czech Republic France Greece
Guatemala Hungary Italy Japan Poland Portugal Singapore
South Korea Switzerland Thailand Turkey Ukraine Vietnam

Published by Oxford University Press, Inc.
198 Madison Avenue, New York, New York 10016

www.oup.com

Oxford is a registered trademark of Oxford University Press

Library of Congress Cataloging-in-Publication Data
Sulmasy, Glenn M., 1966–
The national security court system : a natural evolution
of justice in an age of terror / Glenn Sulmasy.
p. cm.
Includes bibliographical references and index.
ISBN 978-0-19-537981-5
1. Criminal justice, Administration of—United States.
2. National security—Law and legislation—United States.
3. Military courts—United States.
4. Courts-martial and courts of inquiry—United States.
5. Terrorism—United States—Prevention.
6. Jurisdiction—United States.
I. Title.
KF9223.S85 2009
343.73'0143—dc22   2008050775

1 3 5 7 9 8 6 4 2

Printed in the United States of America
on acid-free paper

FOR THE SULMASY FAMILY

Contents

Introduction   1

ONE   Military Justice and the Original Intent
       of Military Commissions   14

TWO   Military Commissions in U.S. History   30

THREE The Second World War Military
       Commission—*Ex Parte Quirin* et al.   47

FOUR   The War on al Qaeda and the Military
       Order of November 13, 2001   67

FIVE   *Hamdan* and the Military Commissions
       Act of 2006   93

SIX   The Legal Landscape after *Boumediene*   127

SEVEN The National Security Court System   157

       Conclusion: The Way Ahead   194

       Notes   207

       Index   227

Preface

THROUGHOUT THE WRITING of this manuscript, military commissions have remained in the media and the controversy has continued. Despite the questionable legitimacy and lack of credibility associated with the military commissions in the global democratic community by 2008, the Bush administration continued to push the use of military commissions to adjudicate terrorist suspects throughout the writing of this text. No prosecutions had occurred other than the plea bargain of Australian citizen David Hicks through late September of 2008.

As my editors have continually reminded me, this project has truly been a moving target. And this target continues to move: as of November 2008, two cases have now been tried before military commissions, Barack Obama was elected president of the United States, his transition team is feverishly working on the details of closing Guantanamo Bay as a detention center, and the Bush administration was reportedly considering closure of the facility (or set the process in motion) before departing in January of 2009.

The two defendants who have been tried are Salim Hamdan, the personal aide of Osama bin Laden, and Ali Hamza al Bahlul, bin Laden's media chief (or as some would call, his chief propaganda aide). Ironically, the trial of Salim Hamdan became the first real "war trial" in the commissions' process. (Hamdan is the detainee who became famous for his success before the Supreme Court in 2006 in *Hamdan v. Rumsfeld* when the Supreme Court declared that military commissions originally ordered in November of 2001 were illegal.) Interestingly, although both cases concluded with little controversy, they both revealed the intricate problems with using war tribunals to try international terrorists. Both cases highlighted the inadequacy of the military tribunals.

The military commission for Hamdan, the first real war crimes tribunal since the Nazi tribunals in the immediate aftermath of the Second World War, resulted in a conviction handed down by a panel of six military officers on August 6, 2008. The commission convicted Hamdan of the charge of providing material support for terrorism, but in a clear setback to government prosecutors, acquitted him of the more serious conspiracy charge. The *New York Times* reported, "Supporters said the system's fairness was illustrated by the careful verdict, while critics said the trial, which featured secret evidence and closed proceedings, demonstrated the injustice of the Bush administration's military commission system." While the conviction was a victory for the government, such a victory was short in measure and still clearly lacked the credibility hoped for by many within the Bush administration. Interestingly, on the same day that Hamdan's conviction was issued, the presiding military judge, Captain Allred, U.S. Navy, ordered that the five years Hamdan had been detained at the Guantanamo Bay prison would be applied to any sentence ordered at the sentencing hearing.

The sentencing, a separate hearing as part of the bifurcated military justice process, was a clear blow to the prosecution team. Hamdan received only sixty-six months in jail—essentially only six months beyond the five years' credit awarded the previous day. This relatively light sentence could not possibly have been what the prosecutors were seeking, particularly in regard to the time, money, and resources expended on the case. Regardless of the resultant sentence, human rights groups such as Amnesty International immediately argued that the conviction itself was obtained under military commission procedures "that do not meet international fair standards [and this] compounds the injustice of his more than five years' unlawful detention in Guantanamo."

Ali Hamza al Bahlul, however, was not as fortunate. Al Bahlul was convicted of conspiracy, solicitation to commit murder, providing material support for terrorism, and other significant charges. Prosecutors argued that he had made a recruiting film, "The Destruction of the American Destroyer U.S.S. Cole," which depicted the vicious attack on the U.S. Navy ship at anchor on the Yemen coast. Still, although this was indisputably a victory for the government prosecution, the reputation of the commissions has so terribly eroded in the seven years since their inception that any conviction or sentence garnered little credibility. Al Bahlul's life sentence has done little to reenergize support for the process or reaffirm the legitimacy of the tribunals.

Thus, an "evolution of justice in an age of terror" is appropriate. Although policy makers within the United States have slowly altered the process over the past seven years, it seems as though the need for immediate change strengthens daily. Other military commissions are likely to be completed by the date of this book's publication (even after the end of President Obama's 120-day suspension of the use of military commissions). While some measure of victory may be declared by the Bush administration, the legitimacy of the process is so tainted at this point that the results of any "justice" achieved are minimal. Any future military commissions will most probably be viewed as nothing more than tactical victories. If the United States continues to embrace this system seen as flawed by the general public and the global community, the impact will be a strategic defeat for American influence and prestige.

Having returned from Washington, D.C., just two days after the historic election of Barack Obama as president, I am tremendously hopeful that he will, in a true bipartisan fashion, commit to the real change so many of his constituents within the United States are hoping for. A move toward a sea change in the national security law arena would be to close the Guantanamo Bay detention center and adopt the "third way" I discuss within this book—the creation of a national security court that will embrace human rights and support the rule of law.

Acknowledgments

THIS BOOK HAS been an exciting journey for me. In late 2001, I was strongly in favor of using military commissions. However, over the past few years I have come to realize that it is simply not the right legal system to employ in the War on al Qaeda. Military commissions, although used throughout U.S. history, were never intended to be a vehicle to create a preventive detention system. Rather, they have been used to try cases against alleged illegal belligerents. In the twenty-first century, and in a unique war such as this, the United States can not hope to engage the support of our allies or even the support of a coalition of U.S. citizens if we engage in the preventive detention of our enemies. We must create a system that is adjudicatory in nature. The National Security Court System offers just such a vehicle.

As I have progressed in my thinking on this topic through the past seven years, many people have helped me to better understand the realities of the legal issues associated with fighting international terrorism. This book is the culmination of an education gleaned from the intellectual energy and learned experience of numerous colleagues, friends, and family. They, like me, saw that the situation demands a "third way." We are doomed to ongoing dissension if we remain trapped in the policies of the past.

First, teaching at one of the nation's four military academies, the U.S. Coast Guard Academy, has provided me the chance to explore new ways of thinking through these issues. It has allowed me to work with the Corps of Cadets who, more often than not, educate me more than I teach them. Additionally, my colleagues have been superbly supportive of this effort. In particular, I would like to thank Dean Kurt J. Colella; Captain Anne Flammang, USCG; Professor Judith Youngman; Commander Jim Carlson, USCG; and the rest of the Department of Humanities for their input, support, and guidance. It has proven invaluable. It is an honor every day to be on the faculty with such dedicated public servants and academics.

I have attended numerous conferences that provided excellent platforms to exchange ideas and refine my proposals. My participation at them has been instrumental in the creation of this book. I would like to thank the New York City Bar Association, the American Civil Liberties Union, the American Bar Association, the Federalist Society, the U.S. Military Academy at West Point, and the International Law Association, among others. These organizations have all dedicated time, resources, and research support to exploring the issues associated with the military commissions at Guantanamo Bay.

During the past two years I have had the wonderful opportunity to research, study, and write while living on the opposite coasts of the United States—I spent one year at Berkeley Law School (Boalt Hall) and one year at the Harvard Kennedy School (HKS). Working with scholars at these superb institutions has prompted me to pursue new avenues and to think "outside the box." The faculty and staff at both universities afforded me opportunities I could never have anticipated. I am truly grateful to the University of California, Berkeley, and Harvard University for their support in my pursuit of this project.

At Berkeley Law, I had the occasion to study under such distinguished intellectuals as Professor Harry Scheiber, Professor David Caron, and Professor John Yoo. The diversity in scholarship and political thought at Boalt Hall was truly stimulating. My time in Berkeley was a unique chance for a New Englander to spend time on the "left coast" and to begin serious contemplation of divergent and emerging legal approaches to the current armed conflict. Berkeley Law School provided the opportunity to really explore the global perspective of this book's subject matter with fellow LL.M. students from around the world.

The time I spent at Harvard exceeded all of my expectations. My fellowship at the Carr Center for Human Rights Policy at HKS afforded me the chance to ensure that this book and the proposals contained herein were infused with a human rights perspective. The Carr Center's support of this project has been incredible. While I was at Harvard, I benefited greatly from the opportunity to teach classes at the school of government as well as the law school. I received valuable input from the faculty, staff, and students. I would particularly like to thank Professor Sarah Sewall for her support and guidance as this project moved forward. Others from the Carr Center who deserve my sincere and special thanks are Tyler Moselle, Professor Samantha Power, Jemma McPherson, and Lois Andreasen. Their talents in providing advice and guidance have been exceptional, and I am grateful to have had the opportunity to work alongside so many of the esteemed faculty and staff at Harvard University.

Obviously, there are many others who were of invaluable assistance in the creation of this book. They have helped to review, revise, and, most important, challenge me to think in a more complex manner about many of the issues addressed herein. In particular, my most sincere thanks go to my editor, David McBride, for his support and patience. I could never thank him enough for believing in me as well as this project. Other major influences and supporters have been Professor M.N.S. Sellers, Andy McCarthy, Professor Kate Stith, Professor Chris Borgen, Professor Harvey Rishikof, the Honorable Kevin O'Connor, General Charles Dunlap, USAF, David Rivkin, Commander John Dettleff, Professor Margaret Stock, Lee Casey, Dr. Lou Fisher, Dean Reuter, Timothy Griswold, Norman Paulhus, the Honorable Robert R. Simmons, Professor John Yoo, Richard Roncone, Todd Gaziano, Ben Wittes, John Marrella, Captain Rob Kutz, USCG (Ret.), Vincent Vitkowsky, Professor Jeremy Waldron, Professor Geoffrey Corn, and Gene Hamilton. Of note, I also wish to acknowledge a special debt to the late Keith Ryan and my distinguished colleagues at the Institute for International Humanitarian Law in San Remo, Italy. They, along with many others, provided valuable assistance in the formulation of my ideas concerning the National Security Court System and the resultant creation of this manuscript.

As with any project, there are those closest to you that help you in countless other ways. My family provided me with invaluable insights as to how such a new legal system might be perceived by the general public. I would like to thank my parents, Warren and Peggy Sulmasy, for always reminding me what a very special place America is. They were tireless in their efforts to instill in me the deep desire to "step into the arena." Their patriotism and love of freedom has impacted me beyond what they could ever imagine. I must also thank my brothers, Danny, Warren, and Pete, for their input, guidance, and support throughout this project. And, of course, a special thanks to my sisters, Cathy and Dawn, for their constant emotional support of all of my professional endeavors.

My sisters and brothers have always reminded me of what is truly important in life, my family.

Last, I would like to thank my wife Lori and my daughters, Shannon and Alexandra, for putting up with my time away from the family during the many early mornings and late nights spent working on this book. I often read, researched, wrote, and reviewed drafts and notes on the periphery of the family action. They were very patient with my frequently preoccupied participation in the events of their lives during the book's evolution. They have been a constant source of inspiration and comfort. My deepest appreciation goes to Lori and my girls for being there for me—no matter what. Lori has always been supportive of my writing and my pursuit of learning. I could truly never thank her enough for her patience with my often crazy schedules and spur-of-the-moment opportunities for educational adventures. I thank God for the blessing of being here with her to watch our two daughters grow up to be such fine young ladies with good hearts, strong ethics, and curious intellects. They remind me every day why a book such as this is important: in the final analysis, it is about the America of their future.

THE NATIONAL SECURITY COURT SYSTEM

Introduction

IT IS SOMETIMES easy to forget how very close the communist nation of Cuba is to the American homeland. Cuba sits in the Caribbean Sea, a scant hundred miles as the crow flies from Key West to the northern coast of Cuba. Approximately 500 miles from mainland Florida, there is a small U.S. military installation located on both sides of the mouth of Guantanamo Bay on the south eastern tip of Cuba. The forty-five-square-mile naval base was formally established by treaty following the Spanish-American War through an "Agreement between the United States and Cuba for the Lease of Lands for Coaling and Naval Stations." The agreement was formalized in February of 1903, under the auspices of Article VII of the Platt Amendment.[1] U.S. Naval Station Guantanamo Bay has remained a United States military installation despite the Cuban revolution in 1959 and the establishment of a communist government under Fidel Castro. It is the oldest U.S. base located in overseas territory; it was obtained after the end of the Spanish-American War. And the lease is perpetual; it may be broken only upon the agreement of both signatories or the abandonment of the base by the United States.

The base will clearly not be abandoned anytime soon. However, the Guantanamo Bay detention center is the center in a storm of controversy. The current public perception of Guantanamo Bay (often abbreviated to GTMO and colloquially referred to as "Gitmo") is particularly ironic. Once regarded as an "oasis of freedom" in the midst of tyranny, the U.S. Naval Station Guantanamo Bay was symbolic as a beacon of human rights and democracy shining through the ugly forces of state-imposed communism so prevalent in the latter half of the twentieth century. The military value of Guantanamo Bay as a forward-based station for regional security, which includes targeting drug trafficking and sea-based terrorist attacks and protecting migrants who attempt to make their way through the surrounding waters in unseaworthy vessels, has been proven time and again. Historically, this small piece of perpetually leased real estate has proven vitally important to the long-term security of the United States and the stability of the Caribbean region, particularly when viewed through the lens of the Soviet Missile Crisis and the massive Haitian refugee migration in 1991.

While President Fidel Castro restricted free trade, embraced the communist sociopolitical policies, and denied basic freedoms to his citizens, the U.S. Naval Station Guantanamo Bay stood for an intangible good—the strength of the rule of law against the backdrop of the dark humanistic failures of the Marxist-Leninist model. It became a vision of hope, human rights, and freedom. It represented the altruistic side of America, and by extension the capitalistic economic model used in democratic societies. Beyond its symbolic global perceptions, Guantanamo Bay also served as a reminder to those in the U.S. armed forces of a warrior ideal—a drive to serve something greater and nobler than the survival of the self. The desire to be guardians of basic human rights and defend the inherent dignity of each person is an ideal that drives countless young women and men to join the U.S. armed forces—they want to serve the greater good and protect this American vision of freedom and dignity. Once an oasis, the U.S. Naval Station Guantanamo Bay now inspires visions of fear, unlawful detention, lawlessness, and worst of all, torture in the twenty-first century.

It is often mistakenly assumed that the U.S. Naval Station Guantanamo Bay was created expressly in response to the attacks of September 11, 2001. Historically, the base at Guantanamo Bay was a training center for virtually all United States Coast Guard cutters and United States Navy vessels operating along the eastern coast of the United States. The ships and their crews received intensive warfare training in a grueling tropical environment. They were subsequently tested and graded on their expertise in navigation and ship handling and during various combat weapons exercises in anti-air, antisubmarine, and antisurface warfare. Crews were even readied for mass conflagrations (MASSCONFLAGS)—devastating warfare scenarios such as the launching of nuclear, chemical, and/or biological weapons—against U.S. vessels. This Gitmo of the Cold War and late twentieth-century era developed into a "center for training excellence" with wonderful opportunities for military personnel to relax after a hard day at sea. The tropical base had terrific recreational facilities for enlisted personnel, a beautiful officers' club overlooking the water, splendid beaches with some of the finest scuba diving in the world, a riding stable, and the chance to see classic American automobiles frozen in time. Local Cubans who worked on the base were retroactively permitted by Castro to continue their jobs after the Cuban Revolution before Castro closed access permanently to the Americans. Since everything on the base had to be shipped in, automobiles were at a premium and the locals worked hard to make them last. Gitmo often seemed an island frozen in time.

Unfortunately, the past seven years have remade the image of Guantanamo Bay by some into "the gulag" of our times.[2] The Fleet Training Group, the largest tenant command on the base, had relocated to Mayport, Florida, in 1995. The installation shrank in personnel size and fleet importance during the base realignment and closure (BRAC) evolutions of the 1990s. However, this all changed on the fateful day of September 11, 2001. It is tragic that the image now associated with Guantanamo has come from the worst extremes of enforced communist domination and subordination of the individual spirit. Many other nations, nongovernmental organizations, and even American citizens have come to view this naval base as a negative—such a contrast to the vision of the military installation that tangibly embodied American freedom to the Cubans. After the horrific attacks of 9/11 ushered in the realities of asymmetrical terrorist warfare in the twenty-first century, the U.S. Naval Station Guantanamo Bay, Cuba, was chosen by the Bush administration to detain those who were alleged members of the al Qaeda network or part of the Taliban regime. The model selected to adjudicate the detainees there was the established wartime justice system of military commissions. Detention of these alleged international terrorists and the presumptive goal of using military commissions to adjudicate their cases in sequestered camps on the base has, rightly or wrongly, destroyed the formerly positive American military image of Guantanamo Bay.

It is hard to assign blame but it is undeniably easy to acknowledge that the image of the United States has also been tarnished by the detention of alleged al Qaeda fighters on the base.[3] The Bush administration's decision to proceed with military commissions as the best means to adjudicate their crimes against the United States, although initially altruistic and arguably appropriate, has wreaked havoc with the United States' fight against international terror and has eroded American leadership in other areas throughout the world. It has impacted the ability of the United States to lead in areas such as trade, the environment, and, most important, the promotion of the rule of law and the spread of democracy. It has tarnished world opinion of the United States of America—both at home and abroad. Regrettably, other nation-states, nongovernmental organizations, and many American citizens have come to see Guantanamo Bay as a symbol of prejudice, lawlessness, arbitrary detention, and the type of coercive interrogation that has been described as torture. The ambiguity surrounding the status of the detainees, as compared to established global norms for dealing with traditional prisoners of war (POWs), has also led to widespread cynicism, both domestically and internationally, about the true mission of the facility. Questions have been constantly raised about whom we are detaining, whom we might detain in the future, and what kind of oblique justice will be applied to them. These concerns are indeed undermining the U.S. ability to lead the fight against international terrorism.

This book addresses an achievable and effective means to regain a positive world image of a just and judicious United States. It is possible to restore both American and international faith that a fair and effective system of United States justice can prevail in the "War on Terror." In many ways, the manner in which the United States detains, interrogates, and adjudicates the al Qaeda fighters is the seminal issue of this era. Many Americans long for their country once again to enjoy the status of a benevolent global superpower that we once were and that we strive to be in the future. It is critical that the United States government handle this problem quickly and efficiently. It has become clear that the military commissions, used throughout U.S. history since the Colonial era to prosecute war crimes, are not the appropriate venue for this unique armed conflict. The War on Terror is itself a hybrid—a mix of law enforcement and military warfare. The enemy we fight is also a hybrid—a blend of international criminal and insurgent warrior. Thus, this book proposes as a solution a hybrid court—a court created by taking the most appropriate aspects of our own Article III (of the U.S. Constitution) federal courts and military commissions to address the pressing needs of national and international security and balance the scales of justice.[4]

A special hybrid court system, now commonly referred to as a national security court, is the answer. It can be crafted as part of evolving

Foreign Intelligence Surveillance Act (FISA) legislation to address the requirements of preserving national security and intelligence sources with the preservation of fundamental human rights within an appropriate and civilian-controlled American justice system. While most policy makers in America today agree that Guantanamo Bay as a detention facility must close, there are currently no serious proposals on what to do once that occurs. This dearth of options, however, is reasonable when one contemplates that the United States has had to constantly adjust to a rapidly evolving terrorist threat and a type of warfare that is now being waged against traditional nation-states.

The current U.S. policy is trapped between two existing paradigms—the law enforcement approach and the law of war response. Some policy makers remain in a pre-9/11 mentality, arguing that the existing criminal law system is the right way to address international terrorism and the best means available to showcase the American way of justice. Others, although avid supporters dwindle daily, cling to the belief that military commissions, based on the model of those used in the Second World War, are the most appropriate vehicle. Neither paradigm is adequate to address this unique challenge. The reality is that neither is constructed to handle the intricacies of adjudicating both multinational and U.S. citizens.

It is crucial to remember that terrorist agents and volunteers are working for an international "organization" striving to commit acts of extreme anarchy while exploiting the democratic prosecution of justice and rule of law to preserve legal rights they themselves would unhesitatingly deny to citizens of the Western world if the roles were reversed. The inability of current legal systems to adapt to this stark paradigm stems not only from a lack of consensus but also fundamentally begs for a "third way" that upholds the rule of law, brings justice to the detainees on behalf of the victims of international terrorism, and prevents future terrorist attacks. A court system must be developed that affords due process and satisfies universally recognized human rights obligations while it still protects the security of the homeland and those personnel charged with executing security strategy, such as the military and the Central Intelligence Agency (CIA). To that end, I most strongly assert the need for the creation of a National Security Court System (NSCS).

In order to lay the foundation for creating a new court system to detain and adjudicate the al Qaeda fighters, this book begins with a look at the original intent of both the military justice system and military commissions. The Founding Fathers anticipated that the military, when war began, would function as an arm of the executive branch of government. The executive branch (since George Washington's presidency), Congress, and even the courts have agreed that once fighting commences, the decision making is best left to the commander in chief. The Founding Fathers, relying heavily on the ideas of the political theorists Blackstone and Montesquieu, wrote the *Federalist Papers* following this theory; the Constitution was ratified with this division of power in mind, and our courts have generally embraced the "military deference doctrine" throughout United States history.

I further examine the historical context by reviewing the actual use of military commissions throughout U.S. history—with particular emphasis on both the eighteenth and nineteenth centuries. Examples from the presidential periods of Andrew Jackson and Abraham Lincoln detail the need to have and use military commissions to detain, try, and adjudicate illegal belligerents during periods of armed conflict. Warfare of the twentieth century evolved rapidly with incredible advancements in armament and technology. There is also a discussion of the now famous case (or rather infamous case, depending upon your point of view) of *Ex Parte Quirin*.[5] This seminal case occurred during World War II. It is worth close examination for its insight into the challenges nations face in war and the resultant decision by President Franklin Roosevelt to use military commissions (even for United States citizens).

To provide a legal foundation for the National Security Court System, the book then explores the first decade of this century and the Bush administration's decision to use military commissions both in November of 2001 and as a result of the Military Commissions Act of 2006. It is crucial to understand the rationale of why the government chose to use military commissions for adjudicating war crimes in the current armed conflict with al Qaeda. My interviews with key players in the administration provide some insights into what policy makers were thinking and why military commissions were chosen as the appropriate venue to try al Qaeda detainees. I also examine the evolution of the public's perceptions of military justice and why using these legal procedures to try the "hybrid fighter" detainees has led to such divisions in public opinion. Provided is a snapshot of the United States' evolving standards of justice as this nation struggles with how best to subdue the threat to national security while grasping the intricacies of the "Muslim cultural warrior" psychology.

Legal mechanisms of the twentieth century have been rendered ineffective to handle these unique, unlawful belligerents. The established judicial systems are not able to address all the aspects of terrorist suspect adjudication, and none of them is supported by a domestic or international consensus. Not only is the trial aspect in controversy; the issues of preventative detention, appropriate punishment, post-sentencing imprisonment, and eventual release to the public remain unresolved items of contention. When reflected through the prism of national security evidentiary issues and habeas corpus protections, the complexity of the entire adjudication process is almost overwhelming. It is imperative that policy makers entertain a new approach that can reasonably accommodate these complexities and provide a fair and stable platform for justice. The trials and named defendants currently under debate are only the beginning; terrorists will continue to be captured in this long war. It is a war that many experts predict will dominate, at a minimum, the first two decades of the twenty-first century.

As of the summer of 2008, the president of the United States, Secretary of Defense Gates, Secretary of State Rice, five former secretaries of state, and both presumptive presidential party candidates called for the closing of the Guantanamo Bay detention facility. The Obama administration has now ordered the facility closed by January of 2010. But there remains great uncertainty about how to replace it. It is logical to assume that prior to closing the camps at Guantanamo Bay, the United States will establish a new system for detaining and adjudicating the captured fighters. It would have been optimum if such a system had been proactively created three or four years ago. Hindsight aside, all political branches of the United States must now cooperate quickly and effectively in outlining the future of Guantanamo Bay and the current detainees while simultaneously striving for the creation of an appropriate system of justice to regain a position of moral authority in world affairs.

The necessary proposal must develop and implement a process that upholds the rule of law, affords adequate due process, and satisfies fundamental human rights obligations—all the while protecting the security of the homeland and preserving the ability to wage effective war against terrorists. Certainly, this is no easy task. The two prevailing paradigms for how to proceed that existed over the past two decades—either using the law enforcement model to try al Qaeda fighters in Article III courts in the United States or using the law of war model to employ military commissions—are simply not working. In light of the U.S. Supreme Court's holding in the *Boumediene v. Bush*[6] decision regarding habeas corpus rights for the detainees, the situation now demands a specialized court, similar to bankruptcy or immigration court, which has a specially trained judiciary and distinct evidentiary requirements to appropriately handle the sensitive nature of such proceedings.

The National Security Court System offers such an opportunity for policy makers. A hybrid court that will validate executive branch wartime powers and policy through the cooperation of multiple federal agencies such as the Department of Justice, the Department of Defense, the CIA, the Federal Bureau of Investigation (FBI), and the Department of Homeland Security can ensure that justice is served as well as promote the traditional U.S. adherence to the rule of law. With the legislative oversight and support of Congress and the infusion of judicial branch resources and expertise, the policy, procedures, and funding necessary for the National Security Court System (NSCS) can become a reality.

A proposal for this new court system is explored in detail. The NSCS requires civilian oversight of the system by the Department of Justice instead of the Department of Defense. It offers specifics about myriad aspects of the National Security Court System process, composition of the court, evidentiary issue resolutions, and proposed duties and specialized backgrounds for the assigned judges. As a counterpoint, there is a discussion of reasons that the civilian U.S. criminal court system should not be considered for detention and adjudication of the current, or any future, cases. Although the need for a new court system has been called into question and there are those who would rather use existing "open and operating" U.S. federal courts, I most strongly disagree. I see this option as being as problematic as the commissions themselves have been—albeit for vastly different reasons.[7]

The success of any proposal that responds to this pressing need depends upon its appeal to a broad spectrum of interests, both domestic and international. My suggestions are designed to address concerns across the political spectrum. During the past four years, I have been quite fortunate to have had many opportunities to present variations on this National Security Court System proposal to diverse groups around the country in settings ranging from general public gatherings to scholarly legal and policy symposia. The input I have received from academics, human rights activists, military judge advocates, law students, and members of various advocacy and political groups has helped me to rework key ideas and incorporate various safeguards into the new system. Over the course of the past few years, I have modified many tenets of my proposal based on their learned input.

The National Security Court System proposal provides an apolitical response to the clearly flawed applications of the law enforcement model and the law of war model. In the course of many open presentations, I have become deeply troubled by the destructive nature of public discourse that has evolved surrounding this subject. As a nation of concerned citizens, we should be open to recognizing that the twentieth-century law enforcement approach, as was detailed in the report of the bipartisan 9/11 Commission,[8] manifestly failed. It was a contributing factor to the unprecedented success of devastating attacks on civilians in New York City and against the Pentagon.[9] We must be prepared to recognize that the post–9/11 response of employing the traditional tenets of the law of armed conflict has clearly failed to win public acceptance.

As public debate on this topic continues, it is imperative to recognize that proponents of both paradigms are indeed patriots. Advocates of international human rights on one side should not be labeled "soft on terror" nor should advocates who maintain the legitimacy of the military justice system be cast as "war criminals." Academics, lawyers, policy makers, and other concerned parties argue for what they earnestly believe to be the proper means to detain and adjudicate the detainees in the War on Terror. Supporters of the existing paradigms have been seeking the best solutions to painfully difficult problems through established models, thereby trying to make this situation fall in line with military and juridical precedent. Instead, in addressing the rapidly evolving conflict, these efforts have often raised more questions than they have provided decisive responses. By forcing the present situation to conform to historical norms, it often seems both sides are trying to jam a square peg in a round hole.

Some commentators have been critical of any suggestion for creating an NSCS by referring to specialized terror courts as nothing more than "star chambers." Interestingly, these attacks have come from both the political Left and the Right. Some argue there is no need to create something new. They would prefer to use the existing federal court system. I do find that view most unfortunate. It is the responsibility of all citizens within a republic to inject fresh ideas into the policy arena when the existing system is failing to control the situation. For lawyers and academics in particular, one could even propose that it is in fact a civic duty to do so. The very dearth of new proposals in the "marketplace of ideas" regarding this mass detention was the catalyst that promoted my interest in exploring new ways to approach the problem. Unless a new paradigm is adopted, the United States will continue to be divided (and will remain so in the foreseeable future) on the issue of the detainees. Despite such deep divisions, I am encouraged that many serious people have become increasingly supportive of exploring a new solution, and momentum is growing to find a compromise to this crisis.

National security experts, from all jurisprudential perspectives, have recently become enamored with the concept of creating a new national security court system. Specific proposals have been issued from representatives of all sides of the political spectrum: Professor Neal Katyal (who represented Salim Hamdan in *Hamdan v. Rumsfeld*), former Bush appointee Jack Goldsmith, Professor Harvey Rishikof of the National War College and former dean of Roger Williams School of Law, author Stuart Taylor, Israeli scholar and University of Utah Law School professor Amos Guiora, Brookings scholar Benjamin Wittes, conservative commentator and former federal prosecutor Andy McCarthy, and national security scholar, Professor Bobby Chesney of Wake Forest Law School. This broad appeal is certainly indicative of the possibilities that policy makers are ready to embrace the NSCS.[10] Although each of these supporters has proposed a security/terrorism court model, there is obvious diversity in each proposal and distinct guidelines for implementation.

Different from these other proposals, the National Security Court System will be adjudicatory in nature. The concepts of preventative detention are not suitable to the current hybrid war. If properly created, the NSCS will function to ensure that long-term detention is not necessary in the War on al Qaeda. Along that line of reasoning, there are two critical presumptions within this "third way" proposal. First, we are, in fact, a nation-state engaged in armed conflict against the international terrorist organization al Qaeda and its affiliated entities. Thus, there is a recognized need for limitations concerning who may be classified, in effect, as unlawful combatants. It recognizes the very real distinction between al Qaeda fighters and traditional guerrilla soldiers as specified in the Geneva Conventions. Second, my proposal assumes that the political branches of the United States government, namely, Congress and the executive branch, are the most appropriate branches to decide the means and methods in prosecuting this war.

It is of primary importance to remember that we are actively engaged in armed conflict against al Qaeda (and other loosely affiliated entities). As such, the National Security Court System is based on the premise that we are a nation at war. However, this war is a unique armed conflict and different from any other we have ever fought. The asymmetrical, amorphous, and evolving War on Terror has confused many observers. In dealing with such a complex paradigm of armed conflict against terrorists, the NSCS can not operate in a vacuum. The armed conflict we are engaged in is not, as has been argued over the last seven years, a general "war on terror" against all global terrorists. It has been refined into a new type of conflict against a new type of warrior. In concert with the creation of an NSCS, we must redefine the war itself and name it for what it has become—the War on al Qaeda. This small semantic change, if conducted on a grand scale and widely accepted, will help remove a great deal of cynicism, both domestically and internationally, about who we are detaining and will detain in the future.[11]

The critical second tenet is that the political branches are the appropriate branches to decide the means and methods of warfare, although I strongly believe, and assert within this book, that the executive is the best equipped (as the Founding Fathers intended) to respond to foreign threats and function as commander in chief during war or national emergency. In prosecuting the War on al Qaeda, the Congress (more so than in traditional wars) must exercise its necessary function of oversight. It must create legislation necessary to most effectively engage the enemy in this armed conflict. Intrusions by the judiciary over the past five years—often referred to as legislating from the bench—are undesirable, unnecessary, and unprecedented. The U.S. Supreme Court's rulings have not clarified the legal ambiguity but rather have contributed to a situation that is increasingly chaotic. These rulings have the potential for unprecedented ramifications on the operation of the entire American court system.

The judicial branch has now "muddied the waters" for an established and rather simple tenet: in times of armed conflict, the commander in chief has the inherent right and authority to establish a system best suited for detaining fighters captured in warfare. These intrusions upon precedent not only adversely impact a commander in chief's ability in this area but will likely open the door to legal challenges in other areas of the prosecution of warfare, namely, strategy and tactics. They will also create new constitutional protections for the detainees, including the application of the Fourth Amendment, the Fifth Amendment, and other constitutional provisions. This would, in effect, give the detainees the same rights of U.S. citizens; it certainly provides more rights than prisoners of war now receive under the Geneva Conventions in traditional armed conflict. This is not hyperbole. Unless there is appropriate political response, this is indeed where we are headed.

Unfortunately, since the executive and legislative branches remain deadlocked in the paradigms of the past, the U.S. Supreme Court has intervened in the *Rasul v. Bush*,[12] *Hamdi v. Rumsfeld*,[13] *Hamdan v. Rumsfeld*,[14] and most recently, *Boumediene v. Bush* in June of 2008.[15] The Republican-led Congress consistently deferred to Bush administration requests and never took charge of addressing eroding public support and vicious criticisms of the commissions. Even after the Democrats took control of the Congress in 2006, rhetorical invective coupled with legislative inaction has been the norm. Perhaps now, after *Boumediene*, the political branches will band together in solidarity against our terrorist foes and will finally function in a "proactive mode." The Democrat-led Congress can begin in the spring and summer of 2009 to lay foundations for an unprecedented, change-oriented policy toward the detainees and Guantanamo Bay itself. With the election of President Obama and large Democrat majorities elected in both the House and the Senate in the elections of 2008, the political branches now enjoy a historic opportunity to lay the groundwork for resolution of this most pressing problem in 2009.

I had hoped that such proactive measures and studies would have been conducted in the intervening years since 9/11. Instead, we have a sitting court of nine justices, learned legal scholars but also unelected and life-tenured judges, who are now deciding upon the *jus in bello*[16] of this conflict. Inaction by the political branches will potentially lead to additional military decisions being made by the Supreme Court—decisions that could be disastrous for our national security. True political courage will prod this debate forward toward real compromise and eventual resolution.

This book has been a labor of love. As my editors constantly reminded me, this timely topic is also a moving target. The *Boumediene* case, in particular, has catapulted this issue into the presidential election of 2008. President Obama has repeatedly, as both candidate and now as president, called for the closure of the Guantanamo Bay detention center. While many other articles have been written on the topic of the Guantanamo Bay detention center and the War on Terror, I am hopeful that this book will become a resource to all sides in this dialogue and it will help lay the framework to enable the next administration to create a new system of justice to meet the challenges of the twenty-first century. The devil is in the details, and I remain optimistic that this is not an end in and of itself but rather a catalyst for debate.

This complex issue was obviously not resolved during the waning days of the Bush administration. The executive branch has performed admirably and has reacted as well as can possibly be expected under the extreme conditions of this unprecedented armed conflict. However, there simply was not enough time, or political will, for the Bush administration (in conjunction with the sitting Congress) to advocate real change in Guantanamo Bay. They unfortunately were forced to leave this pressing issue for the new administration to develop solutions. Truly, it is up to the 111th Congress and the 44th president of the United States to effect real change in the adjudication of detainees in the War on al Qaeda. I remain sanguine, however, that the case will be made for the value of a National Security Court System.

The Guantanamo Bay detention center must close, and a new court system must be designed and implemented. The U.S. Naval Station Guantanamo Bay must shed its negative connotations and once again become a source of inspiration. It can resume its status as a beacon of freedom in the midst of tyranny to future generations of American military members. The treatment of alleged al Qaeda fighters is, and will continue to be, the issue that best defines what U.S. justice is all about. Rightly or wrongly, lawfully or illegally, the implementation of military commissions in the War on al Qaeda has been clearly unsuccessful as a matter of policy. Our ability to humanely detain and effectively prosecute those who wish to undermine the democratic ideals of the United States will inevitably become a defining issue for the next administration.

ONE

Military Justice and the Original Intent of Military Commissions

THE BUSH ADMINISTRATION's decision to use military commissions as the preferred means of adjudicating al Qaeda was not new for the United States government. Throughout our relatively short history, U.S. military commanders and presidents have relied upon this type of "special tribunal" as the best means to try crimes committed by unlawful belligerents during periods of armed conflict. In 2001, President Bush and his lawyers looked to this established practice as well as the relatively ambiguous statutory provisions provided within the Uniform Code of Military Justice (UCMJ), and determined this was the most flexible option to employ.

Historically, numerous military commissions were convened to prosecute unlawful belligerents, such as spies, saboteurs, and persons fighting out of uniform; they were used during George Washington's tenure, during the Civil War, and during the Second World War.[1] The most notable early case was Washington's use of the "military commissions" during the Revolution against Major Andre after the Benedict Arnold spy plot was uncovered. A review of the original understanding reveals that the Founders were intent on ensuring that foreign policy decisions (including military operations and thus, the military commissions) were left to the executive branch alone.[2] This was especially so in wartime, because the Founders intended the executive to retain the authority to quickly respond with speed and dispatch to national security threats both at home and abroad. This reliance was based upon their experiences under British rule, the Colonial era, the Revolution itself, and the British Articles of War, and their reliance, in creating the Constitution, on the great thinkers of their era, most notably Locke, Montesquieu, and Blackstone.

U.S. Military Jurisprudence and the Uniform Code of Military Justice (UCMJ)

As background to a discussion of the Founders' original understanding, it is important to distinguish between military trials for members of the U.S. armed forces today and "military commissions" currently employed for violations of the laws of war by illegal belligerents. Partially as a result of the publicity surrounding the military commissions in the U.S. Naval Station Guantanamo Bay (Gitmo), there are numerous commentators today discussing the merits and demerits of the military system.[3] It can be said there has never been as much interest in the Judge Advocate General's (JAG) Corps or the military justice system as there is today. Unfortunately, much of the information being disseminated is often incorrect.

The courts-martial system (as is well known throughout the West today) is the court process and procedure for the federal criminal system employed exclusively by the U.S. armed forces predominantly to adjudicate crimes committed by its own members. The system contains a decreased expectation of constitutional protections for those under its jurisdiction. Military justice became increasingly progressive throughout the twentieth century, most notably after the enactment of the Uniform Code of Military Justice (UCMJ) in 1950.[4] The military justice system is a federal criminal system distinct from the civilian federal court system. Its jurisdiction is over crimes committed by members of the armed forces (although it does have other limited jurisdiction over others), both for common law crimes and military specific crimes. The need for a unique system of justice for the armed forces has long been recognized in American jurisprudence and has been affirmed by all three branches of government since the founding of the Republic. It is generally understood that the unique structure and society of the armed forces necessitates its own form of justice. The best known military law expert of his day and referred to by the U.S. Supreme Court as the "Blackstone of military law," Colonel William Winthrop, wrote of military justice in 1896, "Military law, in its ordinary and most restricted sense, is the specific law governing the Army as a separate community," adding, "Military law proper is that branch of the public law which is enacted or ordained for the government exclusively of the military state and is operative equally in peace and in war." In teaching military law to undergraduates at the Coast Guard Academy and to law students, I have always emphasized the importance of recognizing military law as existing to serve a unique subset of society, the armed forces. The role of the military is to fight and win wars and thus it requires a separate system to adequately balance the needs of justice while still ensuring that the military is not hampered from achieving its unique objectives. Discipline, with often rapid results, is a vital component within the military justice system.

Beyond courts-martial (the trials of military members), there are also provisions for non-lawyers to administer justice under what is known as nonjudicial punishment. In the past, and to a more limited extent today, the military was uncomfortable with having "justice" or "lawyers" involved in matters that might impact the mission accomplishment. Until the twenty-first century, warriors and operational commanders were often suspicious of too much legal involvement and intrusion into the power of the commanders. As would be expected, many operational commanders did not want "nonwarriors" impacting discipline or reducing some of the awesome powers the commander inherently retains within the armed forces. Thus, the structure of military justice was, and remains, an instrument of the command.[5]

Originally, the military justice system was quite harsh and earned a reputation within the United States as a severe form of discipline— much more so than would be administered under the civilian federal criminal system. Caning, whippings, and other severe punishments were routinely administered throughout the first century of the Republic. During the American Revolution, the Continental forces were essentially governed by the 1774 British Articles of War.[6] The courts-martial or hearings then were without judges and completely command oriented in nature.

From the end of the Revolution until the early part of the First World War, the Congress adopted British Articles to be used as the system employed by the American forces. Some amendments and updates were made during the years 1913–1916, initiated by two major figures in the history of U.S. military law: General Enoch Crowder and General Samuel T. Ansell. In particular, it was Ansell's proposals and efforts at updating and implementing more process into the military justice system that eventually gained traction, and major reforms were implemented at the end of the First World War.

The 1920 Articles of War, strongly advocated by General Ansell, now included the same three types of courts-martial used today—summary, special, and general. The right to counsel was incorporated into the latter two "trials," and even double jeopardy was recognized.[7] Still, from this period until the eventual adoption of the Uniform Code in the mid-twentieth century, the Navy, Marine Corps, and Coast Guard all maintained different systems of justice, distinct from the Army code. They were in many regards similar to each other, but yet in many ways quite distinct. For example, even today, the Navy and Coast Guard retain an exception to the right to refuse nonjudicial punishment—otherwise provided for within the UCMJ for other members of the armed forces not "embarked" on a vessel. As a result of this sort of sweeping power within the Coast Guard and Navy, some refer to command of a U.S. Coast Guard cutter or U.S. naval warship as the "last great monarchy in the world." Although an overstatement, there is some truth in this notion of a "distrust" of lawyers by Navy and Coast Guard officers who are often skeptical of too much process within their commands. They perceive such notions as negatively impacting the military commander's otherwise complete and utter control of all aspects of his subordinates' work product as well as unit mission accomplishment. As Dr. William Generous noted during the 1970s,

> Like the Articles of War, the AGN [Articles for the Government of the Navy] were borrowed wholesale from the British....the Navy court-martial system was very much the same as the Army's. The power of the commanding officer to initiate charges, convene courts, appoint members, and officers and conduct a review of the proceedings was the same....Like the Army's, the Navy system included three different types of courts-martial. Each was identified by its power to punish and number of members....[T]he navy provided that the Judge Advocate General review the record of trial for legal errors and that the Bureau of Naval Personnel review it "for comment and recommendation as to disciplinary features." But this apparently thorough system did not guarantee due process to the accused....The Navy has never placed a high premium on lawyers in uniform, and the JAG review was most often done by non-lawyers.[8]

Interestingly, after every major war since the Civil War, the military justice system has become increasingly progressive and more in line with the ordinary punishments and process of the civilian justice system and federal courts. The catalyst for a major overhaul of military justice, however, was provided predominantly by General Ansell while he served as the judge advocate general of the Army. The twentieth century, in particular, witnessed dramatic changes in how the military justice system functioned. This is, in large part (similar to the post–Civil War improvements in military justice after many of those drafted returned home), due to the effects of the draft. Professor Fred Lederer notes this as beginning with the adoption of the 1920 Articles of War: "In amending the Articles of War in 1920, Congress created what appears to be legislative precedent; the experience of large numbers of citizen soldiers at war compels Congressional review of military criminal law and substantial legislative revision."[9] Ordinary lawyers, doctors, milkmen, printers, and many others were drafted into the military, and as such, were subject to the harsh realities of military justice of the day. Many of these draftees, upon returning to civilian life, in the United States demanded changes in how the military conducted its legal affairs. The draftees' concerns mostly revolved around the amount of due process afforded military members. Congress, as Lederer notes, reacted to these concerns of ordinary citizens.[10] They adjusted the military law codes after both World War I and World War II and began to transition the laws governing the armed forces from their draconian origins to a more rights-oriented, progressive military justice system.

Changes in military law were dramatic at the conclusion of the Second World War. The numbers of American citizens fighting in this war are astonishing—over 16,000,000 men served in the armed forces.[11] At the conclusion of the war in 1945, still cognizant of the need for a different system from the existing civilian systems, Congress worked hard to adopt a uniform, formal legislative code by which the armed forces all would now operate. Congress, in conjunction with the newly created Department of Defense (1947), responded to the widespread public displeasure with military justice and worked hard to put all the services processes, laws, and customs under one umbrella code. Additionally, they had to balance the need for progressive justice with the realities of the military structure and nearly absolute authority. As Professor Edmund Morgan, dean of the Harvard Law School and chair of the drafting committee for the new code, noted, "This meant a complete repudiation of a system of military justice conceived of as only an instrumentality of command; on the other hand, it [negative] a system to be administered as the criminal law is administered in a civilian criminal court."[12]

The Congress created a delicate balance of enhancing the due process afforded members of the armed services, but at the same time it ensured that the military was still able to meet its obligations of promoting the national security. They created court systems and even a civilian oversight court of appeals now known as the Court of Appeals of the Armed Forces (CAAF). Although other changes have occurred, such as the creation of military judges in the Military Justice Act of 1968,[13] the balance achieved and the resulting code have remained fairly intact since the code's creation in 1950.[14]

These substantial efforts resulted in the adoption of the Uniform Code of Military Justice in 1950. The Congress understood the need for this distinct subset of society to have its own system of justice. The mission of the armed forces, "to fight and win wars," was incorporated as much as possible in creating this new, formal code of justice. The code now provided specifics on all aspects of both common law crimes as well as uniquely military crimes. It balanced the needs of the military, the needs of the command, and the needs of creating a more justice-based system. Perhaps most significantly, it finally placed all of the five armed services under one, unified legal code.

Thus, common law crimes such as larceny, burglary, rape, drug possession and distribution, and assault and battery are all part of the UCMJ.[15] In addition, strictly military crimes are included and incorporated as part of the code, including laws such as orders violations, disrespect, misbehavior before a sentinel, adultery, fraternization, and other "military crimes."[16] As Professor Fred Lederer has asserted, the military is a unique subset of society and has a distinct mission requiring different rules and duties from ordinary citizens. Additionally, for minor offenses, there are "hearings" conducted by officers that afford limited process to the accused and exist to give commanders a tool to achieve rapid "battlefield justice." For such minor offenses, distinct from the ordinary civilian criminal process, the military justice system permits punishment of an accused without the benefit of counsel, rules of evidence, or a judge.[17] All of these additional provisions make the system unique from the ordinary criminal justice system within the United States. Although the rules and punishments have become progressively less severe since the founding of the Republic, the unique role the armed forces plays still demands a separate system. The entire U.S. military justice system is now embodied in the Manual for Courts-Martial (MCM). It provides for all aspects of rules and procedure for military law. It is worthwhile to first understand this system in greater detail in order to better explore the history and legality of military commissions. The MCM is divided into five parts: (I) The Preamble, (II) Rules for Courts Martial, (III) Military Rules of Evidence, (IV) The Punitive Articles, and (V) Non-Judicial Punishment.[18]

Preamble

The Preamble provides a basic overview of the system and establishes that the military justice system is, de jure, a separate federal criminal justice system operating within the United States. It lays out, in an introductory fashion, the organization and structure of the Manual for Courts-Martial. Perhaps its most important provision, often overlooked by critics of the military justice system (and the military commission specifically), is the Nature and Purpose of Military Law:

> Military law consists of statutes governing the military establishment and regulations issued thereunder, the Constitutional Powers of the President and regulations issued thereunder, and the inherent authority of military commanders. Military law includes jurisdiction exercised by courts-martial and the jurisdiction exercised by commander with respect to non-judicial punishment. The purpose of military law is to promote justice, to assist in maintaining good order and discipline in the armed forces, to promote efficiency and effectiveness in the military establishment, and thereby to strengthen the national security of the United States.[19]

As is the case throughout the MCM, the Preamble is silent on the issue of military commissions. As will become apparent, there is actually very little guidance provided on the rules and procedures of the military tribunals. It appears this was done purposefully to afford the military commander maximum flexibility for trying war criminals during a period of armed conflict.

Rules for Courts-Martial

When a convening authority makes the decision to go to "trial" (referred to in the military justice system as "courts-martial") she has several options: a summary court-martial, a special court-martial, and a general court-martial. All three are applicable depending on the crime committed, the maximum punishment of the alleged crimes, and the rank of the officer conducting the hearings (in special courts-martial [SPCMs] and general courts-martial [GCMs], these are military judges).

Generally, the summary court-martial (SCM) is for minor offenses and the maximum punishment is thirty days. These "hearings" or trials are presided over by a non-lawyer (generally) and there is no defense counsel or prosecution assigned to the "case." The SCM is overseen by one commissioned officer with very little of what is provided for in ordinary trial procedure, either military or civilian. In addition, SCMs are authorized only for enlisted members who are rated E-6 and below and members can only be sent to the brig (prison) for no more than thirty days. Officers can never be taken to an SCM. Essentially it is a "super" nonjudicial punishment. Although still deemed necessary by the military and the Congress, there are some in both military and academic circles who believe these procedures have outlived their usefulness in the twenty-first century and should be removed as an option.[20] Regardless, they remain intact as an option for commanders today.

Special courts-martial (SPCM) are authorized for misdemeanor offenses resulting in punishments not to exceed one year in prison. Only enlisted members can be tried for offenses under the SPCMs. These courts-martial have a military judge presiding and can have three to five members (jury) to hear the case. The accused can choose between having the case decided by a military judge or by the members.

General courts-martial (GCM) are for the most severe offenses and punishments can range from over one year in prison all the way to so-called capital cases resulting in the death penalty. Offenses that are referred to a GCM require an Article 32 hearing before proceeding to trial, and the accused can choose between having a judge alone hear the case or having it heard by members (five or more). An Article 32 hearing is the rough equivalent of the grand jury used for civilian trials. GCMs are used for felonies. This is clearly the court where the most severe punishments are available, and thus, it affords the most process for any accused subject to a court-martial.

Military Rules of Evidence

The Military Rules of Evidence (MRE) are roughly the same as the Federal Rules of Evidence (FRE). They include the hearsay rules and its exceptions, and the beyond-a-reasonable-doubt standard of proof to convict for all levels of courts-martial. They are actually modeled on the Federal Rules of Evidence (FRE) and ensure that adequate rights and process are accorded to the accused.

The Punitive Articles

These are the articles within the UCMJ that are the "crimes" under which one subject to the UCMJ is charged. Each crime is listed with a description of the offense, an example, the elements required, and a sample specification. These so-called punitive articles (Articles 77–134) include all manner of offenses. They include the common law crimes as well as uniquely military crimes such as conduct unbecoming an officer, fraternization, and consensual sodomy.

Nonjudicial Punishment (NJP)

This section describes in detail the requirements as well as the procedures (even including a script for the commanding officer to use) for the NJP. These are not trials but rather nonadversarial administrative hearings. There are no lawyers or judges and no requirement of legal training whatsoever for one to conduct these hearings. These are instruments of the command made available to provide the authority for military officers to administer rapid justice for minor offenses. NJP has different "nicknames" within the different services: "NJP" or "Article 15" for the Army and Air Force, "Captain's Mast" for the Coast Guard and Navy, and "office hours" for the Marine Corps. There are maximum punishments permitted to be administered and exact charts are provided in this section of the MCM to ensure that individual members receive appropriate notice of the charges alleged, knowledge of the procedures that will be employed, and guidance for those actually conducting these uniquely military hearings. The rules of evidence are not applicable, and substantive due process and procedural due process are both extremely limited. There is, however, a right to appeal the punishment received within five days of the hearing. This procedure, along with the summary court-martial, remains a great concern to many lawyers and law students who previously have had little exposure to military life. They are shocked at the lack of process and the quasi-judicial procedures that take place within the armed forces. Most civilians are not aware of these avenues to "prosecute" accused criminals within the armed forces.

The MCM is a comprehensive guide for all members of the armed forces that lists and discusses the myriad crimes and procedures within the American military justice system. In essence, it covers in detail all aspects of the existing military justice system. Congress creates, adapts, amends, and updates the MCM from time to time, with the latest version being updated in 2008. It demonstrates how the military justice system has evolved since the early days of the Republic. It is the product of past practice; the Articles of War provided by General Crowder in the First World War; the codification that took place in 1950 with the first formal, standing documents to govern and regulate the armed forces; and now in its current form as "the code" providing justice and discipline to all uniformed members.

Within this code of military law, as well as within the customary practice of military jurisprudence, there is a court available to a commander that is outside of the established courts-martial process; it is commonly referred to as the military tribunal or military commission. It is distinct in that it does not apply the standard rules, regulations, or process that a court-martial would employ. In fact, although noted in several provisions, there is really quite little offered for guidance or mandated procedure within the Manual for Courts-Martial on the topic. Some scholars suggest, as I do, that this is because it has been long understood within the customary law of war that the use of these procedures for adjudicating crimes committed by unlawful belligerents (or during other emergency situations such as when occupying another country or territory or during periods of martial law) needed to be flexible so they could be administered as the executive branch deems appropriate.[21] The UCMJ provides two key, albeit vague, references for military commissions, Article 21 and Article 36.

Article 21 states:

The provisions in this chapter conferring jurisdiction upon courts-martial do not deprive military commissions, provost courts or other military tribunals of concurrent jurisdiction, with respect to offenders or offenses that by statute or by the law of war may be tried by military commissions, provost courts, or other military tribunals.[22]

Article 36 notes:

(a) Pretrial, trial, and post-trial procedures, including modes of proof, for cases arising under this chapter triable in courts-martial, military commissions, and other military tribunals, and procedures for courts of inquiry, may be prescribed by the President by regulations which shall, so far as he considers practicable, apply the principles of law and the rules of evidence generally recognized in the trial of criminal cases in the United States District Courts, but which may not be contrary to or inconsistent with this Chapter.[23]

Thus, the UCMJ recognizes that the commissions require some statutory authority but otherwise treats these different tribunals as independent from the standard courts-martial. They are more a creature of command or a "tool" of the executive branch. This ambiguity, perhaps, has been at the heart of many of the concerns raised by critics discussed in later chapters.

Most notably, these tribunals (or commissions) today are used to try those who violate the laws of war. Throughout the history of warfare, military commanders have sought some means to rapidly adjudicate crimes committed by illegal belligerents.[24] The term "military commission" itself has had many different names throughout history as well as during the late eighteenth century.[25] Military commissions can be used for (1) crimes committed during occupations, (2) during periods of martial law, and (3) for trying illegal belligerents during times of armed conflict.[26] The military commissions created by the Order of November 13, 2001, as well as the Military Commission Act of 2006, deal with the third type exclusively. Unfortunately, many commentators continue to confuse military courts-martial with military commission and tribunals. Commissions, as currently employed and discussed throughout this book, are an outgrowth of military trials and justice—specifically employed by the executive to be used against those accused of committing war crimes during times of war.

The Original Understanding

The Founders' understanding of military justice was drawn almost exclusively from the British models. General George Washington, as commander in chief of the U.S. armed forces during the Revolution was strongly influenced by his tenure as an officer while employed by the Crown of England. While it remains factually elusive to determine when the first military commission was held, it appears that the first occurred during the Reformation in the early seventeenth century.[27] It was conducted by a field commander to adjudicate "war" crimes committed by an unlawful belligerent.[28] The King of Sweden during the Thirty Years' War, Gustavus Adolphus, also instituted a panel of officers to hear law of war violations and to make recommendations on their proper adjudication.[29]

The British eventually adopted a model similar to that used by King Adolphus. Their model evolved over time as a compromise between the Parliament and the Crown. Initially, the monarch unilaterally promulgated the Articles of War, which governed the conduct of servicemen and formalized military justice procedures. The king was viewed as the primary authority governing the regulation of armed forces discipline at home and abroad.[30] Despite these ancient origins, during the reign of William and Mary, a Scottish regiment refused orders and a crisis evolved—the Crown was not specifically empowered to empanel military trials within England and civil courts could not punish "mutiny." Thus, Parliament created what were known as the Mutiny Acts in 1689. Initially they declared:

> Noe man may be forejudged of Life or Limbe, or subjected to any Kinde of punishment by Martiall Law, or in any other manner than by the judgement of his Peeres, and according the knowne and Established law of this Realme. Yet, nevertheless, it being requisite for retaineing such Forces as are or shall be raised during this exigence of Affairs in the Duty an exact Discipline be observed. And that Soldiers who shal Mutiny or Stirr up Sedition, or shall desert their Majestyes Service be brought to am ore exemplary and speedy Punishment than the usuall forms of Law will allow.[31]

This was the first of many acts detailing the procedures and jurisdiction for prosecution of military members engaging in what would now be understood to be violations of the laws of war. The early act, and the ones that most impressed General Washington and the Founders, made clear the authority of the Crown in promulgating rules governing the army—particularly when the troops were serving abroad.

As an aide to General Craddock in the French and Indian Wars, then Major Washington utilized the authority granted him by the Mutiny Acts then in place. During this time, the Crown was authorized to promulgate the laws of war abroad. For war crimes committed within the domestic province of the kingdom, however, the Parliament retained requisite legal authority. Such understanding of the roles of the Parliament and the Crown was still in force at the time the colonies gained their independence. Reviewing this history and his actions taken during the period, it can be said that Washington clearly understood that his authority (while conducting military operations) was executive in nature and that actions taken against officers and enlisted were his decision alone.[32] There are numerous examples of Washington, during this prerevolutionary period, conducting courts-martial and exercising his "executive power." He did however, as some scholars have pointed out, on numerous occasions seek guidance for the proper use of his authority from the House of Burgesses.[33] This advice from the legislature, however, was sought for the proper trial of his subordinate troops (like the system we now use today, as the UCMJ is statutory in nature) and not necessarily for illegal combatants who normally were treated simply as spies and executed.[34] Some confuse Washington's desire for legislative advice on trials of his own troops as historical indicators of the need for legislatures' input on the current military commissions. However, it appears that these scholars equate what was understood as the necessary means for administering justice to subordinate soldiers with what was understood to be the proper means of adjudicating war crimes by illegal belligerents.[35]In reality, they serve two completely different purposes.

During the Revolution itself, the American army (as part of its understood military justice authority and the common laws of war) implemented the use of military commissions against those who violated the laws of war. This often was the preferred method of adjudication for captured British spies. The most famous (and first within the United States), and the first by the United States, was against Major John Andre.[36] He was put before a board of officers and was recommended to be hanged by General Washington. It is important to note the lack of process and General Washington's understanding that he had authority to conduct such a "trial" without any input from the Continental Congress. He relied almost completely upon the laws and custom of war. As noted earlier, Washington, as commander in chief of the Continental Army, functioned as an extension of the executive as a commander in the field and thus retained the requisite authority to conduct such proceedings.

Washington also continued to follow the models established by the British (as both commander of the armed forces and the first president)—including their constitution. The British model, without question, later guided the Founders in their creation of the U.S. Constitution—particularly as it related to military affairs and war making. It established formal roles for both the Parliament and the monarch. Basically, the English system gave the executive leadership the role of initiating and conducting warfare (as well as treaty making) while the Parliament functioned as primarily funding the military campaigns.[37] In order to better understand the eighteenth-century legal authority to conduct military commissions, it is also helpful to look at the Founders' intellectual influences on executive power during this period.

The factual experiences of Washington's conduct as well as the influence of the British Constitution reveal a glimpse into the Founders' intentions regarding the executive power and foreign affairs (including matters such as military commissions for trying unlawful belligerents) during the time leading up to the post-Revolutionary period and the Constitutional Convention. The Founders, however, not only relied upon their British military experiences and government but also were greatly influenced by Western philosophers—specifically Locke, Montesquieu, and Blackstone.

The failures of the Articles of Confederation were, with little doubt, a major catalyst for the Constitutional Convention. As is well known today, one of the Articles' greatest weaknesses was that they lacked a strong executive. This became particularly evident in the arena of foreign affairs—military affairs in particular. Nowhere was the weakness in the Articles more apparent than in the area of executive power. Critics today, such as Louis Fisher and Harold Koh,[38] argue for the need of the legislature to be paramount, even in foreign affairs. They claim support for their arguments is found in the new nation's rejection of the British monarchy as well as the colonists' strong belief and heavy reliance upon legislative supremacy as the best means of securing liberty.[39] Fisher asserts these notions of intended legislative supremacy as support for the reason that military commissions, as constructed prior to the *Hamdan* case, were unconstitutional.[40] It seems here that such reliance is misplaced. The Congress, during the Revolutionary period and the Articles period, in essence functioned as the executive branch. According to Jack Rakove, a leading scholar on the founding of the American Republic, Americans actually referred to the Continental Congress as "The Supreme Executive," or the "Supreme Executive Council."[41] He added, "The idea that Congress was essentially an executive body persisted because its principal functions, war and diplomacy, were traditionally associated with the [C]rown, 'whose executive, political prerogatives, bear a very striking resemblance to the powers of Congress.'"[42] In reality, there was no executive but the commander of the militia fighting the British, General Washington. Thus, to overemphasize the legislature's importance in the area of warfare and military justice seems unnecessary. It is this very weakness of the legislature, in both peace and during the Revolution, in fulfilling these executive functions that was a primary reason for the early American statesmen to gather in both Annapolis and Philadelphia.[43] Among other reasons, they clearly recognized the need for some form of executive to be established in order to best provide for the new nation's national security.

In addition, the Founders looked to the federative power discussed by Locke in his Second Treatise of Government. Locke viewed this power, distinct from executive and legislative powers, as necessary to govern "the power of war and peace, leagues and alliances, and all the transactions with all persons and communities without the commonwealth." Although distinct in a strict sense, he viewed the federative and executive powers as vested together.[44] He said the federative power was focused on the "management of the security and interest of the public without, with all those that it may receive benefit or damage from."[45] He predicted ruin if the federative power were taken away from the executive. He opined that foreign affairs "are much less capable to be directed by antecedent, standing positive laws because what is to be done in reference to foreigners must be left in great part to those who have this power committed to them."[46] Thus, Locke would have been compelled to believe that matters of general foreign affairs should be conducted by the executive, most importantly in times of crisis or war. The military commissions then, as a part of ongoing military operations, would therefore be vested in the executive under the Article II powers. As Alexander Hamilton was to later say in Federalist 74, "The direction of war implies the direction of the common strength, and the power of directing and employing the common strength forms a usual and essential part in the definition of the executive authority."[47] Locke believed such matters could not be governed by the many (through the legislature) but were intended for the executive who could act with discretion, flexibility, and quickness.[48]

Contrary to conventional wisdom today, Locke, although an important influence on the Founders, was not the most influential philosopher in mid-eighteenth-century America. Montesquieu and Blackstone were actually the most widely read and cited by both Federalists and Anti-Federalists during the founding.[49] James Madison declared that Blackstone's commentaries were "a book which is in every man's hand" and that Montesquieu was "the oracle who is always cited and consulted on the separation of powers." Like Locke, they viewed foreign affairs and the conduct of warfare to be best conducted by the executive while matters of domestic concern were better conducted by the legislative branch.[50] Montesquieu observed that "the executive makes peace or war, sends or receives embassies, establishes the public security, and provides against invasions."[51] Once again, he felt military affairs and operations should be exclusively controlled by the executive branch. He wrote, "Once an army is established, it ought not to depend immediately on the legislative, but on the executive power; and this from the very nature of the thing; its business consisting more in action than deliberation." Blackstone had similarly observed, "The

King has the sole prerogative in making war and peace....it would indeed be extremely improper that any number of subjects should have the power of binding the supreme magistrate and putting him against his will in a state of war."[52]

The Founders were clearly impacted by these theories on foreign affairs and military matters by Montesquieu, Blackstone, and Locke. Their consistent and intellectually sound notion that the military affairs are more appropriately placed with the executive clearly had a profound impact on the subsequent creation of the executive powers being vested in the president. This, coupled with the experience of the British as well as George Washington's own experience, reveal the Founders' intent to vest the power of conducting war essentially in the executive.

Military affairs in general, and thereby military justice and military commissions, were intended by the Founders to be creatures of command. This is consistent with the thinking most influential on the Founders, Montesquieu and Blackstone, as well as the Colonial military's experiences during the French and Indian War and the American Revolution. The concept of military commissions was introduced as a means of rapid adjudication of those "warriors" who violate the laws of war. Since the time of Adolphus, the clear intention of retaining these tribunals has been to have swift and severe punishment for illegal belligerents, which fosters a high level of deterrence among other warriors or sovereigns inclined to engage in similar activity. The clear understanding of our Founding Fathers, and thus the original intent, was for such battlefield prosecutions to be conducted as a tool of the command, or by the executive when acting in his or her capacity as commander in chief. Military commissions were viewed in this manner throughout American history by presidents as varied in background and political philosophy as Washington, Jackson, Lincoln, and Roosevelt.

❧❦❧

TWO

Military Commissions
in U.S. History

Beyond the unique Colonial experience and the Founders' intentions, military commissions have been used by American presidents numerous times over the past 200 years. Field commanders
or presidents in the War of 1812, the Mexican-American War, the Civil
War, and the Second World War all used these procedures to try illegal
belligerents for war crimes or crimes committed during periods of martial
law. Although there are many examples available, the most celebrated and
well-known military commissions employed during the nineteenth century were used by General Andrew Jackson, General Winfield Scott, and
President Abraham Lincoln. All seemed to have acted upon the lack of
specificity afforded by the existing statutes (articles of war) and the laws of
war as well as past historical use to support their implementation of these
military trials during ongoing armed conflict. These commissions, in various forms, were generally supported by the judicial branch and understood
by most, if not all, to be a part of the American military jurisprudence.

Andrew Jackson

During the War of 1812, General Andrew Jackson used military tribunals incident to his authority as a military commander. His use of

commissions, however, was predicated upon his declaration of martial law upon the city of New Orleans.[1] His exercise of power in ordering commissions is distinct and different from the way commissions were employed in both the twentieth and twenty-first centuries. But these early types of commissions offer a glimpse into the perspectives on executive power, the flexibility of the military tribunal during wartime, and the appeal of continuing their use to confront the prosecution of agents who threatened U.S. national security during the period of the Bush administration. Both American and British citizens had expected General Jackson to rescind his declaration of martial law after the United States' decisive military victory during the Battle of New Orleans. Jackson, however, had a different perspective. Aware that a state of armed conflict still existed between Great Britain and the United States despite cessation of actively engaged combat, Jackson kept the martial law order in place until after the negotiations for a "legal" truce were completed and signed.

During this interim period between the cessation of active combat and the signing of the Treaty of Ghent, a noteworthy case emerged concerning the use of military commissions. The following sets the stage for this situation (striking in its details for its parallels to ongoing events): a newspaper article surfaced criticizing the application of military law and the employment of military commissions for adjudicating crimes committed. The article demanded that Jackson close the tribunals down and use civilian courts instead. It further asserted that the use of tribunals and most of Jackson's recent and ongoing policies were "no longer compatible with our dignity and our oath of making the Constitution respected."[2] As was the accepted practice of the period (and obviously not permitted today, except on the blogs, the Internet, and newspaper lead editorials), the article was penned anonymously. Interestingly, by either ingenuity or unnamed sources, Jackson was able to determine the drafter of the piece as a Mr. Louis Louallier. He immediately had Louallier (an American citizen) arrested for "inciting mutiny and disaffection in the Army."[3] While imprisoned, the author sought a writ of habeas corpus. It was granted by a Judge Hall. Jackson directed his officers to arrest and confine any person seeking to serve the writ on Louallier. In defiance, Judge Hall issued the writ and ordered Louallier immediately released. General Jackson quickly responded to the judge's decision and proceeded to have Judge Hall arrested as well. The judge was charged with "aiding, abetting, and exciting mutiny." General Jackson took these steps unilaterally and deemed them necessary under the current order of martial law. His actions were born out of caution and his mistrust of the British to actually sign the truce.[4] These steps, shocking to most observers today, were viewed as quite harsh by many of Jackson's contemporaries as well. The citizens of New Orleans believed the civilian courts were open and operating and available. They thought that once the fighting had ended, the need for military tribunals should have ceased. Most commentators today would likely agree with this legal and political analysis. It can be interpreted that Jackson's use of military commissions at this point and his continued enforcement of martial law were at best overreactions to perceived threats. Although negotiations for peace were under way, he had not received any authority from the executive branch or the Congress for repealing the order of martial law.

It is interesting to note that then (and likewise now, as some would argue) the legislature did not act to curtail his power and authority. Regardless of General Jackson's arguably legitimate safety concerns as a military officer, it should be obvious to even the most casual observer that this situation concerned (1) a U.S. citizen, (2) the exercise by a U.S. citizen of his First Amendment right to free speech, and (3) an incident location within the continental United States. Louallier's article was a missive condemning the practices of the U.S. government after fighting had ceased. No military crime was committed that necessitated a military tribunal, and negotiations were well under way for a formal peace treaty.

Regardless, the very concept of imprisoning a U.S. citizen for speaking his mind and then placing a sitting judge under arrest for merely fulfilling his duty as a member of the judiciary shocks the conscience. In order to be fair, it should be noted that the military commissions Jackson employed were a legal remedy during the imposition of martial law. However, these particular commissions must necessarily be distinguished from the tribunals established later during the Second World War as well as the controversial tribunals of the twenty-first century. Also, some could argue in Jackson's defense that he technically had every right to maintain the martial law until the hostilities had formally ended. The job of a military officer, particularly one of flag rank (general or admiral), is to lead the cause of national security. This is even truer during periods of armed conflict. Although we all can second guess his decisions then (and to most, if not all, they seem indefensible), it seems that Jackson would attempt to justify his actions by stating he was just doing his duty as a general in a time of war.

Of note, when tried before the military tribunal, Louallier was acquitted since the tribunal determined he was not a member of an armed force in any capacity and the charge of being a spy was baseless. He had simply written his opinion in a newspaper. The military commission decided there was no other evidence that he was working for the British or any indication whatsoever that he was sympathetic to the British war effort. Thus, justice was seemingly obtained by adjudicating this case before a military commission. It was a fair "trial" regardless of the forum. Disregarding the verdict, however, Jackson ordered Louallier be "detained" in jail until formal peace was declared. He declared that a state of armed conflict still existed and British troops were still encamped within New Orleans and throughout the South. The judge, however, was released but still "asked" to remain outside of the city until after peace was official.

Once Jackson received official word of the peace, he did indeed lift martial law, released the writer, and permitted Judge Hall to reenter the city. This all had occurred—the article, arrest, trial, detention, and release—in just three short weeks since the original arrest of Louallier.[5] General Jackson, as is well known by historians and the general public today, was hailed a hero for his efforts in the war. But his actions—still employing tribunals and against U.S. citizens even after the war had concluded—are certainly not written about in children's history books and almost never referred to by commentators.

Upon his return to the city and taking his seat back on the bench, Judge Hall fined Jackson $1,000 for contempt. Jackson quickly paid the fine. His popularity, however, remained quite high throughout this episode, predominantly as result of his heroics in combat. Public sentiment favored the actions of Jackson, even when many believed them to be illegal.[6] This case is yet another illustration of the precious "tug and pull" when the government attempts to balance national security and civil liberties during periods of armed conflict. Subsequently, Congress deliberated over whether to sanction Jackson for his actions regarding Hall and Louallier. The Congress understood the need and use of the military commissions he had employed throughout the War of 1812 and did not dispute their use during the war. The legislature instead focused on the specifics of this case of a military commander unilaterally deciding to jail a U.S. citizen and a judge who were otherwise engaging in lawful conduct and in accord with the U.S. Constitution. Perhaps in large measure because of the difficult political realities of condemning a hero in the war with the British, congressional votes never sanctioned Jackson for his actions against Louallier and Judge Hall. In fact, amazingly, the Congress actually later reimbursed Jackson the $1,000 he had been fined.[7] Additionally, as is well known, he was later elected the seventh president of the United States. His actions, although thought to be and actually deemed illegal, were viewed by most as simply part of the "fog of war." I doubt such a forgiving analysis would be politically palatable in today's media-dominated culture. Such actions, regardless of the popularity of a particular person, should never be construed as acceptable.

Seminole War of 1818

The military commissions of two British citizens, Alexander Arbuthnot and Robert Christy Ambrister, are other noteworthy examples of the use of military commissions in times of armed conflict. These cases, distinct from those employed during the War of 1812, were military commissions (similar to today's use of the tribunals) used to detain noncitizens and adjudicate crimes committed by them. However they were, once again, utilized as a function of the executive branch without express or implied authorization from the U.S. Congress.

Arbuthnot and Ambrister were working on behalf of the British government in the Indian-controlled regions. They were charged with aiding and inciting the Creek Indians into war against the United States. Arbuthnot was also charged as a spy, and specifically for supporting the Indians to murder two U.S. citizens. Because they were British subjects then, Arbuthnot and Ambrister were essentially unlawful belligerents in a zone of combat during an ongoing armed conflict with the Indians.[8]

Arbuthnot pleaded not guilty to all charges. Ambrister, however, pled not guilty to aiding and abetting but guilty that he led and commanded the lower Creeks in carrying out war with the United States.[9] The military tribunal found Arbuthnot guilty and sentenced him to hang. Ambrister was also found guilty but he was sentenced to be shot. This difference in the sentences ordered is significant. During this period in U.S. history, a "gentleman" would not be hanged.[10] Presumably, since Ambrister admitted to acting in a "warrior" capacity and that he had pled guilty to at least one charge, the military tribunal found him to be more honorable than his cohort. Regardless of the sentence awarded, Ambrister still requested review of his death sentence. The tribunal, upon reconsideration, reduced the death penalty sentence to fifty lashings and hard labor for twelve months. As the "convening authority" for the tribunals, Jackson reviewed their sentences. He disagreed with the tribunal and ordered Ambrister shot. The order was carried out and thus, both men were put to death—Ambrister shot and Arbruthot hanged. Again, the executive (President Monroe) as well as the Congress were initially silent in their response to Jackson's outrageous actions and he remained in command.

Later, a congressional committee did take up the case and reviewed Jackson's actions. The Committee on Military Affairs, by a majority, found Jackson's use of a tribunal to try the cases as well as the executions improper. Once out of committee and put before the full House and Senate, however, the desire of the committee to punish Jackson never received sufficient support for action, and once again, by large majorities in both houses, the actions of General Jackson were undisturbed by the Congress.[11] His use of military commissions, even his unilateral actions to change the finding of the military commission, thus remained valid since the Congress as well as the executive branch did nothing formally (outside of minor committees) to even verbally condemn his actions.

The Mexican War

In this conflict, American generals, as members of the executive branch, sought a legal procedure to carry out justice during a period of armed conflict. Once again, they looked to the "vague" military commissions as the best means available to ensure justice without impacting ongoing military operations. The authority to use these lay almost solely in the customs inherited from the British army. General Winfield Scott sought to employ the military commissions more out of a concern for the lawlessness in an area where no courts were operating. Instead of using the existing Articles of War (permitting courts-martial hearings), he desired a system for both his troops (U.S. citizens) as well as the Mexicans who might commit common law crimes or function as illegal belligerents. Here, different from previous episodes, General Scott did seek authority from the Congress as well as the president for his actions before implementing the legal procedures and trials. Perhaps sensitive to the issues associated with Jackson, he was particularly concerned about acts committed that were not covered by the Articles of War and outside of his understood jurisdictional boundaries.[12] In fact, before even leaving Washington, D.C., for his assignment to command, he wrote Congress seeking legislation to approve his use of military tribunals. Although this authority was tacitly authorized by the president (presumably by virtue of his role in command), Scott never did receive any legislative response, let alone authority or even specific guidance from either of the political branches about employing military commissions. The Congress and the White House remained silent and thus it fell upon the operational military commander in the field to do as he deemed most appropriate and lawful in setting up the tribunals. Without any oral or written authority, he issued General Order No. 20 declaring martial law in Tapico. He had decided military tribunals would be the appropriate venue to try crimes committed by both U.S. citizens and Mexican citizens accused of violating the law.[13] His motivation, different from others in the past, was to ensure order and proper behavior by his own troops. He was actually less concerned about the enemy or Mexican citizens. Thus, Scott, as distinct from Generals Washington or Jackson, was not primarily motivated by specific wartime pressures and finding a way to try unlawful belligerents; his concern was to ensure that the occupation of certain portions of Mexico was orderly and efficient. He wanted order in an essentially lawless province that the U.S. Army was "occupying." Further, he did not want the men under his command, through their commission of criminal acts, to promote greater resistance from the Mexican nationals. Thus, under General Order 20, General Scott stated, "All offenders, Mexican and American, were alike punished, with death for murder or rape and for other crimes proportionally."[14]

This concept of not exciting enemy passions but still ensuring a strong message of deterrence through the occupation forces' use of military justice was progressive, to say the least. Scott himself later remarked that his order resulted in "the highest moral deportment and discipline ever known to an invading army." The threat of using the presumably more severe military commissions resulted in a strong display of both general and specific deterrence. Such deterrence is of even greater importance when an invading army is within another nation's borders and culture. For Scott, it is now widely recognized, the military commissions clearly worked.

The idea of using the tribunals in the same fashion with the same procedural protections (or lack thereof) for both citizens and noncitizens was the means by which to display fairness, consistency, and justice. Notably, Scott did all of this *sua sponte* (on his own initiative) with no guidance from either of the political branches. He used the inherent authority of command to exercise his views of how the commissions should be used. Scott not only used the commissions to prevent insurrection but also as the best means available for rapid, efficient, tough adjudication of crimes with virtually no interference from the due process rights normally afforded civilians.

Civil War

Military tribunals were used extensively during the Civil War. These tribunals, distinct from the courts-martial process and the existing Article III civilian courts, were utilized to adjudicate common law crimes and military offenses that were "not triable...by courts-martial...and not within the jurisdiction of any civil court." Without question, President Lincoln viewed military commissions as the best available forum to prosecute those who committed violations of the laws of war.[15] Although military commissions had been used in previous armed conflicts, the state of emergency resulting from the dissolution of the union led to a more robust, and aggressive, use of these commissions during the 1860s. President Lincoln, as in most aspects of his efforts as commander in chief while serving as president, acted unilaterally in authorizing their use. He sought little, if any, input from Congress on most of his decisions about tactics or other aspects of the war effort. His use of military commissions was no different. Lincoln, however, made every effort to ensure that they were conducted as fairly as possible—but also as rapidly as possible. He ensured, along with his judge advocate general, complete oversight of the process. Additionally, the president himself had final say as to punishment.[16]

Prior to implementing the commissions as the legal forum for war crimes and other common law crimes committed during the Civil War, President Lincoln suspended the writ of habeas corpus. Although the Constitution provides only the Congress with the authority to suspend the writ, Lincoln believed the national emergency under way required him to take measures such as this to ensure the safety of the nation. He was aware of the risk he was taking in acting on the fringes of legality but was comfortable in implementing such bold measures. Lincoln was ready to accept the full responsibility if his decisions were later determined to be flawed, or were illegal. Referring to the steps he had taken, he noted, "Whether strictly legal or not, [these actions] were ventured upon under what appeared to be a popular demand and a public necessity, trusting then, as now, that Congress would readily ratify them."[17] Similar to the debates of today, Lincoln's decision to act unilaterally, without input or consent from the Congress, was largely based upon a legal opinion by his attorney general.[18] The opinion made it clear that the president was well within his authority to act, as commander in chief, in times of crisis as he deemed appropriate. This opinion put the executive, during times of crisis or emergency, above the other two branches in the arena of national security. The Supreme Court was not involved whatsoever. Instead, the executive branch made the decisions and ordered the commissions as a matter of perceived military necessity.

Although not authorized prior to Lincoln's orders, several laws were later enacted supporting the use of military commissions against military members as well as spies.[19] The Congress thus "legalized" the president's decision to use tribunals. During the Civil War, military commissions were used more than in any other period in U.S. history. The numbers are dizzying. During the struggle, there were over 4,200 military commissions and courts-martial and another 1,400 during Reconstruction.[20] Military commissions were to be employed for violations of the laws of war and courts-martial used for common law crimes committed by members of the armed forces in violation of the Articles of War.[21]

During this period, two key cases on military commissions were reviewed by the Supreme Court both during the War and immediately following the conclusion of hostilities, *Ex Parte Vallandigham* and *Ex Parte Milligan*, respectively. Both cases have been widely cited in favor of, and against, the Bush administration's use of military commissions. Supporters of the Bush commissions, such as David Rivkin, believe these cases reveal the unique nature of the commissions in military law and argue that the current cases against alleged al Qaeda fighters are distinguished from the precedent of either of these cases because the Guantanamo detainees are not on U.S. soil and the actions presumptively deal with noncitizens.[22] Thoughtful critics, such as former career naval officer and now law professor David Glazier, assert that these decisions by the Supreme Court make clear that the Bush administration's use of military commissions is clearly in violation of the Constitution in part because the civilian courts are "open and functioning."[23] The reality is that in both cases, the Civil War era decisions are not on point from either perspective. This is because one cannot analogize these cases to the twenty-first-century war against international terrorists.

Ex Parte Vallandigham

Although most in Lincoln's ideologically diverse cabinet believe the use of a commission against Vallandigham was inappropriate, the Supreme Court eventually upheld its validity. Vallandigham, a former congressman from Ohio, was arrested for giving a speech that was in support of the Confederacy and against Union actions. This action violated General Order No. 138 issued by General Burnside. It resulted in Vallandigham's arrest and eventual trial by a military commission. He was charged with speaking out in violation of the general order. This order imposed the death penalty not only upon those who gave physical support to the Confederacy but even for those who merely expressed sympathy for the Confederate cause.[24] Vallandigham, a trial lawyer by trade, mounted a vigorous defense challenging jurisdiction, witnesses, and even the general order itself as being unconstitutional. Objectively, his "talk" was made in public, in an open space, and appropriate notice of the talk had been given.[25] It would seem Vallandigham was doing nothing other than exercising his First Amendment right of free speech. Some today assert that his arrest was clearly an infringement on this constitutional right. This natural tension between liberty and national security always occurs when a democracy goes to war. Critics of the Vallandigham decision do not give sufficient weight on the need to limit such traditional protections during an armed conflict— particularly a civil war being fought within the continental United States. Vallandigham's talk, during a time of open rebellion (and the period of greatest threat to the Union since its founding a century earlier), was, at the very least, inflammatory. Specifically, the former congressman's remarks described the Civil War as "wicked, cruel and unnecessary...and for the purpose of crushing our liberty...to free blacks and enslave whites."[26] Although it is often uncomfortable to discuss such issues within American society today, the delicate balance between liberty and security does, in fact, tip toward security when the nation is at war. The reality is that certain infringements upon liberty often must occur during armed conflict. This was particularly true during the nineteenth-century civil war. This reality can be distasteful in progressive twenty-first-century culture, but it is an unintended consequence when a nation goes to war, even within a republic such as ours. Examples today are abundant: the struggles over the Terrorist Surveillance Program (TSP) or domestic wiretapping, the USA PATRIOT ACT, and even the use of additional security measures in airports and on trains. However, this delicate balance between liberty and security must be achieved by the government. Thus, when analyzing the Vallandigham case, it is critical to understand the context in which the military orders were given and the circumstances surrounding the actions taken by the military.

The military tribunal found Vallandigham guilty and ordered confinement until the end of the war. This reasonable punishment, after a trial by the military, was given even though the maximum punishment for his offenses was death. Fortunately, reason prevailed and the military officers assigned to serve on the commission obviously remained objective; they did not decide the case on emotion alone. Lincoln and his team, although not supportive of the use of the military commission against Vallandigham because they believed a civilian court would have been the preferred forum for judging his actions, did not tamper with the result. They affirmed the decision of the tribunal and justified its actions by rationalizing that the former congressman's talk went well beyond the protections of the First Amendment. His words not only supported Confederate actions but also had a negative impact on raising the Union Army within Ohio.[27] Of note, Vallandigham did seek a writ of habeas corpus from the Supreme Court. The petition was heard, but after argument, denied on the grounds the Supreme Court believed they did not have the jurisdiction to even hear the case as a matter of constitutional law. The Court refrained from interfering in what was understood to be the province of the executive branch and the armed forces.

Ex Parte Milligan

This case,[28] decided in 1866, is often cited by critics of the Bush administration's use of military commissions.[29] In general, the Supreme Court in *Milligan* decided that Mr. Milligan, a civilian U.S. citizen accused of war crimes within a Union-occupied area, should not be brought before a military tribunal when the civilian, federal courts were open and operating. Although the case was properly decided, it seems that critics of modern military commissions confuse, or simply misinterpret, the holding to fit their interests or political agendas.

The fact remains that the Court's ruling is logical, well written, and insightful. It notes the continuous evolution of military justice and commissions over the years—and particularly for crimes committed by U.S. citizens within the territory of the United States. It is not, contrary to critics' assertions, directly on point with the current environment in which the U.S. armed forces are operating. It does not determine that military commissions, de jure, are unlawful or somehow unconstitutional. *Milligan* is very limited in its application. The holding specifically impacts U.S. citizens or those captured on American soil. As such, lawyers have successfully used the holding to support the *Padilla, Moussaoui, Lindh,* and *al Mari* cases being tried in U.S. federal court. These were all cases of U.S. citizens or those captured within the United States who were suspected of being affiliated with al Qaeda (and thus, designated as enemy combatants) and were subsequently tried in open U.S. federal courts.

Lamden P. Milligan was charged and found guilty of conspiracy and sentenced to hang. He, along with four others, was accused of plotting to steal weapons and then to invade Union prisoner of war (POW) camps and set Confederate POWs free.[30] They were accused of plotting to attack and fight the government of Indiana in support of the Confederacy. Milligan was not a soldier, did not wear a uniform, and was labeled what is now referred to as an "enemy combatant." Additionally, Milligan and the three others (including the freed POWs) were also planning to attack the governments of Michigan and Ohio. Upon discovery of the plot, the alleged were charged, found guilty by a military tribunal, and sentenced to hang in 1864.

On appeal, the Supreme Court held that military tribunals cannot be employed to try U.S. civilians in areas where the Article III federal courts are open and functional—even during periods of armed conflict. Even though Milligan was a member of a secret society known as the Order of the American Knights (a group that advocated overthrowing the Union government), the Court stated he was a U.S. citizen operating in Union territory and was not a member of any armed force, and thus the Court held he was merely lobbying against Union policies. The Court reasoned that the military commissions, therefore, were not the appropriate forum in which to try him with the facts provided. The Court stated that Milligan had been apprehended away from the "field of battle," had (to their knowledge) never actually communicated with the Confederate government, and was merely a partisan of the Confederate cause.[31] The Court also concluded that Milligan had not engaged in any illegal acts of hostility against the government. He was not an unlawful belligerent but rather merely a supporter of the Confederate cause. With these facts before the Court, and again deciding the case after the actual War between the States had concluded, the Supreme Court cautioned that Milligan could have been any citizen of the Confederacy—not necessarily an unlawful belligerent. Therefore, a military tribunal was not appropriate for this case. Beyond all of these facts, he was a United States citizen and should have been entitled to have the ordinary civilian courts determine his status and adjudicate his crimes.

Civil libertarians and those who support the use of civilian courts to try the al Qaeda fighter view this as the foundation of their arguments against the current employment of military tribunals.[32] They view the current conflict as somehow analogous to the Civil War and often use this case to support trying all of the captured al Qaeda fighters in civilian court. This seems to be an overreach and a great expansion of the actual holding. This case should not be taken out of context and used to support the sweeping use of federal courts to try all al Qaeda suspects today. The current armed conflict is international in character and not a civil war. The Court in *Milligan* was also in the tough position of trying "Americans" (even though Confederate Americans) as well as hearing the case after hostilities had ceased. It seems likely the Court would have decided differently if the nation had still been engaged in its civil war when the opinion was delivered. There were also serious policy considerations taken into account in this decision. The government wanted to ensure that the newly reunited nation would not be retaliatory toward former members of the Confederacy. The greater good was served by bringing the nation together, fostering unity, healing the nation's wounds, and refraining from being vindictive toward former enemies. Thus, there was much more involved in deciding *Milligan* than is portrayed by some who merely emphasize the "courts are open and operating" language contained in the opinion.

The 5–4 decision by the Court, however, does show (in the nineteenth century) the divisions over the use of commissions—even during this period and after the cessation of open hostilities (of note, the chief justice wrote the dissent in this case). As is the case today, people were divided over whether civilians who engage in unlawful belligerency, regardless of location, should be afforded the many rights associated with being tried in U.S. courts. Regardless, *Milligan* does stand for this principle now ingrained within U.S. military law jurisprudence: U.S. citizens can not be detained and tried by the U.S. armed forces if (1) they have not joined the enemy, (2) are captured away from the battlefield, or (3) are captured when the civilian Article III federal courts remain open and operating.[33] These three prongs, however, as will be discussed in greater detail in later chapters, are not directly applicable to the enemies the United States faces today. Most are detained awaiting prosecution for going well beyond mere statements and committing actions in support of international terrorism or for having some "association" or "affiliation" with al Qaeda operations.[34]

Perhaps the best known, or most infamous, military commissions of the Civil War were conducted against the conspirators involved in Lincoln's assassination. In May of 1865, President Johnson ordered nine military officers to serve on the tribunal. There were eight accused, seven men and one young woman. They were charged with conspiring with the intent to kill President Lincoln, Vice President Johnson (who convened the tribunals), Secretary of State Seward, and General Ulysses Grant. All eight were convicted: four were given prison sentences and the other four were sentenced to public hanging. When an appeal was made for a writ of habeas corpus, it was denied, with the court relying on the fact that President Johnson had already ordered suspension of the writ.

Lou Fisher, among others, has stated that these commissions were decided more on emotion than reason. To some, they appeared preordained to order conviction and were carried out, not in the spirit of justice, but rather with vengeance. Johnson did seek an opinion from his attorney general as to whether military commissions were the appropriate forum for the trials. There remains ambiguity as to when Johnson actually asked for the opinion; some assert it was done after the fact to ensure that legality was preserved. Regardless, Attorney General Speed opined that the accused "not only may but ought to be tried by a military tribunal." He went further and asserted, "When war comes, the laws of war come with it," and "Presidents have substantial constitutional authority to act under the laws of war." Such reasoning sounds awfully similar to the reasoning of the Justice Department under the Bush administration. Of note, the accused were punished within a little over two months after their capture.

Another well-known commission during the Civil War was that employed against eight southerners in August 1865. A nine-member tribunal was convened in Washington, D.C., to hear the case against the eight who oversaw the Andersonville, Georgia, prison. They were charged with conspiracy and murder. Alleged atrocities at the prison included overcrowding, sun overexposure, providing polluted water, maltreatment, and abuse. When Judge Advocate General Holt reviewed the trial record, he was horrified at the atrocities committed by Confederate prison officials and guards. He angrily denounced the actions of the accused in saying he could find nothing in criminal history "parallel to this monstrous atrocity." He further alluded to their "diabolical combination for the destruction and death, by cruel and fiendishly ingenious processes, of helpless prisoners of war." Most of the blame fell upon the officer in charge of the prison, Captain Harry Stirz. Although evidence was presented that he might not have been guilty of the crimes but rather that he had been trying to improve conditions at the prison during the year he was there (1864–1865), he was found guilty on almost all of the charges against him. Some have asserted that, similar to the Lincoln assassination tribunals, the commissions employed here performed more like a court of vengeance toward the South than a court of law. Regardless, Stirz was hanged on November 10, 1865.

Other tribunals took place during the Civil War that offer a perspective on the potential for abuse when these tribunals are solely authorized in the field of battle by military commanders. Many of the tribunals used against the Indians display the illegitimacy that could arise from legal mechanisms that did not have the necessary input (or a "check" in this case) from the civilian leadership. The most infamous of the Indian tribunals were the commissions used against the Dakota Indians in Minnesota in 1862. The Dakota, now better known as the Sioux tribe, had waged war against settlers in the Western territories. The Dakota Indians had suffered under American expansion and lost significant land holdings as a result of questionable "treaties" signed during the 1850s and the early 1860s. Additionally, Congress had been slow in paying money that was intended for the tribe as a result of such treaties.[35] During the month of fighting, heavy losses were incurred by both sides but importantly, the Dakota tribe had killed nearly 358 American settlers.

A five-member military tribunal was formed to hear the charges against the Indians, in particular for their killing of civilian settlers. The commissions lasted slightly over a month and 392 members of the tribe were charged. Importantly, the commission was created, organized, and held all under the sole authority of Colonel H. Sibley.[36] There was no authorization from the president, let alone Congress. The commissions convicted 323 and sentenced 303 to hang.[37] President Lincoln, upon hearing of these actions, immediately inserted himself and reminded the military that under existing federal law only he had the authority to approve sentences of death. After deliberations and consultation with his attorney general and judge advocate general, he recommended only those who participated in "massacres" rather than merely battles be put to death. Many of the soldiers and civilians in the territory sent letters to Lincoln pleading with him to execute all sentenced to death by the commissions. Lincoln, to his credit, remained steadfast that only those who engaged in "atrocities" (or what we would call "war crimes") be subject to death. To do otherwise would be putting legitimate soldiers of the Dakota tribe to death from merely engaging in armed conflict against the United States. As a result, only thirty-eight members actually were hanged.

As Dr. Fisher, the highly regarded constitutional law scholar and expert on military commissions, has noted,

> The military tribunal for the Dakota trials has been the subject of several critiques, partly because of the accelerated nature of the proceedings and the prejudice of the tribunal members. In addition, the tribunal could have granted, as a privilege and not as a right, counsel to the defendants, to assure that they understood the charges and could respond adequately. This was particularly necessary for defendants who had little command of English. In later military trials against Indians, counsel was provided.[38]

The Dakota trials represent the potential abuse by commissions if not properly overseen by the civilian leadership. In this case, the military decided without seeking any authorization whatsoever to employ tribunals and to order death if necessary. Although tribunals would have been appropriate for those who engaged in the massacres of settlers, Colonel Sibley instead chose to use them in the inappropriate fashion of essentially ordering the death penalty against all who were captured. Clearly, civilian oversight of wartime commissions is necessary, and Lincoln fortunately inserted himself into the process, thereby ensuring that those who employed the military commissions did not themselves commit "war crimes." Although there were still some commissions employed that resulted in death sentences, Lincoln's intervention and restraint ensured that the commissions (and the severe penalties afforded such nineteenth-century tribunals) were not used arbitrarily or capriciously by the U.S. Army.

In different ways, then, military commissions were used throughout the nineteenth century. They have been employed, almost exclusively, by military commanders in the field of battle or by the commander in chief in times of armed conflict. While some specific cases, such as *Milligan*, were found unconstitutional as applied, the commissions remained part of military law jurisprudence. Until later in the mid-twentieth century, the legal support for these unique "military trials" was primarily based upon the customary laws of war. Since the Revolution and up to the current era, they have remained a forum distinct from ordinary courts-martial proceedings. Due to their flexible nature, they were implemented as the best available option during times of martial law, in occupied territories, on the front lines of a war, and of course to try "unlawful belligerents." Their use during the eighteenth and nineteenth centuries normally afforded a unique, less rights-oriented procedure to meet the needs of the U.S. government during periods of armed conflict. It seems that the goal of the commanders and presidents during this period was primarily to provide a system of justice that would strongly deter violations of martial law, the laws of war, or other actions deemed to have a negative impact on military operations. This emphasis on deterrence continued into the twentieth century. Even as military justice was becoming increasingly progressive, the military commissions remained a flexible tool of justice for commanders in the field as well as the commander in chief.

❧✕❧

THREE

The Second World War Military Commission—*Ex Parte Quirin* et al.

MILITARY COMMISSIONS WERE also used to a limited degree in the 1898 Spanish-American War, particularly in the Philippines until the peace treaty was signed in April 1899. During this period, they were generally viewed as accepted legal practice during ongoing military operations (when conducted overseas). They were not, however, employed as part of the First World War. During the Second World War and its aftermath, military commissions were predominantly used to try illegal belligerents and to prosecute war criminals. The two most noteworthy cases of this period were *In re Yamashita*[1] and *Ex Parte Quirin*.[2] Although most of this chapter is devoted to reviewing the facts and issues confronting the Roosevelt administration in the *Quirin* case, it is still important to discuss *Yamashita* briefly at the conclusion. Although the Bush administration lawyers in the twenty-first century relied on *Yamashita* far less heavily than *Quirin*, the case is still also cited as support for the use of military commissions by the executive branch in times of armed conflict.

The most noteworthy case during the Second World War era and during the twentieth century was *Ex Parte Quirin*. It is also referred to as the Nazi saboteur case.[3] This case was cited repeatedly by the Bush administration to support its decision to use military commissions in 2001 and beyond. It was, after all, a legal precedent from a unanimous Supreme Court. It had generally been accepted as "good law" by academics, politicians, and the bar. Although some parts of the decision were later questioned by the noted legal expert Professor Weiner of Harvard and even by Justice Frankfurter himself,[4] it seems reasonable that the administration relied upon this case for guidance in constructing its Presidential Order of November, 2001.

This case is fascinating. The facts surrounding it are a mixture of history, politics, intrigue, suspense, terror, and a bit of luck. It is unfortunate that more attention had not been given to this case prior to September 11, 2001, and that the politics of the current cases often distract scholars and students from enjoying its fascinating details. The real hero who initiated the process of catching the saboteurs was a "Coastie"—or a U.S. Coast Guardsman, named John C. Cullen. He had the job that many Coasties in the mid-twentieth century dreamed of—patrol on the beaches of the uber-affluent Hamptons on eastern Long Island. His interdiction and confrontation of the saboteurs occurred on the famous Amagansett Beach. In all likelihood, his alertness prevented various attacks from occurring within the United States. Although not as significant as the attacks and battles under way at the time in Russia, Germany, the United Kingdom, Japan, Italy, and North Africa, this sort of sabotage within the continental United States would have had a major impact on the nation's interest and motivation to fight. Although clearly distinguishable from the detention and trial(s) for alleged al Qaeda fighters in the twenty-first century, Roosevelt's decision to use military commissions to try alleged illegal belligerents who were plotting terrorist acts on U.S. soil, not wearing a standard military uniforms, all during a period of armed conflict, sounds eerily similar to decisions made by the Bush administration sixty years later.

In June of 1942, eight enemies of the United States came ashore within days of one another on Long Island, New York, and in North Florida after being transported by submarines from Hamburg, Germany. While each had trained and studied in Germany, two were American citizens. The intent of the Germans was to wreak terror and havoc upon the United States by attacking infrastructure, railroads, factories, bridges, tourist sites, and major buildings.[5] Hitler was intent on hurting the U.S. war effort; he wanted to undermine U.S. morale. Additionally, he was furious that thirty Germans had been caught and arrested several years before for spying within the United States. He instructed his staff to ensure that the mistakes made in espionage were corrected and that this time the infiltration of America was done properly.[6] So motivated, Hitler and his immediate staff instructed the saboteurs to damage both production and the support elements of the United States. Sabotage attacks such as these, he anticipated, were critical to winning the war in Europe without ever formally invading the continental United States. Presumably, he believed the citizens of the United States were "weak" and that a democracy such as ours would collapse once attacked in this fashion—by saboteurs attacking from within. Thus, the saboteurs were acting as (and should be now appropriately labeled) unlawful belligerents. Dr. Lou Fisher, perhaps the foremost scholar on *Quirin* and of U.S. military tribunals, has argued that this case is one of the worst in U.S. history. In his book on the German saboteurs and in various law review articles, he questions the legality of the decision and, in particular, the Bush administration's reliance on *Quirin* as sufficient precedent for the employment of military commissions in the twenty-first century. I differ with my esteemed colleague. I see the case as logical, legally sound, and consistent with past precedent, and in accord with the military laws of the era.[7]

The eight men selected for the mission all had lived in America and were at least conversant in English. The Nazi government had placed them in training camps outside of Berlin in Brandenburg. They were trained to use the tools of sabotage—explosives, fuses, timing devices.[8] Additionally, they visited aluminum plants, railroads, and canals to become familiar with possible targets.

The plan was to split the eight men up and have them enter the United States in different locations. Each group was transported to the U.S. coastline by submarine. The group directed to land in New York was commanded by George John Dasch; the other group, assigned to land in Florida, was led by Edward John Kerling. Quirin, the named litigant, was under the Dasch command.[9] Once offshore and within easy landing distance of both Florida and New York, the two groups each took two separate small boats to get ashore. Once ashore, they took off their frogman suits and changed into "American civilian" clothes. In doing so, at that point (in accordance with international law conventions and the customary law of war), they lost any wartime protections associated with being members of an armed force.

Patrolling the shores of Amagansett in the Hamptons area of Long Island, a one-person U.S. Coast Guard patrol noticed, stopped, and questioned the men as to their intentions. Coast Guardsman Cullen confronted the men on the beach and was surprised at their awkward reaction to his inquiry. Immediately, Cullen became suspicious of the group. Dasch proceeded to get angry, and then offered Cullen $260 to keep quiet. At that point, Cullen ordered the group of four back to the local U.S. Coast Guard Station for further questioning. The men refused. Cullen then proceeded to head back to the station for additional support and asked the men to stay in place. As he departed, the Germans quickly defied orders and went to bury their uniforms (apparently this was not in their original plans), and then hurriedly left for the train station. The train from eastern Long Island would eventually land them in Manhattan.

Upon his return to the station, Cullen immediately contacted the Coast Guard members of the OSS (now known as the Coast Guard Investigative Service (CGIS)). CGIS, upon notification, then contacted the Federal Bureau of Investigation (FBI) for further inquiry. The FBI opened up an intense investigation into what had just occurred on the beaches of Long Island. Within hours of the report, the FBI discovered the buried German uniforms. While the FBI was conducting a massive manhunt, Dasch became increasingly nervous about the operation. He turned himself in to law enforcement authorities. While this was happening in New York, the four who had come ashore in Florida had successfully landed as planned and were already in and around Chicago and Cincinnati. Ironically, the other group led by Kerling was soon thereafter arrested as well. After being informed by his mother (who resided within the United States) that the FBI was asking questions and that he should sign up for the draft, Herbert Haupt (one of the group that landed in Florida) actually stopped by the Chicago FBI field office to let them know he had returned from a trip to Mexico City. Of course, with the other manhunt under way, the FBI became very suspicious of any German national returning to the United States at about the same time. The FBI later arrested him as well. Now all eight "terrorists" were in custody and being classified as unlawful belligerents under the common law of war. The "attack" on the United States had been foiled. Coast Guardsman Cullen's initial confrontation on the beach led to the capture and arrest of eight men who had planned to strike terror within the country and severely hamper support for continued operations overseas. He is truly the hero of the *Quirin* case.[10]

The Tribunals

There was great debate both inside and outside Franklin Delano Roosevelt's administration on how to try these men for conspiracy to commit acts of terror on U.S. soil. Obviously, there were strategic as well as tactical considerations involved. American citizens' support for the fighting overseas was strong, but it is impossible to gauge how these types of incidents could impact the will of a nation to fight. Roosevelt wanted to send a strong signal that such acts of overt aggression by the enemy—in this case, agents of the Nazi government—would result in swift, harsh punishment for those captured. Some critics allege that the decision to use the military tribunals was motivated more by a concern about public relations than any thoughtful legal analysis.[11] I disagree. Perhaps the decision was motivated in part by such a concern, but this cynicism disregards the realities of warfare. If the facts of the situation were revealed, Germany (which could obviously follow the case in an open criminal court) could adjust its tactics and training of personnel and thereby ensure that its next attempt would prove successful.

It is true that once all the captures had taken place, there were numerous reports, news stories, and other media propaganda hailing the FBI's handling of the spies.[12] Some suggest the propaganda victory would have been significantly diminished if, in open court (i.e., federal criminal court), the real story of the Germans had been revealed. It would show the German agents merely bumbling and making significant mistakes—demonstrating that their capture was more an inevitability than an indication of extraordinary efforts by the U.S. Coast Guard and the FBI. Although this certainly was part of the analysis in deciding to use tribunals, the most prudent way to analyze the decision to use military tribunals focused on one issue—deterrence, both specific and general.

It was general deterrence in that Germany (as well as the other Axis powers) would now be hesitant about engaging in this sort sabotage against the United States again. Convictions of the attempted saboteurs would send a clear signal that the United States deals with such illegal acts swiftly and harshly. Further, it would make individual Germans (and Americans who might sympathize with Germany) less likely to volunteer for such undertakings in the future. Specific deterrence would be satisfied in that the accused would be removed from the "fight" and be subject to the harsh realities of the laws governing military commissions. The eight individuals would now potentially be subject to the death penalty.

The decision was based on myriad other reasons—policy, politics, war support, public relations, propaganda, secrecy, and to reaffirm that the men's actions constituted an illegal act of war—but all of these centered around the need to punish the perpetrators rapidly while still according some level of the American legal process to all of the accused. The administration wanted to prevent recurrence of such attempts but to still adhere to the rule of law in carrying out the prosecutions. President Roosevelt, clearly alarmed at this intrusion into U.S. sovereignty, ordered both Attorney General Biddle and his Judge Advocate General Cramer to meet immediately and recommend to him the best means to proceed.[13]

Reasons against the use of civilian courts were numerous. For example, the maximum punishment under the federal laws for sabotage was only thirty years' imprisonment; the men being charged were not civilians but unlawful belligerents; there was a perceived need to ensure that the Axis governments received a strong message as to what would happen if someone attempted such terrorism again during the war; and there was a need to respond to the public embarrassment at the lack of defense of the U.S. homeland. The Roosevelt administration did not want to reveal in open court how easy it was for two German submarines to come so close to U.S. shores without any interference from the U.S. Coast Guard or the U.S. Navy (until the USCG confronted the saboteurs ashore). There were legitimate concerns about due process issues and evidentiary issues. However, these concerns were complicated by the question of whether the naturalized U.S. citizens (Mr. Burger and Mr. Haupt) would have to be distinguished from the others and tried in civilian courts. Moreover, the war effort seemed to demand rapid trials and severe punishment that might not be possible within the civilian U.S. justice system.[14] These issues confronting the Roosevelt administration are virtually identical to the ones confronting the Bush administration after the attacks of 9/11. Lou Fisher's historical account is outstanding, but it is unfortunate that other detailed studies of the similarities of the decision-making process in the two administrations have not been seriously undertaken. The similarities, both positive and negative, are startling. The most obvious distinction between Roosevelt's 1942 commission and the twenty-first-century commissions, however, is that Roosevelt clearly desired an adjudicatory process that would be rapid, with fewer constitutional protections than would be afforded in civilian courts, and based on the laws of war, but still a trial. He remained convinced of the need to try the individuals rather than "detain" them for the duration of the war. This "detention" would have been the case if they were POWs, which they clearly were not. They were unlawful belligerents, or saboteurs.

Three key members of the Roosevelt cabinet engaged in dialogue, argument, and debate about the relative merits/demerits of each system to best adjudicate the war crimes committed. Secretary of War Henry

L. Stimson, Attorney General Francis Biddle, and Major General Myron C. Cramer all met immediately to discuss their options. They did have some help up front. Initial advice was offered by the convening authority and Commander in Chief Roosevelt himself: he made clear that he wanted convictions of all eight.[15] General Cramer and the Department of Justice attorneys all felt a civilian trial would be too likely to offer the possibility of light sentences—something they all felt uncomfortable with and that was clearly not what President Roosevelt desired. Biddle, the lead federal civilian prosecutor for the nation, was strongly in support of using military trials. That the attorney general favored military tribunals actually surprised Secretary Stimson, who wrote in his notes, "Instead of straining every nerve to retain civilian jurisdiction of these saboteurs, [he] was quite ready to turn them over to a military court."[16] The decision was, in part, based upon a distinction between the current case and the *Milligan* case described in chapter 2. The decision makers agreed these German unlawful belligerents were not ordinary citizens engaging in protected First Amendment speech. In fact, they saw this case as completely different from the accused in *Milligan*. Once again, the arguments within the Roosevelt administration sound extraordinarily similar to those that occurred within the Bush administration in 2001. Roosevelt, as commander in chief, weighed in demanding that the death penalty be an option for those trying the case. This would not be possible if the administration opted to use civilian courts. He saw no difference in this case from the first use of an American military commission against an unlawful belligerent, the case against Major Andre.[17] Thus, the influence of President Roosevelt, as commander in chief during an ongoing war, was quite pronounced. He made that clear to staff on several occasions during their brief discussions regarding the available options. While others may assert the primary motivation for using the military tribunals was to keep quiet the specific facts of the case—the ease with which the saboteurs had entered U.S. waters and the continental United States and the less than accurate portrayal of the FBI as heroic, as the agents were being presented by the bureau and within the media—the reality appears to be that the decision was pushed by Biddle and Cramer in an effort to support Roosevelt's analysis of the case. An avid reader of history, the president seems to have reached this conclusion with little influence from anyone else.

After a short few days of discussion over the specifics of any proposed tribunal, the administration decided to appoint a seven-member military commission to try the saboteurs. Interestingly, noting that the case was something of a hybrid of both Article III courts and military trials, Roosevelt retained both Biddle as attorney general and Major General Cramer to oversee the process. In appointing his attorney general and the judge advocate of the army as the "prosecution team," Roosevelt ensured expertise in both trial litigation and military law. This decision foreshadows the proposal discussed later in this book on a Department of Justice–led National Security Court System.

One cannot overemphasize the importance Roosevelt placed on alacrity in his decision to employ military commissions. The president wanted these cases handled as rapidly as possible and knew that one of the great hallmarks of the military justice system is its rapid adjudication of crimes. During ongoing combat, the need for rapid adjudication of crimes is particularly important. Speed is even more important when the military trials are for unlawful combatants who have conspired to wreak havoc within the continental United States. In 1942, the country was in a declared war with Germany and had been infiltrated by the enemy. The commander in chief wanted results. The conversations between Roosevelt and his national security team, particularly those not recorded, were (to say the least) quite heated. Civilian courts could not provide what the administration desired. The last thing the Roosevelt administration wanted was long, drawn-out trials that would invariably have some negative impact on U.S. support for the war. Additionally, his administration believed the civilian courts (and their lighter sentences) would not send the signal of deterrence they intended to show the world.

Within one week of the men's capture, on July 2, Roosevelt, without input from the Congress, issued Proclamation 2561 (hereafter the Order) creating the tribunal.[18] The Order was titled, "Denying Certain Enemies Access to the Courts of the United States." Up front, the Order stated that "the safety of the United States demands that all enemies who have entered upon the territory of the United States as part of an invasion or predatory incursion, or who have entered in order to commit sabotage, espionage, or other hostile or warlike acts, should be properly tried in accordance with the laws of war." Importantly, the military tribunal was to be based upon the laws of war. The proclamation did not mention the forerunner to the current Uniform Code of Military Justice (UCMJ), the Articles of War. In creating the tribunal based upon the laws of war, the tribunal was afforded enormous latitude with regard to process, evidentiary issues, and appeals. Further, in ensuring that the tribunal was based on international law, and not statute, the members would not be persuaded or constrained by acts of Congress, notions of due process as traditionally understood in U.S. courts, or by any statutory mandates. Both Attorney General Biddle and President Roosevelt felt strongly that they must not permit access to the federal courts by the prisoners. Thus, they included provisions in the Order that the traditional writ of habeas corpus was not authorized for the saboteurs. On this point, Roosevelt was quite firm. He passionately asserted, "I won't give them up....I won't hand them over to any U.S. Marshal with a writ of *habeas corpus*. Understand?"[19]

Additionally, the Order departed from the courts-martial procedure and sentencing scheme covered by the Articles of War: conviction, even for capital cases, only required a two-thirds vote. The Articles of War (and the current UCMJ today) require a unanimous vote for the sentence of the death penalty. Procedurally, the Order provided for the admission of evidence if deemed to be of "probative value to a reasonable man" by the president of the commission. It also ensured that the final reviewing authority would be the commander in chief (the president himself) instead of the judge advocate general who ordinarily would have retained such authority. Due to concerns for national security, the trial would not be open (in courts-marital and under the Article of War, all courts-martial are presumptively open proceedings). Finally, the commission itself adopted other procedures regarding juror (member) challenges. Specifically, they ensured the right to disregard any challenges by the defense that made reference to, or relied upon, the provisions contained within the Articles of War.[20]

Two defense counsels at senior officer levels, Colonel Cassius Dovall and Colonel Kenneth Royall, were assigned to defend seven of the accused (another JAG officer, with the rank of colonel, was assigned to defend Dasch alone). As remains the case today, military judge advocates (military lawyers), when serving as defense counsel, are ethically bound to "zealously defend" the accused. Both men, from available reports, understandably found this role difficult.[21] As mentioned earlier, the commander in chief had made clear to the prosecution that he had expected guilty verdicts—and, in most cases—the death penalty.[22] These men were asked to defend the saboteurs, enemies of the United States seeking to terrorize the civilian populace, while still remaining in uniform and somehow still appearing loyal to the war effort as well as to the commander in chief. This was clearly not an easy task in America in 1942. It can now be said that both did an incredible job under less than desirable conditions, defending the saboteurs in such a short time frame and with all of the publicity surrounding the case.

They stand tall as great examples for all judge advocates in the armed forces today.

The defense, citing *Milligan*, immediately objected to the jurisdiction of the court. Not surprisingly, they asserted that the courts were open and operating, and drew comparisons between the German "civilians" captured within the borders of the United States and the two American citizens who were part of the group of eight. Biddle responded emphatically with a now famous quote: "This is not a trial of offenses of the law of civil courts but it is a trial of the offenses of the law of war, which is not cognizable to the civil courts."[23] The defense's objection was overruled.

The government proceeded to charge the defendants with the following crimes:

1. *Violating the law of war*
   Specification 1: In that, during the month of 1942, Edward John Kerling (and others) being enemies of the United States and acting on or behalf of the German Reich, a belligerent enemy nation, secretly and covertly passed, in civilian dress, contrary to the law of war, through the military and naval lines and defenses of the Untied States, along the Atlantic Coast, and went behind such lines and defenses in civilian dress within zones of military operations and elsewhere, for the purpose of committing acts of sabotage, espionage, and other hostile acts, and, in particular, to destroy certain war industries, war utilities, and war materials within the United States.

   Specification 2: In that, during the month of June 1942, Edward John Kerling (and others), being enemies of the United States and acting for and on behalf of the German Reich, a belligerent enemy nation, appeared, contrary to the law of war, behind the military and naval defenses and lines of the United States, within the zones of military operations and elsewhere, for the purpose of committing or attempting to commit sabotage, espionage, and other hostile acts, without being in the uniform of the armed forces of the German Reich, and planned and attempted to destroy and sabotage war industries, war utilities, and war materials within the United States, and assembled together within the United States explosives, money, and other supplies in order to accomplish said purposes.

2. *Violation of Article of War 81*—"Whoever relieves or attempts to relieve the enemy with arms, ammunition, supplies, money, or other things, or knowingly harbors or protects or holds correspondence with or gives intelligence to the enemy, either directly or indirectly,

shall suffer death or such other punishment as a courts-martial or military commission shall direct."

Specification: In that during the month of June 1942, Edward John Kerling (and others), being enemies of the United States and acting for and on behalf of the German Reich, a belligerent enemy nation, and without being in the uniform of the armed forces of that nation, relieved or attempted to relieve enemies of the United States with arms, ammunition, supplies, money and other things, and knowingly harbored, protected and held correspondence with and gave intelligence to enemies of the United States by entering the territorial limits of the United States, in the company of other enemies of the United States, with explosives, money and other supplies with which they relieved each other and relieved the German Reich, for the purpose of destroying and sabotaging war industries, transportation facilities, or war materials with the United States, and by harboring, communicating with, and giving intelligence to each other and to other enemies of the United States in the course of such activities.

3. Violations of Articles of War 82d (based on)—"Any person who in time of war shall be found lurking or acting as a spy in or about any of the fortifications or posts, quarters, or encampments of any of the armies of the United States, or elsewhere, shall be tried by a general courts-martial or by a military commission, and shall, upon conviction thereof, suffer death."

Specification: In that, during the month of June 1942, Edward John Kerling (and others), being enemies of the United States and acting for and on behalf of the German Reich, a belligerent enemy nation, were, in time of war, found lurking or acting as spies in or about the fortifications, posts, and encampments of the armies of the United States and elsewhere, and secretly and covertly passed through the military and naval lines and defenses of the United States, along the Atlantic Coast, and went about, through, and behind said lines and defenses and about the fortifications, posts, and encampments of the armies of the United States, in zones of military operations and elsewhere, disguised in civilian clothes and under false names, for the purpose of committing sabotage and other hostile acts against the United States, and for the purpose of communicating intelligence relating to such sabotage and other hostile acts to each other, to the German Reich, and to other enemies of the United States, during the course of such activities and thereafter.

4. *Conspiracy*

    Specification: In that, during the year 1942, Edward John Kerling (and others), being enemies of the United States, and acting for and on behalf of the German Reich, a belligerent enemy nation, did plot, plan, and conspire with each other, with the German Reich, and with other enemies of the United States, to commit each and every one of the above enumerated charges and specifications.

The charges were made, the defense and prosecution were assigned, and the commissions were set to begin.

Colonels Royall and Dovall, remaining in an awkward position, wrote the president himself (as the convening authority) asking for a meeting with him prior to the commencement of the tribunal. They were concerned, as lawyers, about the constitutionality of the court. Roosevelt refused to meet with them.[24] With the tribunal now officially under way, Royall actively pursued getting various justices of the Supreme Court to support a petition as to the constitutionality of the tribunal. He sought to meet various justices, outside of any formal proceeding, to permit him an audience to plead his case. He eventually was successful, after truly "zealous" efforts on his part, in having Chief Justice Stone agree to set an oral argument on the defense concerns on July 29, 1942. Since the case was under way and they had not followed normal procedure to this point, the defense counsels scrambled to file papers in the district court of the District of Columbia prior to the Supreme Court hearing the case. The district court moved quickly, and the court's opinion, authored by Judge Morris, denied permission for the case to be heard before that court. As controlling guidance, Judge Morris relied upon President Roosevelt's Order, which did not permit access to civil courts for the case. Regardless, the defense counsels, by filing with the district court, ensured that proper procedural requirements were met before the oral arguments could be held at the Supreme Court. Although awkward and unconventional, the two defense counsels performed Herculean tasks as military lawyers defending their clients.

The law of war is a niche area of the law. This is true today—a point repeatedly asserted by commentators arguing against using civilian courts to try unlawful belligerents. It was even more striking in the 1940s. The justices of the Supreme Court were not familiar with military law or the law of war and none was up to speed or learned in this area of jurisprudence. They were not as comfortable listening to these arguments and making a decision of this importance during the normal one hour of oral argument afforded for cases that come before them. In addition, they only had a couple of weeks to study the laws involved, they were on their summer recess, and they sensed that this case would have enormous significance in interpretation of the law of the land and would also have a major impact on the domestic war effort. Thus, Chief Justice Stone waived both the normal rules of procedure and the one hour limit on argument. In fact, the oral arguments in the *Quirin* case lasted almost nine hours.[25]

During the extraordinarily long hearing, the defense focused their arguments on the unconstitutionality of the tribunal for this case, citing once again *Ex Parte Milligan* as controlling precedent. They also challenged the appropriateness of several of the justices hearing the case, arguing that they were conflicted out and should have recused themselves for myriad reasons. Some of the justices had already met with Roosevelt and discussed the case; others had personal issues that should have forced them to recuse themselves. Chief Justice Stone had a son on the defense team; Justice Murphy did recuse himself due to his status as a military officer in the reserves; Justice Frankfurter met with President Roosevelt and his team routinely, including Secretary Stimson; and Justice Byrnes had already been working closely with Attorney General Biddle and the legal staff, assisting them in writing memos and orders for the White House during the early part of U.S. involvement in the Second World War. Ironically, none of these objections was successful and the judges remained "seated" and heard the case. I would suggest such glaring conflicts of interests on the Supreme Court would never survive similar scrutiny today. The norms of military justice (and those of the United States as well) have evolved considerably over the past fifty years since this case was decided. Such judicial conflicts of interest, if occurring in the twenty-first century, would be covered by the twenty-four-hour news media as well as by courtroom "watch dog" groups, and the groundswell of concern would be enormous. For example, in the *Hamdan* case, discussed in greater detail in a later chapter, Chief Justice Roberts recused himself from hearing the case simply because he had heard earlier versions of the case while he was still an appellate court judge. But that was not the case in 1942, and all of the Justices (except Murphy) heard and ruled on *Quirin*.

The brief and arguments presented by the defense counsels primarily focused on this issue: "Whether the President of the United States may provide for trial by military commission of offenses which are (with the exception of the charge of spying covered by Article of

War 82) cognizable in the district or other appropriate courts of the United States, at a time when such courts of the U.S. are open and functioning regularly."[26]

They attacked the facts as applicable to the crimes alleged and introduced support for their effort to remove the case into civilian court. Perhaps their most compelling argument, however, was the ex post facto clause concerns. The Order from Roosevelt listing the associated crimes was implemented only after the saboteurs had already been in the country. The Order itself was issued only after the saboteurs had allegedly committed the crimes. Under the existing statutes of the United States, the most severe punishment for their alleged offenses was thirty years. The defense counsel argued for this to be the maximum punishment for their clients—thirty years instead of the possible death penalty. However, in order for this argument to be successful, the commissions would have to be grounded solely in domestic law, or governed by statute. Roosevelt's commissions, however, were governed by the laws of war. Thus, per the Order, the laws of war controlled and this body of law does not have an ex post facto clause. As is well known, the laws of war are predominantly governed by custom, not statute. However interesting the defense arguments were, the justices were not persuaded, and they agreed with the government's position(s).

Another area the defense pursued, similar to today's criticisms of the Bush tribunals by civil libertarians and many academics, was the issue of habeas corpus. The defense argued that the necessity of habeas corpus was deeply entrenched in the Rule of Law and the Western legal tradition. Deviations from such foundational principles of law were not possible. Biddle and Cramer argued, however, that "the great bulwarks of our civil liberties—and the Writ of Habeas Corpus is one of the most important—was never intended to apply in favor of armed invaders sent here by the enemy in time of war."[27] The government argued that application of these well-entrenched standards of civilian law could not have ever been intended for the situation at hand or for any prosecutions of unlawful belligerents in times of armed conflict. They were intended for ordinary, civilian cases to ensure that the rights of a nation's citizens were not denied by an overreaching government. In the finest of Western legal traditions, the purpose was to avoid tyrannical rule. But such notions of justice would seem both impractical and impossible to apply to issues of armed invaders, or more specifically, saboteurs from a nation with which we were at war. Biddle and Cramer went even further, repudiating the applicability of *Milligan* at all by asserting that the German saboteurs had "as agents of the German government crossed our lines secretly in enemy warships for the purpose of committing hostile acts."[28]

Foreshadowing modern arguments, the prosecution emphasized the new nature of warfare. Specifically, they referred to how warfare had evolved over the course of the nineteenth and twentieth centuries, in particular since the Civil War. Warfare had become increasingly rapid, technology had become more advanced, and the ability to inflict massive damage with little effort made the need for decisive action by the commander in chief to prevent such acts, during armed conflict, critical to the national security. They argued that the president's decision to use military commissions was justified because they were essential to the need for rapid justice in an ongoing war. Biddle and Cramer were clearly of the mind-set that decisions such as whether to use tribunals for alleged war criminals were for the executive alone to make. They resisted any notion of bringing the Germans before a civilian court, to which the constitutional protections afforded U.S. citizens would necessarily attach. They were shocked that such notions were still under consideration. Ironically, sixty years later, these same (or similar) debates about the preferred forum for unlawful belligerents still rage on.

After arguments were heard, the Court released its opinion (orally), upholding the jurisdiction of the commissions for the eight belligerents. The lawyers then went back to the military trial, which had been temporarily suspended pending the decision by the Supreme Court, to determine the fate of the accused. Of note, the Supreme Court's written decision was not actually completed until three months after the announcement of its decision. This, to some, indicates the unnecessary sense of haste with which the court made their initial decision to uphold the tribunal's jurisdiction.[29] A decision made almost immediately following an oral argument without the benefit of additional research and reflection was certainly not ordinary. It is easy to look back now and question such decision making and why the Court did not simply wait for the three months in order to render its formal findings, opinion, and decision. Hindsight, however, always supplies a corrective lens. When one analyzes this decision, it is critical to remember the mind-set of the U.S. government and the nation during this period in 1942. There was legitimate concern that this infiltration of the United States was the first in an expected wave of attempts to enter the country via our porous borders. Certainly, America was concerned about the impact such intrusions would have in our ongoing battles with Germany, Italy, and Japan. We were a nation in a declared war, with an identifiable enemy, and the need for rapid decisions and rapid "justice" was deemed paramount. The decision makers recognized that this "wartime" decision was necessarily distinct from ordinary holdings of the Court that do not have such immediate, and important, consequences for our national security. This was a unique case.

The executive and the judicial branches of government moved quite rapidly to respond properly to the legitimate requests of the defense counsel. They promoted the rule of law by ensuring that "trial" and adjudication occurred as rapidly as feasible. The emergency summer session by the Supreme Court and the Order itself both indicate a sense of urgency on the part of the government. The justices felt it critical to send a clear signal to the enemy that those perpetrating these types of violations of the laws of war would be brought to justice swiftly and firmly. Thus, although peculiar to us reviewing the case today anachronistically, if we put ourselves in the mind-set of the middle of the Second World War, an opinion published three months after the decision—although arguably flawed in some respects—was actually an impressive display of service and patriotism considering the circumstances under which the justices were operating. Rather than being criticized, the Court should be commended. Although no additional attacks occurred, one will never know how significant the Court's decision was in ensuring an end to the use of saboteurs by the Axis powers.

When the military commission did resume, the defense now offered impressive and eloquent references to democracy and their belief in how the Republic should respond, particularly when operating during a state of emergency or war. Similar to the arguments raised by the JAGs today, lawyers for the saboteurs asserted that the United States should not "want to win [the case] by throwing away everything we are fighting for, because we will have a mighty empty victory if we destroy the genius and the truth of democratic government and fair administration of the law."[30] The defense was giving everything they had, within their boundaries of ethical standards, to achieve success. From the tribunal record, and reports afterward, it does appear both defense counsels strongly believed, personally, that the tribunals were the wrong way to proceed in this case. Their noble efforts, however, were fruitless. All eight were found guilty by the tribunal. The six German nationals were sentenced to death and the two Americans sentenced to life in prison.

The trial concluded on the first day of August and within a week, on August 8, the six were put to death by electrocution. Roosevelt had achieved his desired result in lightning-like fashion. From the point of capture in June, the Order, the standing up of the commissions, the arguments before the Supreme Court, the trial by military commission, sentencing, and execution had all been achieved in less than two months. The military commissions had achieved their intended purpose. One can suspect the German government took note of the swift response by the United States.

It does seem that much of Roosevelt's motivation to use military commissions was his desire to bring these unlawful belligerents to justice rapidly and to ensure that his preferred punishment by death remained an option for the court that would hear the case(s). His interest in speed was assured by using the military justice system. The following chapters will reveal that similar thinking was employed by the Bush administration in the fall of 2001. They looked to *Quirin* as the "Roosevelt Model" to use for the unlawful belligerents in the War on al Qaeda.

1945 Military Commission

There was, however, as Lou Fisher has repeatedly reminded me, another attempt by Germany to infiltrate the United States later in the war. In this second German infiltrator case, the Nazis used a German-born citizen, Erich Gimpel, and William Colepaugh of Connecticut to enter the United States, once again by submarine, this time onto the shores of Maine. Their primary function, different from the 1942 case, was to engage in intelligence gathering—particularly on the atomic bomb project. The two were eventually apprehended in New York City. Roosevelt once again used the military commission as the forum to try these two saboteurs. However, this time he ordered the commissions for these two unlawful belligerents to be under the direction of the Department of Defense. In this case, Attorney General Biddle had nothing whatsoever to do with these cases. The trial took place not in Main Justice (the fifth floor of Department of Justice headquarters) but rather on the army base located at Governor's Island in New York Harbor. Within two months of the order from Roosevelt, the two were convicted by the commission and sentenced to hang on February 14, 1945. Roosevelt died before the executions were carried out, and President Truman commuted the death sentences to life in prison on May 8, 1945. Thus, the military commissions were used once again. Although these were different from the 1942 commissions, the validity of using military tribunals as a tool of military justice remained intact. Fisher writes that the changes employed in the 1945 cases show that the Roosevelt team had matured in their use of the commissions. He argues that certain changes distinguished the latter tribunals from the *Quirin* case and were significantly more lawful: (1) the Department of Justice was not involved at all; (2) the judge advocate, not the president, was the reviewing authority [as is standard within military justice]; (3) the president did not serve as the appointing authority; and (4) the military commissions were located at a military base instead of the nation's capital. Such changes (or maturation), he suggests, should have been the lesson learned by the Bush team and the model employed, not the *Quirin* case. He argues that the 1945 case was more lawful and applicable in ordering the tribunals against the terrorists. There may be some truth to the claim that the Roosevelt team had "learned" a few lessons from the first tribunal in the 1942 case. Then again, the context in which the decisions were made is significant. Different from *Quirin*, in 1945 there were two infiltrators, primarily here for intelligence gathering. Perhaps more violent activities were part of the plan as well, but they were here predominantly to gather intelligence on the Manhattan project. Thus, the threat was not as imminent as the terror campaign Hitler had hoped for with the 1942 saboteurs. Second, the nation was at a different point in the war; this was toward the end of the conflict in 1945 and the nation had, as Fisher argues, matured in its thinking, was probably less emotional about such activities, and had grown accustomed to the realities of being engaged in a two-front war. Different from 1942, the nation was more battle-ready and more pragmatic when dealing with such threats. So, it seems that the decision to use the 1945 commissions in a different fashion was likely more a combination of the nature of the threat and acts committed by the two conspirators, the government's maturation in dealing with such threats after four years of a two-front war, and some of Fisher's "lessons learned."

Japan: Military Commissions

At the conclusion of hostilities in the Pacific theater, General MacArthur also decided to employ military commissions against three Japanese leaders who, by direct participation or neglect, were involved in atrocities or war crimes committed during the latter part of the war. The decision to use the tribunals was fully supported by President Truman. The three were General Yamashita, General Homma, and Foreign Minister Hirota. Of the three cases, the trial of Yamashita is the best known and most cited.

Yamashita was charged with permitting brutal atrocities against civilians and prisoners of war. He was sent before a military commission and convicted by a five-member panel on December 7, 1945. Yamashita's defense counsel filed a writ of habeas corpus to the Supreme Court because the tribunal was held on U.S. occupied land in the Philippines. Chief Justice Stone, who accepted the validity of military commissions based upon the precedents established in the Nazi saboteur cases of 1942 and 1945, rejected the challenge. He wrote the majority opinion in the 6–2 case. The Supreme Court held, "An important incident to the conduct of war is the adoption of measures by the military commander, not only to repel and defeat the enemy, but to seize and subject to disciplinary measures those enemies, who, in their attempt to thwart or impede our military effort, have violated the law of war."[31] Many commentators disagreed with the use of the commissions against these three enemies for various reasons, but the decision of the court stands as precedent for the use of such military commissions. Although best known for issues dealing with command responsibility (the "should have known" doctrine), *Yamashita* stands as another case used by the Bush administration to support using military commissions against those who violate the laws of war in times of armed conflict.

The military commissions used during this era were found constitutional by the Court. *Quirin*, the 1945 infiltrator cases, and the *Yamashita* case all stand as precedents for the constitutionality of using military tribunals to try unlawful belligerents and war criminals. Although available for use during ensuing armed conflicts—the Korean War, the Vietnam War, the invasions of both Grenada and Panama, Operation Desert Storm, and the Kosovo conflict—they were rarely if ever employed and did not result in any litigation that might provide counsel, precedent, or examples for the Bush administration to consider. Additionally, during this period, from the Second World War until the twenty-first century, military justice continued to evolve and become increasingly progressive, affording more due process to courts-martial and military law in general.

The Bush team clearly relied mostly upon the *Quirin* case as the one most analogous to the current threat from al Qaeda. But the key distinction to note here is that these cases were all adjudicatory in nature.

They were not used for preventive detention, even in a declared war with an identifiable enemy. Thus, although on point, distinctions must be made in applying these cases from the Second World War to the current situation. It appears that the Bush administration, perhaps unintentionally, stretched the lawfulness of the commissions into uncomfortable regions and thereby suffered unintended consequences over the past seven years.

FOUR

The War on al Qaeda and the Military Order of November 13, 2001

THE DAYS, WEEKS, and months immediately following the attacks of 9/11 were the most tense moments I have experienced in my life. This is true, I presume, for most of my generation. It was, as many have stated, "a second Pearl Harbor."[1] In particular, New York City and Washington, D.C., both places I was in and out of routinely before and after 9/11, were extremely tense. We seemed *semper paratus*—the United States was prepared to respond to anticipated additional attacks from al Qaeda—and we expected an attack every moment of every day in that fall and early winter of 2001. Like many Americans, I felt that the attacks were personal to me. I was born in New York City and still have many relatives there, my two older brothers in particular. One was living with his wife and two children in Battery Park City and one was living in the Franciscan Friary at 31st Street. They both were impacted emotionally, spiritually, and personally by the events of that day. In fact, my brother and his wife were at the bottom of the Trade Center when the first plane hit the Twin Towers. They watched in horror as people they knew, and worked with, were killed, some of them jumping from the ninetieth floor to their deaths. Like so many Americans, they vowed never to forget that day.

New Yorkers and Washingtonians, as well as most other Americans, expected additional attacks that day and maintained that mind-set for at least the following year.

Governor Tom Ridge, the first and only director of the Office of Homeland Security within the White House (later in 2003 the first secretary of Homeland Security) reflected the mood of the country. He once remarked to me, "I would wake up every morning and thank God no one had attacked while I was asleep." The intelligence reports being reviewed daily were nothing short of frightening. Citizens routinely looked into the sky with grave concern when hearing an airplane roar overhead or drove nervously by a power plant in Connecticut or over the Golden Gate Bridge. Tourists walked eerily by the Empire State Building in Manhattan or the Sears Tower in Chicago, or anywhere near government buildings in D.C.—particularly the Capitol and the White House. Speculation ran wild about what form the next attack would take, what building, city, or infrastructure the attackers would next target. Fears of attacks were further fueled by reports of anthrax being sent by mail to key members of Congress and to some high-profile news reporters, and even ordinary citizens in places like the Bronx and the small town of Oxford, Connecticut.[2] We all feared the next attack. There was the real sense the "Sleeping Giant" was alert once again responding to the first attack on the United States since the Second World War and the first successful attack on the continental United States since the War of 1812. Flags were seen everywhere, from lapel pins to houses, to cars, even to overpasses on the highways. Americans were determined to not let the "barbarians" who attacked us have yet another opportunity. The nation was cautious and on edge but seemed prepared to fight for what was referred to as the American way of life.[3] And America seemed prepared to tackle this new threat of the twenty-first century—this new armed conflict brought upon us by al Qaeda. President George W. Bush, the forty-third president of the United States, up until then (he had only been in office under eight months) appearing to be administering an otherwise average presidency, was now hailed as "our leader" and the right man for the job, "the right man in the right place at the right point of history."[4] From interviews and discussions I have had with both policy makers and their staffs, I learned that the United States was under constant threat of attack that could produce unimaginable results during this time frame. The chatter being picked up by government intelligence showed al Qaeda in full operational mode on multiple levels and actively undertaking numerous plots against the United States and its interests. It seemed as though the attacks of 9/11 triggered a new cycle of unprecedented violence and terrorism, and no one knew what was next.

It is in this background and mind-set that the president tasked lawyers from the White House, Department of Justice, and Department of Defense to come up with a framework best suited to deal with the detainees who would inevitably be captured in our unexpected war with the nonstate actor—al Qaeda.

Leaders from within the administration were immediately summoned to collaborate and meet to determine the most suitable forum for processing the detainees. The group reviewed the available options: tribunals, courts-martial, the federal court system, Nuremberg-type war tribunals, and others. A few days after the attacks, William Barr, former attorney general under the George H. W. Bush administration, called Timothy Flanigan, then deputy White House counsel, with his thoughts. He strongly recommended the use of the military commissions. Barr had first suggested the use of these types of tribunals for international terrorists a decade earlier to prosecute the suspects in the bombing of Pan Am Flight 103 over Lockerbie, Scotland.[5] Barr referred to the *Quirin* case as "most apt precedent." Flanigan thought it was a "great idea."[6] Both Barr and Flanagan believed the military commissions would provide greater flexibility than the civilian court system. David Addington, the ever influential aide (then counsel) to Vice President Cheney, completely agreed. Beyond the legal benefits, they believed there was a political advantage to be gained by employing the tribunals as well. "From a political stand point, it communicated the message that we were at war, that this was not going to be business as usual."[7] Apparently, White House Counsel Alberto Gonzales agreed as well as did Attorney General John Ashcroft. Flanigan has recalled that no one "was out being cowboys or creating a radical new legal regime. What they wanted to do was to use existing legal models to assist in the process of saving lives, to get information. And the war on terror is all about information."[8] Brad Berenson, then a White House lawyer, noted, "The watchword became forward leaning. We wanted to be aggressive. We want to take risks."[9]

The key players agreed that the way ahead was to use the military commissions modeled after those President Roosevelt had employed in the Second World War; after all, they had been found to be lawful and constitutional by a unanimous Supreme Court in 1942. While some members of the White House administration who were originally part of the interagency group quietly expressed concern about the legality of applying this model to international terrorists, their concerns were apparently rejected either by design or neglect. Thus, the key inner circle for the decisions being made were Gonzales, Addington, Flanigan, Department of Defense General Counsel William "Jim" Haynes, Ashcroft, Deputy Attorney General Larry Thompson, and a young, deputy assistant attorney general named John Yoo. Of note, only Addington and Haynes had experience within the Department of Defense (DoD) or the CIA, or for that matter any background in national security law. Once the decision was made to use the tribunals, apparently Flanigan and Addington drafted the actual order.[10]

Professor John Yoo, a tenured law professor at Berkeley Law School (Boalt Hall), was appointed deputy to the Office of Legal Counsel at the Department of Justice in the summer of 2001. He had been at Boalt Hall since 1993 and had received tenure in 1999. Yoo was held in high regard by the right wing in America for his legal acumen and his theories on executive power. As a young academic beginning a two-year journey as a government lawyer, he could never have anticipated the coming controversy. I am certain that there are many times he now wishes he had passed on this opportunity to serve his government.

A graduate of Harvard University and Yale Law School, Yoo had previously served as chief counsel to the Senate Judiciary Committee during the Clinton presidency and was pleased to serve again in a government position. Of all the "key players" who advised the president on the law of war issues within the Bush administration, he is the only one who has stood by his opinions. Ironically, his outspoken defense of this advice in the ensuing years since he left government service has often led to his own detriment. With the exception of David Addington, the other actors, to a large degree, have either been silent or have retreated from their decisions and issued legal opinions. Yoo's outspokenness and fidelity to his beliefs have indeed made him a lightning rod for criticisms of the Bush administration on these particular issues.

In the fall of 2001, the issue confronting John Yoo, his immediate boss Jay Bybee (now a judge on the Ninth Circuit Court of Appeals), Attorney General Ashcroft, Judge Gonzales, David Addington, and Jim Haynes was similar to what Attorney General Biddle and Army General Cramer faced in the *Quirin* case—simply, what available system is best suited for detention and adjudication of the captured al Qaeda fighters? Vice President Cheney argued strongly that the military commissions were the right venue. He argued that anyone apprehended in connection with an attack was an unlawful combatant and as such does "not deserve to be treated as a prisoner of war."[11] As a constitutional law professor, Yoo was aware of the precedent in *Quirin* and of the historical use of commissions in time of war. All the lawyers involved in the decision making believed the conflict against al Qaeda to be a war, although a new type of war, and that a traditional law enforcement response to a war would be ineffectual. In fact, most thought a law enforcement response was a danger for the nation.[12] The group, known as the "war council,"[13] believed that using the Article III courts would result in acquittals, light penalties, numerous delays, and the release of important and classified information to defendants and defense attorneys. The imminent military operations against al Qaeda within Afghanistan also argued in favor of the use of some type of military tribunal. The use of a law enforcement approach employed against international terrorism during the previous decade seemed, to all of Bush's team, to have proven a manifest failure. Al Qaeda had declared war upon the United States; the U.S. Congress had just enacted the Authorization for the Use of Military Force (AUMF) in late September 2001;[14] and we were a nation at war. Thus, consensus was quickly achieved among the group. They agreed a law of war regime must be adopted by the Bush administration.

Professor Yoo has written that when he (and others in the Justice Department) reviewed the military order drafted by Flanigan and Addington during the standard vetting process,

> we did not think it ran afoul of the Constitution. In fact, we read it just like the Order issued by Franklin Roosevelt in 1942, the constitutionality of which the Supreme Court had upheld in *Ex Parte Quirin*. Military commissions seemed a good choice for bringing terrorists to justice. Trial in open federal court posed obvious national security and secrecy issues. International war crime tribunals for the former Yugoslavia and Rwanda had been slow, costly, and in Slobadan Milosovic's case, susceptible to being used as a platform for grandstanding by the accused. Even with full international sanction, these tribunals have been widely criticized on a number of grounds. Meanwhile military commissions to try enemy combatants enjoyed a long pedigree in American history.[15]

Ironically, Professor Yoo has mentioned to me on several occasions over the years that he never anticipated that he would be advising on military commissions or other law of war analysis when he accepted his presidential appointment at the Office of Legal Counsel (OLC). As of late September 2001, whether he wanted to or not, he was now knee deep in it.

The administration lawyers and staff looked at the Constitution, history, statutes, and case law when determining the appropriate forum in which to try alleged al Qaeda members. As previously stated, *Ex Parte Quirin* seemed on point. The similarities are quite evident, particularly when viewed through the lens of the mind-set of America weeks after the attack. The administration understood the nation to be at war with an unfamiliar enemy: they did not wear uniforms, represented no singular nation-state, and flouted the laws of war as doctrine.[16] Al Qaeda's goal was, and remains so today, at best to destroy Western civilization and establish a worldwide caliphate, or at the least to disrupt the power structure in the Middle East, expel all Western influence from Muslim nations, and destroy Israel. No one inside or outside the administration will deny these facts. The real issue became, as was the case in *Quirin*, whether to use the federal courts or create a tribunal to try the alleged unlawful combatants. On this decision, though the administration was of one mind, the nation itself was split. Great debates ensued between academics, human rights advocates, and media commentators.[17] For example, Ruth Wedgewood (then a Yale Law School professor) and Kenneth Roth, the director of Human Rights Watch, engaged in several written exchanges on whether this was a war or a law enforcement action.[18] The president, feeling pressure to act, was motivated to ensure that other al Qaeda terrorists were deterred from similar attacks in the future. He also wanted to bring justice to those who committed the atrocious acts upon civilians in the Twin Towers and the military in the Pentagon. As some White House aides later recalled, "All of a sudden, the curtain was lifted on this incredibly frightening world. You were spending every day looking at the dossiers of the world's leading terrorists. There was a palpable sense of threat."[19] In many ways, President Bush's analysis and desires closely resembled Roosevelt's in 1942. President Bush saw tribunals as the best way for rapid adjudication of the alleged crimes being committed by the al Qaeda fighters. He understood military justice to be tough, but extremely fair.[20] Through various public statements Bush made it clear the nation was at war and thus he wanted the Department of Defense to oversee the implementation of the tribunals for what the White House was now labeling "enemy combatants."[21] In support of the view that we were at war, recall that the president had received broad authority, arguably indistinguishable from a declaration of war, in Congress's enactment of the Authorization for the Use of Military Force.[22] The president clearly believed he had the requisite authority to unilaterally use the military commissions.

Although Bush and his team relied heavily upon the methodology, words, thoughts, and actions of Roosevelt, there were marked differences between the two decisions to create military tribunals. In *Ex Parte Quirin*, there were eight identifiable suspects who had been captured. There was no tribunal established in perpetuity by Roosevelt's Order to address future cases—it was for the eight captured German saboteurs only. Expecting many detainees now and in the future, President Bush broadened the scope of his Order to "all those members of al Qaeda or associated with al Qaeda." This creation of "associational status" led to concerns almost immediately from academics and civil rights organizations.[23] Second, the current enemies or those subject to military commission under the Bush plan were now from nations all over the world. In fact, no members of al Qaeda represent any nation-state but rather are nonstate actors representing an ideology. But this broad sweep, "all those members of al Qaeda or associated with al Qaeda," touched upon the sovereignty and citizens of numerous nation-states and has caused problems—and continues to—in the implementation of the Bush Order. For Roosevelt, the "saboteurs" were all acting on behalf of Germany—a nation-state the United States was clearly at war with. The al Qaeda detainees, in contrast, hail from and were even citizens of various nation-states, many friendly to the United States. Third, the Order did not take into account the vast liberalization that military justice had undergone since 1942 and the Roosevelt Order. The growth in the desire to "civilianize" military justice had actually been most pronounced during the period following the conclusion of the Second World War. In fact, the Uniform Code of Military Justice (UCMJ), enacted in 1950, codified all of the laws governing the armed services.[24] So, although *Quirin* was on point in many respects, overreliance on this case revealed a lack of true understanding of the current state of military affairs as well as the revolution that had taken place in military justice in the almost sixty years since the Supreme Court had decided the case. Military justice progressed after the Second World War and again after the Korean War; perhaps its greatest liberalization occurred during the Vietnam War. The military justice system of the latter twentieth century had much greater due process, emphasis on rights, and increasing equivalency with the civilian justice system than had existed in Roosevelt's time. Military judges were now required to hear courts-martial, the military rules of evidence now mirrored the federal rules of evidence, and the operational commanders were becoming more aware of the morale benefits to a command by leaders who clearly emphasized fairness when conducting military proceedings. Simply, the twenty-first-century military justice system was both in statute and culture quite different from the military justice used and implemented by Roosevelt's team. The Bush administration legal team never seemed to appreciate these changes and in many ways was simply unaware of the minor revolutions that had occurred in military jurisprudence since the 1940s.

Still, the administration decisions made in late 2001 must necessarily be critiqued and balanced by the existing state of affairs and the mind-set in the immediate post-9/11 environment. As David Addington asserted in congressional testimony in June 2008, "Smoke was still rising...over 3000 Americans who were just killed."[25] Nonetheless, the three major distinctions listed above (among others) led to legitimate criticisms of the Order of 2001 and eventually initiated the process of adjusting, updating, and challenging the Order. Academics, human rights groups, and civil libertarians used these inconsistencies within the Order to open public debate on the decision to use military tribunals. They attacked tribunals as being outdated, unconstitutional, and inappropriate for adjudicating the alleged war crimes by the unique al Qaeda fighter, who had not been seen before on the world stage.[26]

Criticisms

Many of the criticisms from November 2001 onward revolved around (and continue to this day—see *Hamdan v. Rumsfeld* and *Boumediene v. Bush* cases) whether the nation was actually at war with al Qaeda or simply fighting an international criminal entity. How one viewed the struggle with al Qaeda, whether as a war or a law enforcement action, is foundational to the framework for any adjudicatory scheme advocated or implemented. These two paradigms remain in place today. In fact, they form the policy divide over Guantanamo Bay and, as will be discussed in detail in later chapters, continue to divide the body politic.

The director of Human Rights Watch and respected advocate, Ken Roth, argued in 2002 that the al Qaeda were transnational criminals and, as such, should be detained and tried under a criminal justice regime.[27] Others agreed as well that to use "tribunals" in the twenty-first century was actually taking a step backward as they had become the types of military trials in periods of national emergency that the U.S. State Department routinely declares (and annually reports on) as violations of human rights.[28] Congress quickly began to take note of these concerns.

Senator Patrick Leahy of Vermont, then ranking member of the Judiciary Committee, as well as Senator Ted Kennedy of the Armed Services Committee, both complained about the lack of congressional input being sought by the president. They believed issues such as the creation of tribunals constitutionally required the Congress to, at the minimum, consent to their use (and to implementation of orders and regulations that would deal with the governance of the armed forces) by the Department of Defense. The senators were angry at the lack of any consultation by the White House. The White House believed the inherent power contained within the executive branch authorized the creation of these tribunals and that the president was merely acting as commander in chief during armed conflict.[29] They strongly believed the Congress had already provided any necessary input or statutory authority—the Congress had passed the AUMF, which gave the president sweeping powers to "fight" al Qaeda and international terrorism and bring such "terrorists" to justice.[30] The administration understood such broad statutory authority further supported their assertions that the president had the authorization from Congress (if even tacitly) to conduct military commissions. Congress could always have changed or limited these sweeping powers. For reasons, presumably political (not wanting to seem weak on terror), they have chosen not to alter the authorization at all since its enactment. Similarly, the Bush administration could have sought specific guidance, input, and legislation for the commissions from Congress as they did with the AUMF and the PATRIOT ACT. The administration felt this was not necessary, as they believed the decision to employ tribunals was part of the function of the executive branch in wartime and any legislative authorization that might have been deemed necessary was already covered by the passage of the AUMF.[31] And so they opted not to seek further congressional authorization. Liberal Democrats in the Senate were furious and began angrily complaining about an overreaching executive branch. They felt strongly that the president was avoiding them in order enhance the strength of the executive branch.[32]

By December of 2001, commentators within the media from all sides of the political spectrum began raising concerns about the use of military commissions: Thomas Friedman,[33] William Safire,[34] and even former conservative Republican congressman Bob Barr (later the Libertarian Party candidate for president of the United States)[35] expressed serious concerns about the commissions in opinion pieces and other reports. Public opinion still remained on the side of the president with a majority of the nation supporting use of the commissions, but in hindsight it seems the seeds of doubt had been planted in late 2001 and early 2002. While U.S. troops were engaged in active combat operations in Afghanistan against al Qaeda (and capturing thousands of alleged al Qaeda fighters), many on the left openly questioned what they would characterize as the president's rushed decision to adopt military commissions.

The *New York Times* angrily declared, "In his effort to defend America from terrorists, Mr. Bush is eroding the very values and principles he seeks to protect, including the Rule of Law."[36] Learned and well-respected constitutional scholars Laurence Tribe and Neal Katyal published a law review piece declaring that the tribunals were unconstitutional without an explicit declaration of war or a new authorizing statute.[37] In hindsight, these assertions in late 2001 and early 2002 seem to be an overreaction. The hyperbole seems unnecessary and created the great divisions between the two existing paradigms today. Professor Katyal's assertion that a declaration of war was required appears contrary to history and precedent, never mind the Constitution. There have been only five wars in U.S. history with a formal declaration of war from the Congress: the War of 1812, the Mexican War, the War of 1898, the First World War, and the Second World War. Also, the Supreme Court has made clear since 1800 and 1801 that Congress, under the Constitution, can either declare war or authorize it. Besides which, the reality is that the AUMF is arguably indistinguishable in effect from a formal declaration of war. Regardless of the merits or demerits of such critiques, the "great debate" of the new century began and now was quickly becoming embedded in U.S. political culture. The lines had been drawn. The administration was caught off guard at both the substance and the tone of the criticism. They did listen, however, and began to "re-tool" the original order to initiate the process of the military tribunal by morphing, adapting, and adjusting to the realities of military justice and warfare in the twenty-first century. Of crucial note, while the debates raged, the numbers of captured al Qaeda fighters significantly increased.

The Order

Based upon the practice of commanders throughout military history, the powers inherent in the executive branch embodied in Article II of the U.S. Constitution, as enhanced by the Authorization to Use

Military Force (AUMF) enacted by Congress, and his staff's reading of the UCMJ, President Bush issued his Order creating military commissions on November 13, 2001.[38] I was in Washington at the time the Order was issued and to say the least, the city was abuzz. While at the White House for meetings in the days that followed (and in talking to some of those deeply involved in the decision making at the time), I felt a sense of urgency permeating the atmosphere. The *Washington Post* that day carried the headline, "Military May Try Terrorism Cases: Bush Cites Emergency."[39] The era of the military commissions and the use of Guantanamo Bay had formally begun.

Initially, the Order can be read as somewhat analogous to Roosevelt's in its drafting. Of import, this Order, like Roosevelt's, was drafted, and reviewed, as David Addington alluded, during a period when intelligence strongly suggested that additional, massive attacks were imminent. This should not excuse decisions made, justify any flawed legal analysis, or excuse any lack of consultation with the proper members of the government for input, but it does require that we approach the analysis of the period from a reasonable perspective.

Many of the words and prose in both orders are roughly the same. The Bush Order, however, provided for the military commission to have broad jurisdiction over al Qaeda and its affiliates, or other enemy combatants. It states, in part:

Detention, Treatment, and Trial of Certain Non-Citizens in the War Against Terrorism

By the authority vested in me as President and as Commander in Chief of the Armed Forces of the United States by the Constitution and the laws of the United States of America, including the Authorization for Use of Military Force Joint Resolution (Public Law 107–40, 115 Stat. 224) and sections 821 and 836 of title 10, United States Code, it is hereby ordered as follows:

Section 1. Findings.

(a) *International terrorists, including members of al Qaida*, have carried out attacks on United States diplomatic and military personnel and facilities abroad and on citizens and property within the United States on a scale that has created a state of armed conflict that requires the use of the United States Armed Forces.

(b) In light of grave acts of terrorism and threats of terrorism, including the terrorist attacks on September 11, 2001, on the headquarters of the United States Department of Defense in the national capital region, on the World Trade Center in New York, and on civilian aircraft such as in Pennsylvania, I proclaimed a national emergency on September 14, 2001 (Proc. 7463, Declaration of National Emergency by Reason of Certain Terrorist Attacks).

(c) Individuals acting alone and in concert involved in international terrorism possess both the capability and the intention to undertake further terrorist attacks against the United States that, if not detected and prevented, will cause mass deaths, mass injuries, and massive destruction of property, and may place at risk the continuity of the operations of the United States Government.

(d) The ability of the United States to protect the United States and its citizens, and to help its allies and other cooperating nations protect their nations and their citizens, from such further terrorist attacks depends in significant part upon using the United States Armed Forces to identify terrorists and those who support them, to disrupt their activities, and to eliminate their ability to conduct or support such attacks.

(e) To protect the United States and its citizens, and for the effective conduct of military operations and prevention of terrorist attacks, it is necessary for individuals subject to this order pursuant to section 2 hereof to be detained, and, when tried, to be tried for violations of the laws of war and other applicable laws by military tribunals.

(f) Given the danger to the safety of the United States and the nature of international terrorism, and to the extent provided by and under this order, I find consistent with section 836 of title 10, United States Code, that it is not practicable to apply in military commissions under this order the principles of law and the rules of evidence generally recognized in the trial of criminal cases in the United States district courts.

(g) Having fully considered the magnitude of the potential deaths, injuries, and property destruction that would result from potential acts of terrorism against the United States, and the probability that such acts will occur, I have determined that an extraordinary emergency exists for national defense purposes, that this emergency constitutes an urgent and compelling government interest, and that issuance of this order is necessary to meet the emergency.

Section 2. Definition and Policy.

(a) The term "individual subject to this order" shall mean any individual who is not a United States citizen with respect to whom I determine from time to time in writing that:

(1) there is reason to believe that such individual, at the relevant times,

(i) *is or was a member of the organization known as al Qaida;*

(ii) has engaged in, *aided or abettor conspired* to commit, acts of international terrorism, or acts in preparation therefore, that have caused, *threaten to cause, or have as their aim to cause*, injury to or adverse effects on the United States, its citizens, national security, foreign policy, or economy; or

(iii) has knowingly *harbored one or more individuals* described in subparagraphs (i) or (ii) of subsection 2(a)(1) of this order; and (emphasis added)

(2) it is in the interest of the United States that such individual be subject to this order.

(b) It is the policy of the United States that the Secretary of Defense shall take all necessary measures to ensure that any individual subject to this order is detained in accordance with section 3, and, if the individual is to be tried, that such individual is tried only in accordance with section 4.

(c) It is further the policy of the United States that any individual subject to this order who is not already under the control of the Secretary of Defense but who is under the control of any other officer or agent of the United States or any State shall, upon delivery of a copy of such written determination to such officer or agent, forthwith be placed under the control of the Secretary of Defense.[40]

The Order had been quickly issued. Although he did not draft this nearly as quickly as Roosevelt's Order, the president had made his decision to use military commissions within a little over two months from the time of the attacks on the homeland. The italicized text above reveals the broad language used for those who would be subject to a military commission. Critics, upon reading the actual Order, referred to the military tribunals as "kangaroo courts." Many derided the comparisons between Roosevelt and Bush as ludicrous.[41] The Bush administration was caught completely off guard. Many personnel in key positions within the administration had no background in warfare, the military, or the laws of armed conflict. In retrospect, they likely did not know how to respond to many of the criticisms. Some made allegations—and many still believe today—that the attorney general at the time did not fully understand the UCMJ or the difference between courts-martial and a military commission. Irrespective of the accuracy of such assertions, these were indeed novel legal issues to many in the Justice Department, the White House counsel's office, and even the National Security Council Staff.[42] Beyond a lack of real expertise, the 9/11 Commission later noted, many within the administration (or the previous Clinton administration) had never expected al Qaeda to have the means to carry out an attack of the magnitude of the attacks in New York City and Washington, D.C.[43] The Bush White House, just barely getting up to full staffing at this point (again having been in office only a little over eight months), did not have personnel placed with experience or knowledge in this area of policy and law. For example, the national security advisor, Condoleezza Rice, was a Soviet/Russian expert. Others appointed did not have expertise in the niche area of terrorism and the law of war. Instead of proactively anticipating and responding to these allegations and often unfair criticisms of the Order, they bunkered down to support the new policy and became almost reflexively defensive. They did not, or were unable, to launch a public information campaign on the rich history of military commissions and the validity of using such tribunals as a part of U.S. military jurisprudence. Rather, they began to disregard the criticism, some of which was clearly valid. Criticisms of the Order or of administration staff were seen as "hampering our national security" and critics were tacitly characterized as unpatriotic.[44] Attorney General Ashcroft, before a congressional committee in early December 2001, testified that "charges of kangaroo courts and shredding the Constitution give new meaning to the term the 'fog of war.'" He went further in response to criticisms of the commissions and the need for congressional oversight by saying that the critics "scare peace-loving people with phantoms of lost liberty.... your tactics only aid terrorists... erode our national unity and diminish our resolve."[45] The hyperbole generated on the far left that the president was acting like a "king" and unconstitutionally usurping powers vested in Congress now were set against the administration supporters casting doubt on the patriotism of those who disagreed with them.[46] This was the beginning of the downfall of the commissions. Right or wrong, the perception became the reality: the Bush administration was acting unilaterally. The legal, academic, and partisan attacks escalated throughout 2002 and into

2003. The administration, with no cases going to trial as of yet, had to react and adopt some of the recommendations being floated. The Department of Defense began to restrict its earlier broad guidelines for the tribunals. Although some maturation occurred, major sticking points remained between many in Congress and the administration. Some of the points of contention included the constitutionality of using commissions, the powers of the executive during war, and the amount of due process being accorded the detainees. The Bush team remained in their defensive and reactionary mode. They never stayed ahead of the criticisms, for example, offering new ways to move the trials forward. They simply were reacting to mounting concern over the tribunals and the location of the detention center at Guantanamo Bay, Cuba.

In addition to concerns about the specific makeup of the tribunals, Congress was increasingly irate at the administration's unilateral decision to create them. Although such tribunals, as discussed earlier, have been a creature of commanders in the field as well as the executive branch, Congress asserted that in the twenty-first century such actions demanded consultation with Congress—regardless of how tribunals had been executed in the past.[47] Again, the administration felt statutorily empowered by the broad legislation embodied in the AUMF. In the administration's view, the AUMF had been Congress's input and authorization and the tribunals were simply part of the functions of the commander in chief during wartime. The president remained firm that there was no time (nor need) in November for any further consultations and that he, as commander in chief, controlled the armed forces. Ironically, one of President Bush's primary motivations to use tribunals was the rapidity of military justice. There was a sense within the administration team's "War Council" that the civilian courts would take too long and be bogged down in litigation. Roosevelt's tribunal had been completed, from start to finish, in less than two months. President Bush had expected the Department of Defense to move as rapidly for him. But, as is well known now, such sagacity in executing his Order was misplaced naïveté.

By the spring of 2002, the Department of Defense unveiled its draft Military Orders of the military commissions.[48] The administration, in response to now numerous congressional hearings and media attacks on the existing process, seemed to be understanding that some changes in their original order had to occur. One of the biggest changes, in stark contrast to Roosevelt's order and Bush's of 2001, was to establish rules of evidence and procedure. In *Quirin*, no such specificity was ordered. The Department of Defense, including senior judge advocates of all the armed forces, worked hard to create a fair, balanced procedure affording due process while still remaining conscious of the need to promote national security.

Military Order No. 1 issued by the DoD, implementing the 2001 Bush Order, witnessed an incredible level of scrutiny from many lawyers as well as the American Bar Association itself. These critics attacked the rules promulgated. Many questioned various aspects of the military commissions and this first order setting up the commissions: the military court itself, including the membership of the court (judges, members, counsel); whether the Global War on Terror even was a war; about the definition and use of the term "enemy combatant" and where it had originated in military law; the inclusion of those who could be tried merely by association with al Qaeda; the elements of the crimes listed themselves; and concerns about the jurisdictional authority over citizens of nations with whom we were not at "war." The legitimacy of the tribunals was questioned by leading thinkers such as Cass Sunstein, Lou Fisher, Neal Katyal, Harold Koh, and others.[49] Many based their concerns on the administration's overreliance on *Quirin* decided over fifty years earlier. They felt military justice had become increasingly progressive since that decision, and that the specific facts of *Quirin* did not apply to a "war on terror." As mentioned earlier, these criticisms are not without merit. Defenders of the use of military commissions clearly had an uphill battle. Defending their use became increasingly difficult as not a single case had been forwarded for prosecution. Nearly 800 detainees were now in Guantanamo Bay, some of whom had been there since the early stages of Operation Enduring Freedom (OEF). They were being interrogated and held without charges, and the sense of "justice" sought by the president was quickly vanishing. I recall thinking during this period that it was critical for the United States to try the detainees as quickly as possible under an existing military tribunal format. The key was to try cases and see how, and if, the system could work. Keeping detainees sitting on an island without charges or trial was beginning to erode both national and international support for U.S. efforts in fighting terrorism. Regardless, I too was caught off guard at the passionate, almost visceral, reactions of some to the military commissions.

By March of 2003, the Department of Defense had reworked the original drafts and promulgated Military Orders 1–8 of the establishment of the tribunals. These were written under the direction of

Department of Defense General Counsel Jim Haynes, Colonel Bill Litzau of the U.S. Marine Corps, and noted military historian and JAG Colonel Fred Borch. Again, however, these were promulgated without formal input from the Congress. The DoD was acting, they believed, in accord with the constitutional prerogatives of the commander in chief and historical precedent. As Haynes testified, "The President is Commander-in-Chief, we are at war and he has the authority to create these and implement them as he deems fit."[50] Democratic senators such as Kennedy, Leahy, and Feingold were incensed.[51]

In the summer of 2003, I was back in Washington after the conclusion of the academic year, during which I served as a Visiting Fellow at the Heritage Foundation. It was fascinating to work under the guidance of one of the best-known legal minds of the 1980s, Edwin Meese III. He instinctively was in support of the commissions, but he asked me to do some research for him and actually "convince" him that they were an appropriate tool in the War on al Qaeda. Specifically, Meese asked for a paper detailing both the historical background and the legal justifications for ordering a military commission. A former counselor to the president as well as the attorney general of the United States (two cabinet posts in the two terms of the Reagan presidency), he retains enormous influence within the conservative legal community. Anyone who gets to know him is immediately struck by his sense of decency.

In doing my research for Attorney General Meese, I continued to strongly believe that the use of military commissions was, in fact, lawful. There was precedent since the time of Washington; we were at war; the administration was essentially following the guidelines of Roosevelt and the Supreme Court precedent from the *Quirin* case; the Uniform Code of Military Justice authorizes their use in at least two articles; and perhaps most important to me was that once put in place and left alone to do its work, the military justice system could help ensure rapid adjudication of the cases.

In my idealistic (and perhaps naïve) manner, it seemed to me that the real key in using military commissions was their rapidity and flexibility. I remain convinced that once permitted to start, the commissions would, indeed, rapidly adjudicate the cases of the detainees. The use had never, and was never intended, to be part of a means toward indefinite detention. Our military justice system is more than fair enough to afford procedural protection while still ensuring that justice is served. The commissions employed in the past were always used to ensure rapid justice in adjudicating war crimes. Historically, that has always been the commissions' advantage. With Orders now promulgated and members appointed to serve on the commission, rumors circled that the first commissions would begin that July or August of 2003.[52] In my notes and recommendations to Meese I noted the need to try the detainees as quickly as possible in order to ensure the integrity of the process now in place. As a matter of policy, I was also concerned that the longer the delays continued in actually trying the cases, the more defensive the administration would become and the more likely the validity of the commissions would become suspect—both domestically and to our international partners. Speed was of the essence. I was fearful that if trials did not occur, the commissions, as Professor Martin Flaherty predicted, would end up in the ash heap of history.[53] At this point, however, I was still naïvely confident the cases would move forward by the end of the summer. That was July 2003.

Later that summer I was afforded an opportunity to study at Harvard for a few weeks during a seminar focused on the military commissions and their "validity" from an international law perspective. Various scholars, International Committee of the Red Cross (ICRC) representatives, and practitioners met in Cambridge to discuss these issues. While there, I had the chance to meet with two of the earliest JAGs assigned as defense counsel to the detainees, Lieutenant Commander Charlie Swift and Lieutenant Commander Phil Sundell. We disagreed, in sometimes heated exchanges, over the military commissions. They literally had time on their hands. Notwithstanding the delays being afforded to the detainees (e.g., being charged and tried), as advocates for their clients, they were elated at the prospect of still more time delay. They told me this had given them great opportunities to study, research, and prepare a strong defense for their clients as well as sharpen their arguments against the use of military commissions. Their comments stuck in my head, but at the time I truly did not realize how astute their sentiments were or how relevant their assertions would later prove. These two outstanding naval officers convinced me that the detainees were receiving more than just simple advocacy—they truly had zealous advocates representing their interests. Similar to Colonels Dovall and Royall in *Quirin*, they were in a tough spot as active duty officers defending the detainees but more than superbly fulfilled the requirements of this unique military assignment during a time of armed conflict.

The assigned defense counsel, as well as many civilian lawyers and advocacy groups, were by now attacking the commissions and their location at Guantanamo Bay in myriad ways and from all angles. To them, the commissions were invalid as matters of international law, human rights law, and U.S. constitutional law as well as simply being bad policy while fighting an international "war." Through the direct efforts of people such as Deb Pearlstein of Human Rights First (now at Princeton), international lawyer and president of the New York City Bar Association International Law Section Scott Horton, Ken Roth of Human Rights Watch, representatives from the Center for Constitutional Rights, the various JAG defense attorneys, and many other advocates, cases were making their way through the civilian court system challenging the detention of the detainees and the procedures being used to keep detainees at Guantanamo without charges. More often than not by now, civil and human rights groups were challenging the military commissions system altogether. Two cases in particular made it to the Supreme Court in 2004: *Rasul* and *Hamdi*.[54] While these cases were being reviewed by civilian courts, they slowed down the efforts of the Department of Defense in trying the cases by military commission. The ambiguities and lack of specificity relating to the composition and procedures of the military commissions did open the door for many of these challenges. The media covered these cases in great detail and gave the impression the commissions were, in fact, simply "courts of convenience" concocted by administration lawyers and offering little to no process for the accused.[55] This coverage led to great confusion among the citizenry as to who the accused actually were, why they were being detained at Guantanamo, and why the administration chose to use commissions at all. Additionally, the courts were now involved in a process that had previously been viewed as the province of the executive branch, or arguably at least the two political branches. Although in the *Hamdi* case, the plurality accepted that this was an armed conflict and therefore the detainees could be held until the end of hostilities,[56] the Court's decision was still critical of and uncomfortable with the detention policies of the administration. Concern expressed in *Rasul*, and to a lesser extent in *Hamdi* (and some holdings in the lower courts), still gave great support and momentum to many of the critics' allegations. Also, the idea of holding detainees until the end of hostilities in a "war on terror" seemed contrary to the principles of American justice. Questions from the court decisions emerged: What was a war on terror and when would it end? At the end of the ideology? How does one declare an end to "terror?" Was this possible? If it was not, then how long could these detainees be held at Guantanamo Bay? Congress, particularly the minority Democratic Party members, still believed they should be involved in this process and that it could not be simply left to the executive. Things were beginning to spin out of control.

Guantanamo

Beyond the criticisms emerging from within our own domestic legal circles (as well as an increase in U.S. citizen concerns about the commissions both as constructed in 2001 and as modified in 2003), the international community was highly suspect and cynical over this U.S. form of "military justice" being used to handle the detainees.[57] Many nongovernmental organizations (NGOs) and international leaders within and outside the legal academy aggressively questioned why the detainees were being held at Guantanamo. The ICRC, Amnesty International, British governmental leaders, and others began wondering when "hostilities would cease" and therefore, how long detainees would be required to stay at the camp in Cuba. During this time, allegations of torture began to make headlines through the world. Bush responded by simply stating, "We do not torture."[58] Numerous nations were being impacted since the detainees were of many different nationalities. Guantanamo now became a domestic political issue in other nations such as Great Britain and Australia. Many questioned interrogation practices and how the U.S. defined torture. Through the successful efforts of the NGOs and lawyers representing the detainees, public sympathy began to shift toward the al Qaeda (and Taliban) detainees. The more distant the memories of the brutal, vicious attacks of 9/11 became, the more sympathy and concern became centered on the al Qaeda and Taliban members captured and held in Guantanamo. By 2005, many had been at the facility since 2002. Virtually all were being held without charges and none had gone to trial. Guantanamo came to be seen as simply a place to keep the detainees without any recourse to a court of law.[59]

Once opponents of the military commissions and Guantanamo criticized the administration for an attempt to consolidate unprecedented power in the executive branch, it also became possible to plausibly attack even the categorization of the Guantanamo detainees as so-called enemy combatants. The argument ran thus: (1) The president acted unilaterally (without contemporaneous, explicit input or authority from Congress) in establishing military commissions and the Guantanamo detention center. (2) We should therefore be suspicious of other exercises of executive power, particularly as they pertain to the

"War on Terrorism." (3) The president's categorization of the individuals at Guantanamo as "enemy combatants" is in and of itself suspect. (4) Even if we concede that enemy combatants can be detained until the end of hostilities, we cannot be assured that everyone detained at Guantanamo is an "enemy combatant." (5) The process for determining and reviewing who is and who is not an "enemy combatant" and who therefore may be detained cannot be wholly left to the executive branch of government.

The administration wanted to keep the detainees at Guantanamo for three key reasons. First, it wanted to remove some of the detainees from the field of battle to a remote location. Second, the administration wanted to ensure that the al Qaeda fighters did not come to the United States where many constitutional rights would likely attach. The third reason was to keep them from going back to the field of battle by keeping them detained. Obviously, the overarching reason for detention (regardless of location), as has been well documented elsewhere, was to conduct interrogations of the detainees to gain information that could help to prevent another attack.

Although the Bush administration had clearly stated the detainees were not POWs and were not entitled to Geneva Convention protections, the administration still sought to detain the al Qaeda fighters similar to the way prisoners of war would be treated—kept in a camp until the end of hostilities.[60] However, they miscalculated or confused these principles—those detained clearly were not fighters entitled to POW status but they also were not standard warriors. Confusion emerged; did the Geneva Conventions apply or only when it appeared to suit the administration's needs?[61] This dilemma highlighted the confusion of trying to strictly apply the law of war to this new type of warrior. In essence, every al Qaeda fighter was an unlawful belligerent and thus, once captured, held the status of detainee. As a detainee, and not a POW, the individual would not be afforded the gold standard of treatment, but the administration still wanted to assert the same "detaining until the cessation of hostilities" standard ordinarily afforded by the Geneva Conventions.[62] This mixing of non-Geneva standards and Geneva standards led to confusion, ambiguity as to the status of the detainees, and difficulty in determining what rights were triggered by this legal analysis. Such confusion in application of standards unnecessarily exacerbated skepticism of the administration's real intentions.

In keeping the detainees on the island of Guantanamo, administration lawyers had relied on the 1950 *Eisentrager* case.[63] In short, *Eisentrager* made clear that constitutional protections will not be triggered if "alien" captured persons (outside the United States) are not detained within the United States. As the base in Cuba was U.S. territory, but not within the "continental U.S." the administration felt it was more than appropriate to hold the detainees there based on the holding in *Eisentrager*. However, *Rasul* had essentially overruled *Eisenterager*.[64] Lawyers for the detainees, foreshadowing future arguments in *Boumedeine*, argued that the United States actually had de facto sovereignty over the base, and thus, rights to challenge their detentions in U.S. courts attached. In its 6–3 decision, the Supreme Court ruled that federal courts do have jurisdiction to consider challenges to the legality of detaining foreign nationals, being held at Guantanamo Bay, alleged to have committed war crimes.

Justice Stevens, writing for the majority, noted six points regarding *Eisentrager*: (1) the petitioners were enemy aliens; (2) they had never been or resided within the United States; (3) they were captured outside U.S. territory and held as POWs; (4) they were tried and convicted by a military tribunal held outside the borders of the United States; (5) they were convicted for offenses against the laws of war committed outside the United States; (6) they were at all times imprisoned outside of the United States. He contrasted these facts with the alleged al Qaeda fighters. The detainees, such as Rasul, were not nationals of nations with which we were at war; they had not been charged; they had not been before a tribunal; and most important (or controversial), they had been detained for over two years in a region where the United States had exclusive jurisdiction and control. Thus, the court asserted it could hear the petitions by the detainees. Importantly, it did not hold that there were any constitutional flaws but rather distinguished the current detainees' situation from those at issue in *Eisentrager*.

Thus, by the end of 2004, Guantanamo as a "detention facility" had now become even more innocuous. In 2004 and early 2005, critics claimed that the reason for using Guantanamo, a military base where the courts could not necessarily reach and outside entities could not study or question, was its utility as an interrogation facility—or as some acerbically asserted, a torture base.[65] Again, the United States denied that this was the case and it seemed then, to me at least, that most Americans did not believe that to be true and took the president and his advisors at their word: torture was simply not part of the American way of war. It had never been and was not now.

In the summer of 2004, however, pictures emerged from a wing of a prison camp in Iraq at the now famous Abu Ghraib prison. The United States had taken over the prison after toppling the Saddam

Hussein regime in Iraq as part of Operation Iraqi Freedom (OIF). OIF was completely different and essentially distinct from the operations in Afghanistan and the greater "war on terror." The decision to go to war in Iraq was based allegedly on the widely believed (not just U.S. intelligence but intelligence from elsewhere) presumption of Saddam's nuclear ability and his intentions to use weapons of mass destruction against U.S. interests as well as the U.S. ally in the Middle East, Israel. By March of 2003, the United States had invaded Iraq and toppled the Saddam Hussein government. In Operation Iraqi Freedom, American soldiers were (different from operations in the "war on terror") carrying out their operations in accord with the Geneva Conventions. After all, the soldiers the United States fought in OIF were ordinary combatants, wearing uniforms, within an established chain of command, and were, for the most part, abiding by the laws of war.[66] Prisoners captured, then, should have been afforded the protections of Geneva completely—excluding those (e.g., unlawful combatants, or insurgents) who were now operating as al Qaeda in Iraq as part of a greater insurgency after the toppling of the government. Ironically, it was widely known, particularly by the Iraqis and other surrounding Muslim nations, that Abu Ghraib had been used as a torture prison under the Hussein government.

The Abu Ghraib prison was actually notorious under Saddam's rule. It was now under U.S. control. The prisoners held at Abu Ghraib, then, should have been treated with the "gold standard" of dignity and respect afforded POWs. They were, to a large extent, captured lawful belligerents. The pictures that were leaked from the prison and blasted all over the world through the twenty-four-hour news cycle revealed U.S. soldiers torturing Iraqi prisoners with electric devices, forcing them to wear hoods, engage in forced mutual masturbation, and perform sexually perverted acts with one another. These images rightly horrified the world. The pictures sent a shock wave through the United States, our international partners, the Muslim world, and the U.S. military itself. Although these were proven to be isolated incidents in one wing of a prison and appeared more to be the result of faulty leadership than systematic torture by U.S. servicemen of prisoners, the damage had been done. The soldiers involved were court-martialed and convicted. In these trials it became clear the ultimate fault lay with Colonel Karpinski, the commanding officer of the prison. Other accusations went further up the chain to include General Geoffrey Miller and even Secretary of Defense Donald Rumsfeld. Regardless, serious questions now were being legitimately raised about other prisons the United States was operating, notably in Bagram. Guantanamo now became a focus of many international organizations. If the United States would conduct itself this way toward the Iraqis, what was it doing with the detainees in Guantanamo? Obviously, enemies of the United States and the administration used these images to their benefit as well. In my view, the actions of a handful of soldiers at Abu Ghraib did more to set back the U.S. efforts in the War on al Qaeda than any single battle, policy, or event over the past seven years. Al Qaeda, of course, also used this to garner sympathy and to energize its followers, and potential followers, in the days, weeks and months that followed. The United States (and the Bush administration) was now completely on the defensive. Guantanamo was constantly viewed under a microscope.

Rumors and disinformation appeared everywhere. Reports, studies, and news stories emerged almost every day. U.S. citizens, influenced by the realities of the distasteful and un-American activities that occurred in the Abu Ghraib case, began questioning the truthfulness of the administration. Many questioned whether the administration was being straightforward on the realities of Guantanamo and support eroded further. The lack of weapons of mass destruction ever located within Iraq as well as the "we don't torture" comment alongside the pictures from Abu Ghraib created a credibility problem for the administration. Regardless of why weapons of mass destruction were not found or what the realities of Abu Ghraib were, there was a new receptivity to allegations of misbehavior by U.S. troops. Critics of the administration, many of whom were Democratic members of Congress, now asserted that such actions were sanctioned by high-level members of the Bush team.[67] This permitted and gave tacit support to outrageous allegations being made against the noble men and women of the armed forces as well as both low-level and high-level members of the Bush administration. Mistakes, faulty intelligence, and errors were now being cast as criminal acts and in many cases "war crimes."[68] People were now open to believing that the United States had in fact strayed off course. Such increased cynicism allowed for claims such as the *Newsweek* story, not long after Abu Ghraib, that U.S. soldiers were flushing down the toilets at Guantanamo copies of the Koran belonging to the detainees.[69] The "street" was now awash with protests, concerns, and outright anger at the United States. Many who had otherwise thought the United States was acting nobly began to doubt. The media fueled this concern and angst with vast coverage of this story of misbehavior by U.S. troops. It mattered little when

Newsweek eventually withdrew the article. One of the most respected news magazines in the world had asserted that U.S. soldiers were acting this way, and members of the Muslim faith were shocked and horrified. The allegations were never proven and were later retracted by *Newsweek*, but the damage was done.

Another example of the mounting tide of opinion against the military tribunals and holding the detainees at Guantanamo occurred in June 2005. Irene Kahn, president of Amnesty International, declared in the organization's annual report that Guantanamo had become the "Gulag of our time."[70] Senator Dick Durbin (D-IL) echoed her comments on the floor of the Senate, analogizing Guantanamo and the tribunals to the Gulag, the efforts of Pol Pot, and even worse, the Nazis.[71] Politically driven hyperbole such as this led to great divisions within the United States. Yes, there had been mistakes, but to compare U.S. men and women employed in the armed forces of the United States to the KGB and the Nazis was ludicrous. Regardless, many people believed something had to change. Many opponents of the military commissions now believed the commissions were systemically flawed. They were certain the allegations raised by *Newsweek*, Amnesty International, Human Rights Watch, and others of torture and mistreatment of the detainees were the result of policies ordained at the highest levels of the administration, including the president and vice president. Respected members of the international scene, such as the president of Amnesty International and Senator Durbin, sent a disturbing message to the rest of the world. Their outrageous comments, however, were given credibility by the fact that in 2005, not a single alleged international terrorist had gone to trial, while hundreds of others remained detained on the island without charge. Suspicions continued to be fueled by other such allegations both domestically and internationally. What was Guantanamo really all about? Although I still spoke and wrote that analogizing Guantanamo to the Gulag or Nazi concentration camps was irresponsible and disrespectful to the U.S. armed forces, I was becoming painfully aware that the use of Guantanamo and the military tribunals may have suffered a knockout punch. The tide of public opinion had now changed permanently and the administration was having increased difficulty responding to the myriad allegations being made against it and its use of Guantanamo as a detention center. The perception for many was that the horrible acts that occurred in Abu Ghraib were also occurring in Guantanamo. Our national credibility was greatly diminished. Strapped with the difficulties in fighting an insurgency in Iraq, the credibility issues with

Abu Ghraib, the failure to find weapons of mass destruction after the topple of Saddam Hussein, and no real answers as to why no trials had yet occurred at Guantanamo, the administration (and many supporters of their policies) became aware they were losing the battle of public opinion—and losing badly. Yet, they remained on course, and little, if anything changed.

The Order of November 13, 2001, was issued by President Bush in a period of national emergency and of heightened security. It was adapted, often reluctantly, by the administration to better tailor the tribunals and detention to meet the ongoing needs and bring it more in line with twenty-first-century military justice. The Department of Defense went to great lengths to update the commissions through 2005. However, not consulting Congress and not having an aggressive, long-range communications plan to counter the criticisms of the commissions, combined with the inability to produce a single conviction through 2006, eroded the authority and legitimacy of both the detention facility and the tribunals themselves. By late fall 2005, the judiciary was now poised to once again entertain questions on the military commissions and was well aware of the need for additional changes. The political branches had not made substantive changes to their policies since the attacks of 9/11, and the court seemed prepared to "prompt" the inevitable changes to the Order originally issued in November of 2001.

FIVE

◈

Hamdan and the Military Commissions Act of 2006

THE MILITARY COMMISSIONS, as ordered by the president in November of 2001, and modified to a limited degree by the Pentagon, remained in place during the following five years. The "detainees" were still held at Guantanamo Bay, Cuba, and public support for the commissions continued to erode. Although several successful challenges to parts of the commissions occurred in federal district courts, circuit courts, and even the Supreme Court in *Rasul* and *Hamdi*, the holdings did not directly impact the military tribunals themselves. That all changed with the case of Salim Hamdan. By the spring of 2006, not a single military tribunal had been conducted at Guatanamo. Over 700 detainees remained on the naval base in the Guantanamo Bay Detention Center in a state of legal limbo; many of them had been detained without charge since 2001 or early 2002. The military commissions, while still "operating," remained bogged down in civil litigation, and the political branches were still unwilling to commit to any real "change." International criticism of the tribunals increased dramatically throughout 2005 and 2006. Although used throughout U.S. history and lawful in most respects, the current military commissions had not been implemented well. As a matter of policy, the system was not functioning in the manner the Bush administration had intended. During this period and with this backdrop, the Supreme Court for the third time immersed itself into the War on al Qaeda. In March 2006, the Supreme Court heard arguments in *Hamdan v. Rumsfeld*.[1] Apparently, this action by the Court was necessary to finally get the political branches to actively update and modify the existing military commission.

Hamdan v. Rumsfeld

Hamdan was a close confidant of Osama Bin Laden and actually served as his personal driver.[2] He was also alleged to be a full al Qaeda member and actually the bodyguard of Osama Bin Laden. Represented by Lieutenant Commander Charlie Swift of the Navy JAG Corps as well as Professor Neal Katyal of Georgetown Law School, Hamdan challenged the validity and constitutionality of the military commissions as constructed.

Salim Ahmed Hamdan, a citizen of Yemen, was captured by coalition forces during the invasion of Afghanistan. Once turned over to the United States, he was subsequently transported to Guantanamo Bay, Cuba, for detention. In July, 2004, he was charged with conspiracy to commit terrorism.[3] The administration was making preparations for him to be tried by military commission when Hamdan through his lawyers, sought writs of habeas corpus and mandamus to challenge the administration's intended means of prosecuting this charge. Hamdan objected to the authority of the president to convene the military commission for two reasons: first, he claimed that neither any congressional act nor the common law of war supports trial by military commissions for the crime of conspiracy. Second, he argued that the procedures the president had adopted to try him violated the basic tenets of military and international law.[4] Essentially, Hamdan argued that the commissions were not in conformity with the Geneva Conventions or the requirements of Uniform Code of Military Justice (UCMJ).

Procedurally, the courts' rulings as the case made its way through the system varied—mirroring the very real "split" in opinion throughout the country on how, or whether, to proceed with the commissions. The District Court of Columbia ruled on behalf of Hamdan, holding that military commissions are not proper and could not be employed unless the government had clearly ascertained that Hamdan was not a prisoner of war (POW). Judge James Robertson relied upon the requirements of the Third Geneva Convention that requires all captured fighters to be afforded what are referred to as Article 5 Tribunals.[5] These tribunals are used to make status determinations of soldiers captured on the field of battle in a conventional war. Since Hamdan had not been given this hearing, Judge Robertson ruled that the commissions were not appropriate. The district court judge was in the unenviable position of ruling on a unique military case in a different kind of war. His options were limited. Judge Robertson relied upon civilian perspectives of the law of war in deciding this special military case. He applied the Geneva Conventions to a non-Geneva Convention conflict, clearly opposing the commander in chief, who believed the conventions did not apply in this case.[6]

Upon appeal by the government, a three-judge panel of the D.C. Circuit Court of Appeals unanimously reversed the district court holding. The D.C. Circuit asserted the military commissions were legal on the following grounds:

- Military Commissions are legitimate forums to try "enemy combatants" because they have been approved by Congress by both the UCMJ as well as the Authorization to Use Military Force (AUMF);
- The Geneva Convention is a treaty between two nations and does not confer individual rights and remedies;
- Even if Geneva could be enforced in U.S. Courts, it would not be of assistance to Hamdan at the time because the War on al Qaeda is not between nations, the only requirement is that they be tried by competent tribunal, without specificity as to the jurisdiction;
- Under the terms of the Geneva Conventions, al Qaeda and its members are not covered;
- Congress authorized this sort of military court by statute;
- The judicial branch of the U.S. government cannot enforce the Convention, thus invalidating Hamdan's argument that he cannot be tried until ascertaining whether he is a prisoner of war or not.[7]

After the writ of certiorari was issued in late 2005, arguments were held the following March. The Supreme Court announced their decision in late June 2006. By a vote of 5–3 (Justice Roberts recused himself since he had been on the three-judge panel in the D.C. circuit ruling on the same case), the Court reversed the ruling of the court of appeals, holding that the military commissions as constructed were illegal under military law as well as under the Geneva Conventions. Further, the Court held that President Bush did not have the authority to unilaterally set up the tribunals without specific authorization from the Congress.

The Court's opinion, authored by Justice Stevens, declared the president's Order of 2001, and therefore the existing military commission process, illegal and invalid. The *New York Times* hailed the decision as "a victory for the rule of law" and the "latest in a series of rebukes to the Bush administration."[8] Importantly, however, a close reading of the majority opinion reveals that there was never any articulation (supported by a majority) of any constitutional defects. Instead, the majority opinion asserted that the crime of conspiracy charged against Hamdan was not included in any specific statutory provision or within the common law of war. Further, the opinion declared that neither the Authority for the Use of Force (AUMF) nor the Detainee Treatment Act (DTA) "expands the President's authority to convene military commissions."[9] Additionally, the Court held that the charge of conspiracy is not, and never has been, a charge under the laws of war. "None of the overt acts Hamdan is alleged to have committed violates the laws of war . . . international sources confirm that the crime alleged here is not a recognized violation of the law of war . . . none of the major treaties governing the law of war identifies conspiracy as a violation thereof."[10] The majority analysis relied predominantly upon an application of the UCMJ and an apparent preference for courts-martial, international law, and federal treaties relating to the treatment of detainees. The Court rejected the president's authority to unilaterally, even in time of war, create the commissions. However, the justices left an opening to "fix" the current military commission process. Justice Breyer, in a concurrence joined by Justices Kennedy, Souter, and Ginsberg, noted, "Congress has denied the President the legislative authority to create military commissions of the kind at issue here. Nothing prevents the President from returning to Congress to seek the authority he believes necessary."[11] Thus, although the majority held that the statutory requirements contained within the UCMJ prevented the president's current military commission structure and process, they also believed that the administration could go to the Congress to seek the authority necessary for employing the military commissions. The decision made clear, however, that if the administration went back to Congress, two key issues needed to be addressed: (1) the military commissions being employed must be legislatively adopted by Congress and the president could not unilaterally authorize the tribunals; and (2) Common Article 3 of the Geneva Conventions must apply to the detention of the al Qaeda fighter.

In deciding that the administration did not have the legislative authority to conduct the current military commissions, the Court claimed the "tribunals" must be in conformity with the procedures contained within the UCMJ. In particular, Justice Stevens particularly emphasized Articles 21 and 36 of the military legal code. Military commissions, as the majority and dissent both agreed, are only mentioned in a few areas of the Manual for Courts-Martial (MCM) and are generally vague.[12] From past practice and as covered in the earlier Articles of War, it seems as though this purposeful ambiguity was to ensure maximum flexibility for commanders, or the commander in chief, to use these tribunals during periods of armed conflict.[13] The preamble states:

> The agencies through which military jurisdiction is exercised include ... military commissions and provost courts for the trial of cases within their respective jurisdictions. Subject to any applicable rule of international law or to any regulations prescribed by the President or by other competent authority, military commissions and provost courts shall be guided by the appropriate principles of law and rules of procedures and evidence prescribed by courts-martial.[14]

In another section it says:

> The provisions of this code and this manual conferring jurisdiction upon courts-martial do not deprive military commissions, provost courts, or other military tribunals of concurrent jurisdiction with respect to offenders or offenses that by statute or by the law of war may be tried by military commissions, provost courts, or other military tribunals.[15]

Under the UCMJ, there are two key references, but again, both are vague:

> Article 21—The provisions of this chapter conferring jurisdiction upon courts martial do not deprive military commissions, provost courts, or other military tribunals of concurrent jurisdiction with respect to offenders or offenses that by statute or by the law of war may be tried by military commissions, provost courts, or other military tribunals.[16]

The majority believed that neither prong—statute nor the laws of war—was satisfied by the commissions. Regarding the statutory authority, the Court adopted a restrictive reading of the broad statute, asserting there was nothing "even hinting" at expanding the president's war powers to create commissions.[17] They note, "Article 21 incorporated by reference the common law of war, which may render triable by military commission certain offenses not defined by statute."[18] Stevens also argued, "The UCMJ conditions the President's use of military commissions not only on the common law of war, but also with the UCMJ itself."[19] The Supreme Court reasoned that the laws of war require more than is provided for by the current military commissions. The majority wrote of their concern "that the preconditions designed to ensure a military necessity exists to justify the use of this extraordinary tribunal have been satisfied here."[20] Since a "conspiracy" charge was not found within the common law of war, the majority felt strongly that there was no real necessity to use the special tribunals. One presumes the Court was alluding to the fact that Hamdan had already been in captivity for over four years when they heard his case. Stevens went further, pointing out "the Executive's part here to satisfy the most basic precondition—at least in the absence of specific Congressional authorization—for the establishment of military commissions: military necessity. Hamdan's tribunal was appointed not by a military commander in the field of battle, but by a retired Major General stationed away from any active hostilities."[21] The majority of the Court was uncomfortable with the use of a military commission, with its reduced expectations of procedure and process, if the government could have used the court-martial system. Their reasoning was that if there was no "urgency" to use commissions, then the preferred method should be either a court-martial for Hamdan or at the minimum the use of the procedures of a general court-martial within any tribunal established. In the past, military commissions (when employed for "trying" unlawful combatants) were held in the field of battle or as a result of exigency. Since many of the accused, including Hamdan, had been detained for many years and there were no indications or facts in evidence that an attack was imminent, there was no sense of urgency that would prevent a more rigid legal process. If nothing else, this difficult analysis does demonstrate the unique nature of this conflict and how the existing statutory rules, as well as the practice from previous conflicts or the common law of war, do not provide concrete advice on how to proceed. Al Qaeda is not the typical "warrior"—whether unlawful belligerent or not.

The majority then turned to the other provision in question. Article 36 of the UCMJ requires that when possible, military courts or commissions should try to mirror civilian court procedures when practicable, or at least courts-martial and military commissions should be similar or "uniform" whenever possible. Article 36 specifically requires the following:

> (a) Pretrial, trial, and post-trial procedures, including modes of proof, for cases arising under this chapter triable in courts-martial, military commissions, and other military tribunals, and procedures for courts of inquiry, may be prescribed by the President by regulations which shall, so far as he considers practicable, apply the principles of law and the rules of evidence generally recognized in the trial of criminal cases in the United States district courts, but which may be contrary to or inconsistent with this chapter. (b) All rules and regulations made under this article shall be uniform insofar as practicable.[22]

Stevens read Article 36(b) to mandate that the rules in courts-martial and military commissions be uniform insofar as practicable, the majority asserting that the two different procedures, as applied in Hamdan's case, should be presumptively the same. Stevens wrote, "The difference between military commissions and courts-martial originally was a difference of jurisdiction alone and to protect against abuse and ensure evenhandedness under the pressures of war.... [P]rocedures governing trials by military commission have been the same as those governing courts-martial."[23] The majority was arguing that the procedures and practice of the commissions could be "regularized" by simply using the existing general court-martial process.

The Court also discussed the "practicability and uniformity" requirements of part b of Article 36. The plain reading of the article reveals that the president should retain broad authority in how he composes the procedures of the commissions. The Stevens opinion, however, interprets Article 36 to require the president to explain why he would use military commissions instead of courts-martial. The decision states that the government had explained (in their written briefs to the Court) only why civilian courts would not be appropriate but did not justify or delineate their reasons for not using courts-martial instead of military commissions.[24] As some critics of the *Hamdan* decision have written, there is simply no evidence of practice, legislative history, congressional enactments, or presidential decisions to support this new requirement imposed by the Court.[25] In their clear preference for court-martial and discomfort with military commissions, the Court asserted, "Nothing in the record before us demonstrates that it would be impracticable to apply courts-martial rules in this case. There is no suggestion, for example, of any logistical difficulty in securing properly sworn and authenticated evidence or in applying the usual principles of relevance and admissibility."[26]

Common Article 3

The Court further held that the military commissions, and the detention of the alleged al Qaeda fighters, did not comport with Common Article 3 of the Geneva Conventions. It provides the following:

> In the case of armed conflict not of an international character occurring in the territory of one of the High Contracting Parties, each Party to the conflict shall be bound to apply, as a minimum, the following provisions:
>
> (1) Persons taking no active part in the hostilities, including members of armed forces who have laid down their arms and those placed "hors de combat" by sickness, wounds, detention, or any other cause, shall in all circumstances be treated humanely, without any adverse distinction founded on race, colour, religion or faith, sex, birth or wealth, or any other similar criteria.
>
> To this end, the following acts are and shall remain prohibited at any time and in any place whatsoever with respect to the above-mentioned persons:
>
> (a) violence to life and person, in particular murder of all kinds, mutilation, cruel treatment and torture;
> (b) taking of hostages;
> (c) outrages upon personal dignity, in particular humiliating and degrading treatment;
> (d) the passing of sentences and the carrying out of executions without previous judgment pronounced by a regularly constituted court affording all the judicial guarantees which are recognized as indispensable by civilized peoples.
>
> (2) The wounded and sick shall be collected and cared for.
>
> An impartial humanitarian body, such as the International Committee of the Red Cross, may offer its services to the Parties to the conflict.
>
> The Parties to the conflict should further endeavor to bring into force, by means of special agreements, all or part of the other provisions of the present Convention.
>
> The application of the preceding provisions shall not affect the legal status of the Parties to the conflict.[27]

Stevens and the majority believed the courts in Guantanamo did not meet the "regularly constituted court" requirement and that the minimal protections required by the treaty were not being satisfied in Guantanamo. As such, they held that the procedures adopted to try Hamdan were in violation of international law. The majority once again took a broad view of the applicability of Common Article 3. They cited the provision with the Geneva Conventions that states, "Each Party to the conflict shall be bound to apply, at a minimum, certain provisions protecting persons taking no active part in the hostilities, including members of the armed forces who have laid down their arms and those placed hors de combat by...detention."[28] The majority also took issue with the analysis of the government and the circuit court that Common Article 3 applies only to conflicts not incidents of an international character. The government argued that since the war was "global" in nature, Common Article 3 should not apply.[29] Stevens wrote that such reasoning is "erroneous."[30] Further, "Common Article 3...affords some minimal protection falling short of full protection under the Conventions, to individuals associated with neither a signatory nor even a nonsignatory 'Power' who are involved in a conflict 'in the territory of' a signatory." They also held that the commentaries on Common Article 3 made clear that "the scope of the Article must be as wide as possible."[31] In establishing that Common Article 3 applies, then logically, Hamdan should be tried by a "regularly constituted court affording all the judicial guarantees which are recognized as indispensable by civilized peoples."[32] Since the majority felt the commissions were not "regularly constituted" and did not provide adequate protections, they held the commissions violated Common Article 3.

The Dissent in Hamdan

To say the least, the conservative wing of the Court (excluding the chief justice in this case) strongly disputed the reasoning and the conclusions drawn by the majority in this case. The minority in *Hamdan*—Justices Scalia, Alito, and Thomas—all strongly dissented. Justice Scalia did not believe the Court had jurisdiction to hear the case and believed any assertion otherwise was "patently erroneous."[33] He believed the case was not "ripe" and the Court should have refrained from hearing and ruling on the case until after the trial had occurred.[34] Justice Alito concurred with Scalia but also emphasized that the military commission convened was lawful. He argued that even if Common Article 3 applied, it was satisfied since (1) the military commissions qualify as a regularly constituted court, (2) they were appointed and established in accordance with domestic law, and (3) any procedural improprieties that might occur in specific cases could be reviewed then, not before the commissions began.[35] Perhaps the most interesting of the three dissents, however, came from Justice Thomas.

His lengthy dissent read from the bench for the first time since 2000 (*Stenberg v. Carhart*),[36] concurred with Scalia (and Justice Alito) on the question of jurisdiction but went further. In his reaction to the majority's holding, he asserted that Hamdan, as an illegal combatant, was not protected by the Geneva Conventions; therefore, any application of Common Article 3 was unnecessary. Additionally, he wrote that the Court should defer to the decisions of the president, as commander in chief, particularly during a period of ongoing armed conflict. He initially relied upon the inherent powers of the president as commander in chief described within the *Federalist Papers*: "the Executive Branch—namely, the decisiveness, activity, secrecy and dispatch, that flow from the Executive's unity" led the Founders to conclude that the "President has primary responsibility—along with the necessary power—to protect the national security and to conduct the Nation's foreign relations."[37] Justice Thomas strongly disagreed that Congress had to "bless" the military commissions. Citing the 1980s Supreme Court case that specifically addresses congressional and executive power in *Dames & More v. Regan*[38] he wrote, "Congress can not anticipate and legislate with regard to every action the President may find it necessary to take or every possible situation in which he might act.... [S]uch failure of Congress...does not especially...in the areas of foreign policy and national security, imply 'congressional disapproval' of action taken by the Executive."[39] Thomas also argued that even if the president did need statutory authority, he had received it in the AUMF.[40] Referring to the plurality in *Hamdi*, decided just two years earlier, he noted that the issues of detainees are, in fact, part of the war effort: "The capture, detention and trial of unlawful combatants, by universal agreement and practice," are incidental to war.[41] The dissent also took issue with the majority's assertions that the military commissions should essentially be mirrors of the courts-martial process. As he noted, members of the administration had stated that "the commissions are intended to be different because the President recognized that there had to be differences to deal with the unusual situation we face and that a different approach was needed."[42] Thomas, in his dissent, also took issue with the court's analysis of the requirements of Common Article 3 stating, "Hamdan's military commission complies with the requirements of Common Article 3. It is plainly 'regularly constituted' because such commissions have been employed throughout our history to try unlawful combatants for crimes against the laws of war."[43] His dissent cites *Madsen* for support: "Military commissions have become adopted as authorized tribunals in this country in time of war, recognized not only in acts of Congress, but in executive proclamations, in rulings of the courts, and in the opinions of the Attorneys General."[44] Thomas was alarmed that the majority had decided the commissions were unlawful, in large measure, because they deviated from the "regularly constituted court" of a general court-martial and their procedures—mostly because there is no requirement (either in history or Supreme Court precedent) for the military commissions to be in conformity with the ordinary military criminal process. The dissent argued strongly that the military commission, as structured for *Hamdan*, met the requirements of Common Article 3. In essence, Thomas and the other dissenters took issue with virtually every aspect of the majority analysis. They believed the commissions, as evidenced in the *Hamdan* case, were clearly lawful.

After a review of the case, it can be argued *Hamdan* was incorrectly decided on several grounds: first, it disregarded altogether existing Supreme Court precedent and United States history on military commissions; second, it did not accord the traditional deference to the executive branch in a time of war (in previous decisions the Court had held that the War on al Qaeda was an armed conflict of some sort); and third, it did not fully distinguish the reasons for, or differences between, military commissions and courts-martial. Regardless of the merits/demerits of the holding, as a matter of policy, the decision in *Hamdan* reflected the serious concerns many within the United States and the international community now had over the situation in Guantanamo. *Hamdan* was now the law of the land and the commissions, as constructed, were unlawful. It was now up the political branches to respond to the concerns raised by the Supreme Court to ensure that there was a process more suitable to trying the alleged al Qaeda detainees.

The Military Commissions Act of 2006

The administration and the Congress were now in the situation of having hundreds of detainees located in Guantanamo Bay without an acceptable process by which to prosecute them. The *Hamdan* decision did not change the detainees' status or "free" them; rather, the ruling held that the "trial" process in place since 2001–2002 was illegal as constructed. To say the least, there was concern in how this would impact the war. It was, unequivocally, a major blow to the Bush administration's legal policies.[45]

The political branches were aware that they had to act quickly. The military, Congress, and the president immediately went to work on creating an acceptable system. There were numerous meetings between congressional leaders from both political parties and the White House, hearings on Capitol Hill, and numerous planning sessions at the Pentagon during the summer of 2006.[46] The different constituencies grappled with determining the preferred legal system to use in response to *Hamdan*. The hearings exposed sometimes deep divisions in perceptions of what had taken place and widely divergent recommendations for the future of the military commissions. The options essentially were these: (1) shut down the military process altogether and use civilian courts within the United States, (2) statutorily create a national security court, (3) use the military courts-martial process, (4) reconstruct the military commissions and obtain specific legislative authority from the Congress for using the tribunals.

Civilian courts were generally viewed by most lawmakers, at this juncture, as impractical and unworkable. Although several critics of the commissions advocated their use, there was simply not the political will to use the federal courts to combat this problem.[47] Additionally, the Bush administration was completely against using the ordinary criminal process in the "War on Terror" to adjudicate the alleged "war crimes" committed by al Qaeda and the detainees.

Creating a special terrorism court was considered and actually advocated by one congressman at an armed services committee hearing, but there was never much traction for a national security court.[48] Creating something completely new would have required an enormous amount of manpower and time—something the political branches would have likely preferred, but that was not the case with the 2006 elections looming less than three months away. They needed to move quickly to get the legal system for the detainees back on track as soon as possible, or—as some asserted—before the November congressional elections.[49] Time was of the essence.

Military courts-martial were strongly considered by the political branches. The White House was not comfortable using the regular military law system for myriad reasons. In many ways, the administration did not want to equate the al Qaeda fighter with our own men and women in uniform. They felt that using the system our own forces are subject to somehow "legitimized" the unlawful combatants (al Qaeda).[50] The White House emphasized the distinctions between the military trials accorded to members of the armed forces and those tribunals specifically available to the president during times of war for unlawful belligerents. A court-martial is entirely separate from Article III courts and therefore not subject to the rules applied in federal courts.[51] Winthrop described them as "instrumentalities of the executive power, provided by Congress for the President as Commander-in-Chief, to aid him in properly commanding the army and navy and discipline therein."[52] It is a trial employed for members of the U.S. armed forces on active duty, POWs, and persons accompanying the armed forces during a time of war. Also, in some limited cases, courts-martial can be used against violators of the laws of war."[53] As discussed in greater detail in chapter 1, the military trials certainly offer a decreased expectation of constitutional protections to the accused and are not nearly the same as the civilian U.S. courts, but they are not nearly as flexible as the military commissions are, or have they ever been. The court-martial system uses the Military Rules of Evidence, virtually identical to the Federal Rules of Evidence and is now completely a creature of statute (the Manual for Courts-Martial); the trials permit juries (although not nearly the same as the civilian courts in terms of a "jury of your peers");[54] require a two-thirds majority to convict (unanimous vote required for death penalty cases) instead of unanimous votes; have decreased expectations of due process (e.g., Fourth Amendment, Fifth Amendment issues [art. 31b, UCMJ] as well as the exclusionary rule); and are heavily regulated and inflexible, as required in the Rules for Courts-Martial.[55] Over the past fifty years, the courts-martial process has been considerably liberalized and has become more rights-oriented than in the past. There are now military judges overseeing the trials, the right to not incriminate oneself is embodied in military justice (even before *Miranda*), the powers of the convening authority (while still great) have been reduced, and the Military Rules of Evidence now mirror the Federal Rules of Evidence.[56] However, even as the courts-martial have become more progressive, the Congress has still ensured that there is a distinct federal criminal justice system and procedures for this "unique subset of society." Importantly, the primary intention of using courts-martial has always been to try "legitimate" warriors for crimes committed under the military's code of laws, the Uniform Code of Military Justice. The reason military tribunals (or commissions) exist and are available to the military has been to provide the executive branch and commanders in the field with a system more flexible and distinct from the one that would be applied to our own soldiers, sailors, and airmen. It seems that the strength of using military commissions is their lack of specificity and procedure. One can presume that this explains why they were drafted in this fashion. Although some argued in favor of using the standard military system already in existence for the detainees (Professor Scott Silliman of Duke Law School has in the past and continues to do so now—and certainly the Supreme Court hinted at this in *Hamdan*), ironically many of the same evidentiary issues associated with the civilian court system would have also manifested themselves if courts-martial were employed.[57] For many reasons, although they considered it, the political branches passed on using the pure military justice system as the means to prosecute the detainees.

A revamped military commissions system was eventually adopted. The political branches determined that the military commissions were, if modified in myriad ways, the best option available to try the unlawful belligerents in Guatanamo.[58] As noted in *Hamdan*, such commissions have jurisdiction over persons who would not be likely to respect the laws of war.[59] According to the "founding father" of military law, Colonel William Winthrop, these "detainees" are not "within the protection of the laws of war and were liable to be shot, imprisoned, or banished, either summarily where the guilt was clear or upon trial and conviction by military commission."[60] He also noted that military commissions have jurisdiction over an "individual of the enemy's army who has been guilty of illegitimate warfare or other offenses in violation of the laws of war."[61] From this, the al Qaeda fighter, although not representing a nation but rather an ideology or movement, clearly meets these requirements. As earlier discussed in chapters 1 and 2, throughout U.S. history these "tribunals" have been used just for "war" crimes such as those committed by al Qaeda. These individuals are enemies in an armed conflict; they are certainly outside the bounds of responsible, ethical war fighting and do not comply whatsoever with the laws of war. The power of the president to convene military commissions is derived from his authority as commander in chief.[62] Rather than having the internal focus of the court-martial, the military commission is "externally directed at the enemy as a means of waging successful war by punishing and deterring offenses against the laws of war."[63] Beyond the customary law of war, when enacting the UCMJ, Congress ensured the inclusion of military commissions as a separate entity distinct from the courts-martial. They have consistently been used as tools during armed conflict to deter "unlawful belligerency" by enemy forces and are ordinarily intended to be faster than civilian courts or courts-martial in dispensing justice. Where the court-martial system offers fewer ordinary protections than would a civilian court, military commissions afford even less protection than would a court-martial. There are ordinarily no juries; a panel of military officers presides in judgment; the commissions have relaxed evidentiary standards; historically, they have had no strict guidelines so as to ensure that the military and executive branch have maximum flexibility; and they have traditionally been creatures of the customary law of war for centuries. The political branches, after considering all possibilities, opted to use a military commission system. In an apparent nod to the majority in *Hamdan*, however, they included many aspects of the courts-martial system, but still created a distinct, wartime tribunal to try al Qaeda fighters who allegedly violated the laws of war.

After vigorous debate on both sides of the political spectrum, large bipartisan majorities in both the House and the Senate reacted to the *Hamdan* decision and the need for modifications to the commission's process, and supported the enactment of the Military Commissions Act of 2006.[64] After this significant negotiation between the White House, the Congress, the Pentagon, and the senior judge advocates, the bill was passed 65–34 in the Senate and 250–170 in the House. The new updated Military Commissions Act was signed into law in October 2006.

The Military Commissions Act (MCA) ensured that trials could proceed against the detainees. Of particular importance at this juncture, no prosecutions of the detainees at Guatanamo had occurred. However, the process was at least now back on track and the opportunity to try the cases seemed, once again, imminent. The political branches had agreed to make changes, to liberalize the commissions, and to a large degree, to utilize many aspects of the courts-martial process. The MCA now did, in fact, afford a laundry list of rights to the detainees; it provided more due process and more judicial involvement in the various aspects of policies related to the war on terror than is required by either the U.S. Constitution or American international law obligations. In fact, the MCA offered protections that exceed the due process standards provided by many democratic countries in their own domestic court systems as well as other ad hoc tribunals or international courts.[65] Importantly, these rights go well beyond those afforded saboteurs in the Second World War during the last military commissions conducted in 1942 and 1945. As a result of the passage of the MCA, each detainee now would enjoy

- the right to a full and fair trial
- the right to know the charges against him as soon as practicable
- a presumption of innocence
- the right to counsel, government-provided defense counsel, and civilian counsel (at own expense)
- an opportunity to obtain witnesses, and other evidence, including government evidence
- an obligation on the government to disclose exculpatory evidence to the defense
- the right to cross-examine witnesses
- the right to not testify against himself
- limitations on the admission of hearsay evidence, focusing on its probity and the danger of unfair prejudice
- ban on statements obtained by torture
- limitations on statements obtained through coercion, focusing on their reliability and probity
- assurance that no undue influence or coercion of a Commission itself or members of a Commission can be exercised
- assurance that Commission proceedings will be open, unless extraordinary circumstances are present
- right to, at a minimum, two appeals, one through the military justice system, and the other through the civilian justice system, beginning with the D.C. Circuit
- assurance against double jeopardy—accused cannot be tried twice for the same offense[66]

The Military Commissions Act was a compromise between the political branches as the best means to proceed in trying the detainees. This is not to say there was not passionate resistance by some to the newly "reconstituted" military commissions. Many academics, lawyers, and policy makers were furious with what they perceived as the lack of real change created by the Congress.[67] Immediately following the enactment, several human rights groups, academics, and some politicians condemned the MCA. Within weeks, Senator Chris Dodd introduced legislation, "Restoring the Constitution Act," to essentially gut the MCA just enacted.[68] The anti-MCA sentiment ranged from criticisms of the unseemly speed with which the legislation was enacted,[69] to claims that Congress should have specifically responded to the portions of the MCA struck down by the *Hamdan* case instead of coming up with comprehensive legislation.

Some critics found the bill thoroughly inadequate, with some portraying it as the embodiment of tyrannical governance.[70] The most oft-cited concerns about the MCA were these: introducing classified material without the accused being able to see the material in its entirety deprives him of a fair trial and violates both the U.S. Constitution and international law; introducing hearsay evidence denies the accused the right to confront witnesses against him; standard habeas corpus petitions are denied under the procedure; evidence obtained by torture or under duress will be admissible, thereby both prejudicing the right of the accused to a fair trial and, at least implicitly, legitimizing coercive interrogation techniques that do not adhere to Common Article 3 of the Geneva Conventions. More generally, most of the critics maintained that the commissions should have become a mirror image of the United States' own court-martial system. The administration thought it had obtained a victory; others, however, still believed the commissions should be closed down for good.

Regardless of the criticisms, a large majority of Congress concluded that the legislation struck the proper balance between upholding U.S. international law obligations while taking into account the realities of the ongoing conflict with al Qaeda and affiliated groups. These realities included the fact that in the current "war," the United States (and its allies) confronts mostly unlawful belligerents, and the need for human intelligence in the War on al Qaeda, much of which can be derived only from the interrogation of captured enemy personnel, is more critical in this conflict than has been the case in most other wars the United States has fought.[71] Further, some seem to disregard the history of military commissions in American jurisprudence since the time of the Revolution. They neglect the Founders' intent regarding executive power. This is particularly true in the contexts of war powers authority, military justice, and military commission implementation during war or other national emergencies.[72]

I had hoped the *Hamdan* decision would have been the catalyst for Congress to really rethink our procedures in how we detain, interrogate, and try the alleged al Qaeda being held at Guatanamo rather than being simply an opportunity to update the commissions process. It was an opportunity to recognize that although military commissions have been used throughout our history, they are not the appropriate forum to try these unlawful belligerents. However, the MCA did make some changes, not the least of which was an unequivocal ban on torture. It seemed that the political branches once again partially responded to critics and allowed for some gradual changes to take place. The morphing of the military commissions continued through the adoption of the MCA. To be fair, however, the MCA still retained many of the inherent flaws in the system that called into question its legitimacy and continued to erode support for it. Although the MCA is clearly acceptable—and in most respects lawful—the political branches still decided to enact a strict law of war paradigm (military commissions) in a very unconventional war. There was simply no political will, particularly during a congressional election year of 2006, to make the real changes necessary to a system deeply flawed as a matter of both policy as well as implementation.

Analysis of the Military Commissions Act and Criticisms

In the following, each of the major criticisms of the Military Commissions Act will be discussed, with a brief response to each. To be certain, some of the criticisms were valid at the time and remain so (as has been proven over the past two years since its enactment). Others, however, were often more grounded in partisanship than fact. There is no question, however, that the procedures enacted in the MCA go far beyond what have been the practices of military commissions used in the past. In the final analysis, the holding in *Hamdan v. Rumsfeld*,[73] rather than eliminating the debate, only further confused the legal landscape. The MCA did little to alleviate many of the policy concerns still being raised. The seminal question remained: do we apply a law of war approach to the trials, or do we employ the civilian courts? Although the military commissions remain appropriate *de jure belli* in traditional armed conflict, it was becoming increasingly evident they were not the appropriate fit for the quasi-warrior, international terrorist al Qaeda fighter. Many of the critics' concerns, in essence, argued for a law enforcement approach affording the detainees ordinary process and procedures by using our civilian federal civilian courts. Unfortunately, in doing so, the government would not have the flexibility it desired or has enjoyed in past practice during armed conflict. This debate raged before and after *Hamdan* was decided and continued even after the enactment of the MCA. While the nation debated, and remained divided, the detainees remained in Guatanamo with most still not being charged, let alone tried.

Introduction of Classified Material

A great deal of controversy and criticism remains concerning the introduction of classified material as evidence in the military commissions. Some liberal scholars and commentators argued that since such evidence will not be seen by the accused in its entirety, he will be denied the right to a fair trial. During congressional testimony, several senior military lawyers, as witnesses, declared that this was inappropriate.[74] There is no doubt that impeding, even in limited fashion, the right of the accused to confrontation raises troubling questions. Preventing the accused from even knowing the identity of a witness may well handicap the ability of his lawyers to mount the most effective cross-examination of that witness or introduce evidence that can impeach him.[75]

However, sharing classified material with the accused could very well pose a serious risk to national security, especially if the accused is acquitted and released prior to the end of hostilities. Worse yet, and even more likely, the accused will capitalize on his privileged access to counsel and investigators to pass messages to his fellow al Qaeda operatives on the outside—and recent experience reveals that terrorists, as part of their established written doctrine, have actually done this.[76] This concern is reinforced by the fact that al Qaeda has demonstrated its ability in the past to obtain information gathered during judicial proceedings.[77]

Significantly, the MCA does require that the admission of classified evidence, out of the presence of the accused, "not deprive the accused of a full and fair trial." This prescription, arrived at after an extensive review of the results of military commission proceedings through both the military and the civilian justice systems, ensures that the use of classified evidence would be exceedingly rare and that such evidence could not possibly be the sole basis upon which the accused is found guilty. Furthermore, the accused's U.S. government-provided military lawyer (who would have the requisite security clearance) would be permitted to view the classified material in its entirety, as would the military jury and the judge. As an additional process for the accused, the classified information provisions cannot be triggered casually. The act ensures that the federal agency that classified the material in issue would have to certify that such material needs to remain classified; the judge would have to certify that a redacted version of that material would not suffice; and the accused would be provided a redacted copy of the transcript so as to be generally aware of the evidence being introduced.

Regardless, this whole issue was extensively debated during the congressional consideration of the MCA and, largely as a result of the efforts by Republican Senator Lindsey Graham, the administration's original language underwent a significant change.[78] Thus, the MCA as enacted reveals that a careful balance has been struck between the legitimate desire of the government to protect classified information and consideration of the due process rights of the accused—especially during an ongoing war. Those struggling with this balancing had to be ever mindful that these tribunals are taking place during—and not after—an ongoing armed conflict. They are therefore distinct from other tribunals of the past, such as the Nuremburg war crimes tribunals, in that the impact and effect of the commission's decisions can have an immediate impact on the current war. This is why the MCA, in recognition of the potential damage that could be caused by the revelation of classified material during the commission proceedings, specifically provides (in extraordinary circumstances) for the possibility of using classified evidence without allowing the accused to have full knowledge of all of the material, but still requiring that he see a redacted version of this material.[79]

Introduction of Hearsay Evidence

The MCA's provisions for introducing hearsay evidence, as has traditionally been the case with military commissions on American soil, provide for the introduction of all probative evidence during the commission proceedings. This is an overt recognition that (given the ongoing nature of this war) many witnesses will not be available to testify. Soldiers, marines, and others involved in the war are likely to be unavailable as a direct result of their duties. Significantly, in the past and currently, most international tribunals similarly provide for the introduction of hearsay evidence as well in those situations where witnesses are unavailable or for certain other reasons.[80] Indeed, the introduction of hearsay evidence is not an unheard of event even in regular judicial proceedings in federal courts. Incorporated into Federal Rules of Evidence (and Military Rules of Evidence)[81] are nearly twenty-four exceptions to what is known as the "hearsay rule." These allow a trial to proceed and justice to be served in circumstances in which a witness will be unavailable to testify—for many reasons, including death. Indeed, it is worth observing that these rules are generally reciprocal: defendants who can satisfy their admissibility predicates may also exploit them to present evidence favorable to them that would otherwise be unavailable. This reliance on hearsay is even more crucial in this war because many witnesses are likely to be foreign nationals, and compelling them to appear at the commission might be difficult; also, many will be unavailable due to imprisonment or even death at the hands of al Qaeda, or in other cases, their own governments. While showing cognizance of these extraordinary circumstances, the MCA does provide protections to the accused by ensuring that the judge must believe introduction of such evidence is probative before entering it into evidence. Thus, although not ideal, there is a "check" on potential abuse at the trial level of the military commissions.

Judicial Review

At the time the MCA was enacted, some scholars alleged that it effectively abolishes the writ of habeas corpus, in violation of the Suspension Clause of the Constitution.[82] As is well known, these concerns were later the issue that came before the Supreme Court in *Boumediene*. The Court, as described in detail in later chapters, held these specific provisions of the MCA to be unconstitutional.[83] Thus, the detainees at Guatanamo now will have, presumably prior to being charged, the right to have U.S. civilian courts determine the appropriateness of their detention. The provisions in the MCA, adopted from the Detainee Treatment Act of 2005, were held to be legally insufficient by the Court.

However, it is not as though the MCA did not provide any means to determine the validity of the alleged al Qaeda member's detention. In fact, the Department of Defense had gone to great lengths to provide some process to the unlawful belligerents. Again, this is unprecedented in U.S. history. Many found these procedures inadequate, however, and in some cases, a complete sham.[84] But the reality is that the statute provided the detainees with judicial review opportunities that exceeded existing requirements under international law and more than the United States had ever granted previously. They were clearly not what is provided for U.S. citizens, but nonetheless they allowed for more than has often been portrayed by the media.

The MCA built upon the judicial review procedures set forth in the DTA. Together, they provided a set of judicial review strictures that were streamlined, yet fair, and provide detainees with limited due process opportunities. Additionally, these were, in many ways greater than the Article 5 Tribunals provided for by the Third Geneva Convention.[85] These provisions comport with the United States Constitution and members of Congress thought they would withstand any legal challenges made.

The DTA made the United States Court of Appeals for the District of Columbia Circuit, (the "D.C. Circuit") the second most influential court in the land, the exclusive venue for handling any legal challenges by detainees and limited the court's jurisdiction to two sets of circumstances: (1) review of the validity of the final decision of a

Combatant Status Review Tribunal (CSRT) that an alien has been properly detained as an enemy combatant, and (2) review of the validity of the final decision by a military commission.[86]

In both instances, the scope of review was precisely defined and limited to essentially two questions: First, was the CSRT or military commission operated in a way that was consistent with the standards and procedures adopted by these respective bodies? Second, was the use of such standards and procedures by either the CSRT or a military commission "to reach the final decision...consistent with the Constitution and laws of the United States" (to the extent that the Constitution and laws of the United States apply)?

There was significant debate about the ambiguity of this language—specifically, whether any factual issues arising out of the CSRT or military commission proceedings can be reviewed by the D.C. Circuit Court (and, ultimately, by the Supreme Court). There was, however, one key factual issue susceptible to review. Under the holding of *Ex Parte Milligan*,[87] it is unconstitutional to bring civilians before military commissions if the Article III courts are "open and functioning." Thus, an enemy civilian who has been subjected to the military commissions procedures could appear (to some) to be in a situation in which the application of such procedures to him is inconsistent with provisions of the United States Constitution. Clearly, Justice Kennedy and four other justices were persuaded by this logic in *Boumediene*. The *Milligan* case, however, is not necessarily applicable to the current situation and confuses the different types of military commissions that can be employed and when they are appropriately used.[88] Regardless of the difficulties in identifying the status of such captured fighters, al Qaeda (and the current use of military commissions envisioned by the MCA) are recognized (and intended to be detained and adjudicated) as illegal belligerents captured for committing war crimes during a period of armed conflict—distinct from the *Milligan* military commission case, which dealt with what was essentially a civilian American citizen (Milligan was not actually a part of the Confederacy) before the Supreme Court after the cessation of hostilities. This distinction, by the way, is exactly what the Court made in *Ex Parte Quirin*[89] by rejecting the petitioners' contention that they were civilians and therefore not subject to military jurisdiction.

The *Milligan* case dealt with an American citizen who was tried by a military commission on American soil. By contrast, even in the aftermath of *Rasul v. Bush*,[90] an enemy alien held at Guantanamo or elsewhere outside of the United States was not expected by the administration (or the Congress after the MCA) to be eligible for the substantive constitutional protections implicated by *Milligan*, as distinct from being merely eligible under 28 U.S.C. § 2241 for access to a federal court in the context of a habeas proceeding.[91] In any case, prior to *Boumediene*, the judicial review options featured in the DTA were consonant with the constitutional requirements as construed by the Supreme Court in such leading cases as *Milligan*, *Quirin*, and *In re Yamashita*.[92]

Under the Military Commissions Act (MCA), while the Combatant Status Review Tribunal procedures remain unchanged, the military commission–related procedures were greatly refined. The MCA established a new appellate body—the Court of Military Commission Review—as the final entity within the military establishment for reviewing and confirming the decisions of military commissions.[93] It further specified that the D.C. Circuit's jurisdiction to determine the final validity of the military commission's judgment does not arise until all of the intramilitary system appeals have been exhausted, or possibly waived. This seemed reasonable and designed to enable the D.C. Circuit Court to step in after the military system has finished its work.[94] It permitted legitimate judicial review while still ensuring some deference to the military's determinations of the status of those they detain. In addition, it provided more appellate rights than many of the illegal enemy combatants would receive within their own nations.

Section 6 of the MCA reaffirmed the proposition that outside the judicial review system provided through the Detainee Treatment Act, "No court, justice or judge shall have jurisdiction to hear or consider an application for a writ of habeas corpus filed by or on behalf of an alien detained by the United States," provided that he has been determined to be an enemy combatant—presumably, through a CSRT-based process. The law also removed any jurisdiction to hear cases for damages or injunctive relief against the United States or any of its agents arising out of any aspect of detention, transfer, trial, or conditions of confinement of an enemy combatant. When combined with the revised War Crimes Act, this provision effectively vitiated any prospect of civil liability in this area by either the United States or its agents. It ensured legal immunity for CIA interrogators or anyone else involved in the interrogation process, provided they comply with these revised War Crimes Act provisions. The administration was particularly concerned that those government personnel tasked with interrogations would be subject to potential crimes if *Hamdan*'s edicts on this issue were strictly adhered to.[95]

In an understandable response to the *Hamdan* court's decision that the Detainee Treatment Act's provisions limiting jurisdiction were not sufficiently clear on the issue of retroactive application, the Military Commissions Act removed any ambiguity on this issue by declaring that such provisions "shall apply to all cases, without exception, pending on or after the date of the enactment of this Act." Clearly, this is all historical now, but one can see problems in how the court in *Boumediene* has now removed the military completely from the process and requires civilian judges to determine whether military confinement is appropriate. I strongly believe this change will result in many problems, both within the civilian-military relations context and actually fighting this armed conflict.

In sum, the DTA and MCA together had afforded opportunities for the accused to be heard and for essential elements of due process to be preserved. Although not exactly the same as what is expected for an ordinary citizen within the domestic United States or for a prisoner of war for that matter, the Congress attempted to meet and balance the needs of the accused and the government as well as practicable by affording what has been determined the appropriate level of judicial review and oversight. As some have argued, the labor and efforts of Congress and the president were unfortunately cast aside by a Court eager to engage in policy making from the bench.[96]

International Law

The Military Commissions Act survived debate over whether it complies with the relevant international law standards. In this regard, under both customary international law and in accordance with the Third Geneva Convention, only those warriors who comply with the requirements of lawful warfare are accorded prisoner-of-war status upon capture. These provisions, granting POW status to captured lawful enemy combatants, are predicated upon important policy imperatives. These imperatives are the need to treat captured legitimate enemy soldiers with the respect they deserve and the desire to ensure that reciprocal treatment is accorded to captured U.S. soldiers.

In the current war, however, the enemy combatants evidence neither honor nor the slightest desire to treat captured U.S. soldiers with respect. Indeed, al Qaeda fighters reject, both in word and action, any notion of compliance with the laws of war and view reciprocity as a weakness in Western war fighting—a "weakness" they intend to continue to exploit. They torture U.S. personnel when captured, behead

Americans on videos that are then publicly distributed, and deny U.S. citizens any protections whatsoever. Thus, the enemies, *de jure belli*, are not themselves entitled to POW-level protections.[97] They are not warriors in the traditional sense and thus, the MCA, in accordance with established military jurisprudence, does not provide them with such status. This, of course, should not impact the treatment (accorded by states that are signatories to the Geneva Conventions) of those who fight wars as lawful combatants and thereby qualify for POW protections. Thus, international law is not impacted, nor superseded, by the MCA. Rather, the MCA reinforces understood principles and American perspectives on the proper handling of illegal combatants during time of war. However, there were and continue to be policy aspects of the commissions that run afoul of international human rights law and customary international law. For example, issues such as the availability of the death penalty as a sentence and other comparative law requirements legitimately continue to cause great concern among many of our allies.[98]

Torture Convention

It is now clear, and has been repeatedly reinforced at various levels of the government, that torture is not part of the American way of war—regardless of whom we fight or what has transpired overseas in isolated incidents. As a member of the armed forces for over twenty years and coming from a military family, I see this as an issue of the greatest import to many in the service. What distinguishes the U.S. military in world history has been its generally noble actions in times of war. Although there have been isolated incidents when U.S. armed forces deviate from this norm (e.g., My Lai during the Vietnam War), in general, the American armed forces pride themselves in their commitment to uphold the law of armed conflict. In the twenty-first century, the U.S. military (as policy) often goes beyond the norm, in every operation, to ensure that during battle, soldiers and officers alike abide by human rights obligations—even emerging international norms. The United States abhors torture and is never interested in seeing its horrific acts or impacts attached to U.S. military efforts. To do otherwise would be contradictory to the ethos of the American warrior, which is to promote human rights during warfare. Thus, Congress, in passing the Military Commissions Act, considered whether the legislation complies with U.S. obligations under the International Convention against Torture.[99] In this regard, the MCA explicitly incorporates language, originally articulated in the McCain amendment (eventually embodied in the Detainee Treatment Act of 2005), which ensures that detainees cannot be tortured. Specifically, the McCain amendment prohibited "cruel, inhuman, or degrading torture or punishment."[100] The MCA supports these obligations and clearly spells out that no evidence obtained through the use of torture will be admissible in commission proceedings.

The MCA goes even further, however, and limits the introduction of coerced statements. Alleged coerced evidence must be scrutinized by the judge to determine whether it is, in fact, reliable and probative before admitting it. This procedure was followed in the commission completed against Hamdan in 2008. The military judge did not admit into evidence several statements of the accused (when introduced by the prosecution) because he deemed them unreliable, as they had been obtained through coercive methods.[101] This process is extremely important both to protect the rights of the accused and to instill respect for the integrity of the commission proceedings. The latter is essential, since many al Qaeda fighters will still claim they were subjected to torture. In fact, as part of al Qaeda's training manuals, when captured, the al Qaeda fighter is ordered, by established doctrine, to claim he was the subject of torture. Despite such provisions, numerous scholars and think tank commentators continue to argue that the United States has, and continues to, engage in torture. Leading legal philosopher Jeremy Waldron has pushed for the United States not to quibble over semantics but to take a strong, clear stand against the authorization of anything close to torture. He writes, "The prohibition on torture is not just one rule among others, but a legal archetype—a provision which is emblematic of our larger commitment to non-brutality in the legal system."[102] Other leading academics and legal scholars have expressed similar concerns. These well-intentioned and reasoned concerns highlight the problems of having quasi-warriors detained in Guatanamo and appearing before military commissions. Such allegations are provided unintentional support (no matter what statutory language is included to prevent torture) when the alleged al Qaeda fighters remain in captivity, most not charged, without trial for six or more years. The perceptions being conveyed are not helpful—and are actually harmful—in maintaining support for the commissions. Such accusations of alleged torture are inevitable in an armed conflict such as this, and the United States gives credence to such accusations by supporting the concept of preventive detention. The solution, however, is simple: try every detainee—regardless of the forum. Opportunities for abuse are exacerbated when extraordinary procedures are implemented, such as seven years of arguably unintended preventive detention. Having said that, the fact remains that the MCA is clear in its prohibition of torture.

Due Process

Military commissions traditionally offered little process whatsoever to "detainees." As noted in Supreme Court jurisprudence and precedent, unlawful belligerents are not normally afforded much process at all. Despite the many who question the procedure, the MCA has ensured that the commissions will be fair. As former military prosecutor Kyndra Rotunda notes in her recent book, *Honor Bound*, the detainees were actually afforded a good deal of support, care, and reasonable process.[103] Others, such as David Glazier, claim that the MCA takes away our long-standing position on promoting the rule of law. One would think, listening to the more strident critics of the MCA, that the United States is unilaterally denying citizens of other nations any rights whatsoever. Although not analogous to the civilian court process and not perfect by any argument, the Military Commissions Act does provide numerous rights and a great deal of process to unlawful belligerents. Despite the myriad policy flaws in having the military conduct these hearings, the commissions are actually rights-laden. The MCA provides rights that often go well beyond the procedures and protections of other systems— including virtually all international systems. There are numerous due process rights clearly afforded through the MCA, and one can argue that these rights actually reinforce the United States' commitment to upholding the rule of law. Rotunda goes so far as to call the camps at Guatanamo analogous to Boy Scout camps. She writes, "To some extent, yes it is Club Gitmo. Detainees live in open bays and have up to 12 hours of exercise time each day...sports including basketball, soccer, and ping pong. They also enjoy an extensive library (Harry Potter translated into Arabic is among the most popular titles)...detainees receive the call to prayer five times a day...one asked the U.S. government to move his entire family to Gitmo."[104] Others continue to disagree— often vehemently.[105] But the military commissions do in fact, as listed earlier, offer generous protections to the accused al Qaeda fighter.

Mirror of the Uniform Code of Military Justice (UCMJ)

As mentioned earlier, during congressional consideration of the Military Commissions Act, many efforts were made to import into the military commission system provisions virtually analogous to those found in the UCMJ. *Hamdan* suggested that the military commission system might be the appropriate venue to best comply with the requirement that alleged unlawful combatants be tried by a "regularly constituted court" found within the Geneva tradition. In fact, many of the congressional proposals (submitted after *Hamdan* was decided) went so far as to attempt to mirror the provisions of the UCMJ. Had they been adopted, such procedures would have elevated the status of the illegal belligerent to a level well beyond his stature envisioned by international law. In fact, by applying what would be applied to our own men and women in the armed forces, these proposals would have raised the legal status of a person who kills civilians indiscriminately, flouts the laws of armed conflict, and engages in torture to that of a lawful combatant. Beyond which, if the United States were to afford the detainees a court-martial, problems would again be inevitable (e.g., evidentiary conflicts as well as difficulties in obtaining an unbiased "jury"). Even so, the MCA adopted most, but not all, of the UCMJ procedures. The MCA responded to the Court's concerns about ensuring that the UCMJ is used as a procedural guide. The MCA incorporated various provisions but did not go so far as to make these commissions identical to the otherwise distinct military courts.

Common Article 3 of the Geneva Conventions

The Supreme Court in the *Hamdan* case stated that Common Article 3 should be applicable to the commission process because Congress incorporated that article into the UCMJ provisions dealing with military commissions. Of note, Common Article 3 specifically applies only to "conflicts not of an international character." It is difficult, as Justice Thomas noted in his *Hamdan* dissent, to characterize the global war on terror as anything less than an international conflict.[106] But the political branches, in seeking compromise, did not tinker or quibble over these requirements.

It is critical to clarify where Common Article 3 really applies and what it actually demands. Under the Geneva Conventions, prisoner of war status is reserved for captured soldiers in the regular armed forces of nations that have signed the Geneva treaties. POWs receive the gold standard of treatment: they cannot be placed in cells; they need only provide name, rank, and serial number; and they are entitled to a great many privileges and benefits, such as retaining their uniforms, unit structures, and chains of command. These rules have in mind the conflicts between the large conscript armies of the First and Second World Wars. They provide protections to those who follow the law of war's prohibition on the deliberate targeting of civilians and its restriction on the employment of violence only against combatants.

The major purpose of these provisions is to ensure, through treaty, that reciprocity is afforded to all nations and their armed forces once engaged in combat. Al Qaeda did not exist at the time the Geneva Conventions were drafted, and affording such protections was never in the minds of the signatories—certainly not the United States. Al Qaeda is not a nation-state and could not be, nor will it ever be, party to such treaties. It has no intention of following any of the laws of war. In fact, its primary tactics—targeting and killing civilians, taking hostages, and executing prisoners—are designed specifically to violate any standards of civilized warfare. Therefore, our conflict with al Qaeda cannot trigger the general POW protections of the Geneva Conventions.

Common Article 3 applies to certain fighters who do not qualify as POWs. It sets minimum standards "in the case of armed conflict not of an international character." Its inclusion in 1949 cured a major gap in the Geneva Conventions, as the original Conventions did not set rules for internal civil wars between a government and resistance or rebel groups. Common Article 3 extends minimum protections to detainees who are not fighting on behalf of the armed forces of another nation, but it does not mandate that they receive the same protections as POWs. It requires, for example, that "persons taking no active part in the hostilities," including the sick, wounded, and captured, "be treated humanely." They are to be protected against "violence to life and person, in particular murder of all kinds, mutilation, cruel treatment and torture."[107]

The basic purpose of Common Article 3—humane treatment—is already the policy of the United States and its armed forces. But Common Article 3 also contains some ambiguous provisions. It prohibits "outrages upon personal dignity, in particular, humiliating and degrading treatment," which it does not define. It only allows the use of a "regularly constituted court affording all the judicial guarantees which are recognized as indispensable by civilized peoples," which it again leaves undefined.

The armed conflict with al Qaeda does not fit within the general Geneva Convention rules for wars between nation-states. Al Qaeda terrorists are not legally eligible for the rights granted to POWs. But the War on al Qaeda does not fall within Common Article 3 either. The United States is not fighting an internal civil war. The battlefield reaches beyond Afghanistan and Iraq, to New York City, Washington, London, Bali, and Madrid. The war that began with the attacks on the World Trade Center and the Pentagon on 9/11 is certainly nothing like the internal civil wars that were in the minds of those who drafted Common Article 3 in 1949. We are not fighting a liberation movement of Americans who want to overthrow the government. We are fighting something that lies completely outside the experience of those who wrote the Geneva Conventions after World War II: an international terrorist organization with the power to inflict destruction on a par with that possible by the armed forces of a nation.[108]

Additionally, *Hamdan* disregarded the distinctions between lawful and illegal combatants. The enemy we now fight does not abide by the laws of war. Any incentive to follow the rules of civilized warfare is removed if that enemy receives the same rights as those who scrupulously obey the Geneva Conventions. As alluded to earlier in this chapter, in applying Common Article 3 to al Qaeda, we equate illegal combatants with ordinary armed forces. By affording Geneva Convention protections to al Qaeda, we are legitimizing its illegal form of warfare.

The MCA reflects the decision by the Bush administration to continue observing both the letter and the spirit of the Common Article 3 requirements. In this regard, the administration proposed detailed language, defining what constitutes compliance with the various requirements of Common Article 3. The need for such definitions is quite palpable, since Common Article 3 contains some well-defined terms, such as "taking of hostages" and "murder," and some extraordinarily broad, vague language, such as "outrages upon personal dignity, in particular, humiliating and degrading treatment." It is also significant that while many of the Article 3 provisions have a universal or near-universal meaning, the concept of humiliation is inherently shaped by one's culture. Ironically, any of these same over-broad requirements would be held unconstitutionally vague in our own domestic jurisprudence. Yet, some scholars still suggest that such indistinct and undefined requirements should be enforced on our military and CIA personnel conducting operations in time of war.[109] They claim that violations of these provisions by U.S. personnel could unintentionally lead to politically motivated prosecutions against U.S. men and women by other nations and international entities.

For example, in American culture (and in most Western cultures), if a person is interrogated by a woman, the occurrence is not viewed as humiliating. It is certainly no more humiliating than an interrogation conducted by a man. By contrast, under the radical versions of Islam, which treat women with disdain, to be interrogated by a woman is viewed as a highly humiliating event, no matter how civil the interrogation procedures might be. Many other well-accepted aspects of an interrogation regime—for example, the standard "good cop/bad cop" routine—while acceptable in Western cultures, may well be viewed as humiliating in a culture that eschews open confrontation. Accordingly, given the inherent subjectivity of such terms as "humiliation" or "outrages against personal dignity," it is entirely appropriate for each state signatory to the Geneva Conventions to translate this language into constitutionally and culturally appropriate domestic law parlance. Doing so certainly does not amount to a repudiation of U.S. international law obligations.[110]

The MCA language essentially defines the interrogation-related strictures of Common Article 3 as being coterminous with the relevant provisions of the Constitution's Bill of Rights, namely, the Fifth, Eighth, and Fourteenth Amendments. These amendments, and the U.S. domestic jurisprudence that construes them, lie at the very heart of the American system of ordered liberty. Criticisms that the United States is being disrespectful to, or worse, disregarding altogether international law appears disingenuous.

Congress determined that the MCA's harmonization of U.S. international and domestic law obligations, including its interpretation of the requirements of Common Article 3, was both reasonable and necessary. There is a broad belief, both within the executive branch and among the American people, that while torture and cruel or inhuman treatment ought not to be deployed, some use of intense interrogation techniques should remain permissible.[111] Even the administration's strongest critics in the Senate have essentially acknowledged that they also support the continuation of aggressive interrogation techniques, at least by the CIA. Yet, to ensure that CIA interrogation programs can continue, it is necessary to assure CIA personnel that their conduct fully comports with the relevant U.S. domestic and international legal obligations. Indeed, the president, on the advice of his senior intelligence officials, has concluded that a mere affirmation that CIA interrogators cannot be prosecuted in the future is not sufficient in the current legal and political climate; what is needed is a clear and compelling public affirmation that the interrogators' conduct is both lawful and appropriate.[112]

During hearings on the MCA, the Senate Armed Services Committee considered a bill that provided the necessary domestic legal protections to the CIA interrogators (by modifying the existing War Crimes Act language), but it did not define what conduct would constitute full compliance with U.S. obligations under Common Article 3. As such, as then drafted, the bill did nothing to protect CIA interrogators from potential future prosecutions in foreign courts or international tribunals. Such ambiguity in this critical statute was both unfair and seemingly derelict in not ensuring protections and clarity for U.S. government personnel charged with conducting interrogations.

In the public debate that ensued in the United States, some asserted that even full compliance with U.S. domestic law (in accord with the revised War Crimes Act) did not constitute compliance with international law (as provided by Common Article 3); they further claimed that this status made foreign prosecutions of CIA interrogators in the future all the more likely. This is true in part because ordinarily such international legal actions are most appropriate where the home state of the accused has manifested an unwillingness to handle the matters itself (or conducted a "sham proceeding" in order to protect the accused). This was certainly a great concern of both the armed forces and members of the CIA. A foreign tribunal could conclude that the revised War Crimes Act has improperly immunized CIA interrogators from their obligation to comply rigorously with Common Article 3 strictures and could order such prosecutions. As a result, the Bush administration persuaded Congress to ensure that the MCA detailed what the United States government understood to be its obligations under international law (Common Article 3). Although a harmonization of U.S. international and domestic law obligations did not absolutely guarantee that no foreign prosecutions would be pursued, it made such prosecutions less likely.[113] The Military Commissions Act wisely provides protections for our CIA members as well as servicemen and servicewomen from politically motivated charges while still upholding our international obligations. It represents the interpretation of the Geneva Conventions by the political branches (the executive and the legislative) vested by our Constitution with interpreting and executing the nation's international obligations.[114]

The purpose and intent of the MCA is that a foreign tribunal will refrain from prosecuting a CIA officer based upon a reading of Common Article 3 that departs from an interpretation that has been publicly and explicitly adopted by both political branches of the United States government. Significantly, the final "compromise" language of the MCA accomplishes this goal, responds to the Supreme Court's guidance and once again, strikes an appropriate balance and removes much of this concern and ambiguity.

After the Military Commissions Act

The enactment of the Military Commissions Act was an important moment in U.S. history. It confirmed that within American law and jurisprudence, military tribunals (in a time of war) can be lawful and just. Maybe even more important, the enactment confirmed that this conflict with international terror is, in fact, a war and thus all laws and actions stemming from the armed conflict must incorporate this fact. The bipartisan MCA was thought to have put to rest, once and for all, the debate over whether this conflict requires a law enforcement response. In *Hamdi* and *Hamdan*, the Supreme Court confirmed that this was a war, and Congress has reaffirmed that the conflict surrounding international terror is a war—and one that is unique, with distinct rules for illegal combatants, habeas corpus, introduction of evidence, and other issues. At the time of the signing of the MCA in October 2006, it seemed to me that all three branches of the United States government had spoken in harmony on the key legal issues involved in this war. Of course, all of this was prior to Justice Kennedy's majority opinion in *Boumediene* in which the Court hints that this is more of a law enforcement action than a war. This opinion that the Court is beginning to view the fight with al Qaeda as more law enforcement than warfare is reinforced by the fact that the holding in *Boumediene* now affords standard U.S. constitutional rights (at least one) to the al Qaeda fighters.[115]

However, some see the MCA and the military commissions as having been harmed permanently through the aggressive political and public relations campaign waged by myriad organizations within and outside the United States. I am one of those. It seems that regardless of the lawfulness of these commissions when applied to a regular enemy in a regular war between nation-states, the unique conflict we are in begs for a new means of detaining and adjudicating the al Qaeda international terrorists. The legitimacy of the commissions, seven years later, remains suspect. Even as several of the commissions do indeed go forward, as Hamdan's did in the summer of 2008, many individuals will still question the legitimacy of the court, and therefore its verdict. Despite providing a lawful, fair trial, the MCA and the commissions are simply not suited for this conflict. Indeed, Secretary of

Defense Robert Gates and Secretary of State Condoleezza Rice have stated that although the commissions are lawful, as a matter of policy the commissions have been tainted to such a degree that the United States should consider looking toward other venues to detain and try the enemy combatants.[116] Thus, fresh ideas and new approaches need to be injected into the debate to ensure that a smooth transition and a coherent long-term policy is in place for this generational war. It seems, as will be discussed in greater detail in chapter 6, that *Boumediene v. Bush* has pushed us further along this path toward real reform and has highlighted the need for a new system that can meet the needs of both due process and national security.

Although the military commissions and the Military Commissions Act are lawful, policy makers need to be looking for a long-term solution—one that is supported both domestically and internationally—by which to properly detain and adjudicate the al Qaeda fighters in this conflict. The Obama administration immediately placed a 120-day hold on the commissions upon taking office in January 2009. As of this writing, the administration is reviewing if any of the military commissions (under the MCA) should go forward. The new administration needs to be mindful that, as a matter of policy, the military commissions and the camp at Guantanamo Bay are not acceptable to many within the United States and have clearly been rejected by our international partners. Although arguably lawful, the legitimacy of the military commission process continues to be questioned—if nothing else, as a matter of U.S. policy. Thus, one can properly view the MCA as a step in a process that is moving toward something more permanent and acceptable from a policy perspective. The process has evolved from the Executive Order of 2001, to the MCA in 2006, and perhaps now to something more permanent in the not too distant future. In essence, the process has been adapting and maturing over the past seven years. This natural maturation of military jurisprudence, however, needs to be considered, debated, and developed by the political branches, and not, as in *Hamdan*, by an overly ambitious, results oriented, judicial branch.

SIX

❧

The Legal Landscape after *Boumediene*

B Y JULY 2008, almost seven years after President Bush's Order establishing the military commissions, there had not been a successful prosecution at Guantanamo Bay. The military commissions achieved only one plea deal, known as a pretrial agreement (PTA) in military law, against an Australian citizen named David Hicks. The first actual "trial" was finally docketed for July 21, 2008, and even so, was still expected to have numerous challenges and procedural difficulties. In fact, although the trial had several surprises and some difficulties, it ran smoothly and resulted in the conviction of Hamdan. Hamdan's sentence was time served with an additional six months. Thus, by December 2008, Hamdan was already released. Other than this one "successful" prosecution, the Department of Defense's implementation of the Bush Order is best characterized as a disaster. For numerous reasons, the military commissions' process is not ideally suited for the twenty-first-century unconventional war the United States is fighting against international terrorism. Although more than ideal for conventional wars against nation-states, and an established component of American military law jurisprudence, the military commissions are clearly not the right forum for trying detainees in the War on al Qaeda. This is a different war with different needs, actions, and procedures. Similar to the changes the United States has made strategically, bureaucratically, militarily, and politically since 2001, it needs to continue morphing the military commissions into something new to better confront the threats we now face.[1] The War on al Qaeda has created ambiguities in the laws of armed conflict and knowledge of how best to fight a war in the twenty-first century. The asymmetric threat in and of itself, the lack of a nation-state to fight against, the relative mess that has resulted from utilizing military commissions in Guantanamo Bay, the political ramifications of preventive detention, allegations of torture, the constitutional issues surrounding the wiretap efforts of the National Security Agency (the Terrorist Surveillance Program, TSP), the updating of the 1978 Foreign Intelligence Surveillance Act (FISA), and recent U.S. Supreme Court jurisprudence all highlight the lack of appropriate laws to govern this new conflict. However, nowhere has the ambiguity of dealing with this conflict—and the rules that apply to it—been more evident than in the United States' handling of the detainees.[2] Congressional hearings on Guantanamo Bay conducted during the summer and early fall of 2008 further complicated the already vague and confusing legal landscape. The political branches need to do more than just hold hearings. They need to find solutions to the quagmire we are immersed in.

The "enemies" in the War on al Qaeda are men and women who do not represent any nation-state but rather an ideology based on extreme religious beliefs; they do not wear standard military uniforms as required by the Geneva Conventions and they do not follow the laws of war. These new "warriors" have proven difficult to categorize since they are not, *de jure belli*, prisoners of war in the traditional sense; because of this, many scholars assert that the Geneva tradition simply does not apply to them.[3] Adjudicating their status and crimes has become increasingly chaotic. As argued earlier, the 2006 U.S. Supreme Court holding in *Hamdan v. Rumsfeld*[4] exacerbated this confusion by declaring the military commissions, as constructed by the Bush administration, to be unlawful.

The landscape became even more confused and uncertain after the Supreme Court decision in *Boumediene v. Bush*,[5] decided in mid-June 2008. While it remains unclear how the political branches will eventually respond, national polls indicate that the majority of citizens in the United States disagree with the decision of the Court.[6] *Boumediene* has only made the legal landscape even murkier by essentially overruling the holding and precedents established in *Hamdan* just two years ago.

Lakhdar Boumediene, a naturalized citizen of Bosnia and Herzegovnia, was suspected by U.S. intelligence agencies of conspiring to blow up the U.S. embassy in Bosnia. He was arrested by the Bosnian police and turned over to U.S. authorities. He was transferred to Guantanamo in 2002. He appealed his confinement through a writ of habeas corpus, and after the case went through a tortured history, the Supreme Court issued the writ and granted review in 2007.

Essentially, the issues in the case were whether alien enemy combatants have a constitutional right of habeas corpus, and if so, if the provisions afforded within the Military Commissions Act meet this constitutional right.[7] In *Boumediene*, Justice Kennedy, writing for the 5–4 majority, held that the detainees do, in fact, have the U.S. constitutional right of habeas corpus and the MCA provisions did not satisfy this requirement. The majority held that the alternative "habeas" procedures set up within the construct of the Detainee Treatment Act (DTA) were not in accord with the U.S. Constitution. The Combatant Status Review Tribunals (CSRTs) that had been used to determine the validity of holding the detainees since 2005 were determined to be flawed procedures. After a lengthy, twenty-page history of the right of habeas corpus within Western legal traditions, Kennedy stated that the CSRTs were "inadequate" as a substitute for traditional challenges of detention.[8] Justice Scalia, in a scathing dissent, thought differently: "The procedures prescribed by Congress in the Detainee Treatment Act provide the essential protections that habeas corpus guarantees; there has thus been no suspension of the writ, and no basis exists for judicial intervention beyond what the Act allows."[9] He went on to discuss the dangers inherent in making determinations about whether a detainee has a propensity to engage in terrorism. He noted the many detainees who, upon release, went back to the "battlefield" and engaged in terrorism once again. These types of examples illustrate "the incredible difficulty of assessing who is and who is not an enemy combatant in a foreign theater of operation where the environment does not lend itself to rigorous evidence collection."[10] Chief Justice Roberts, Justice Thomas, and Justice Alito joined this dissent.

The Court, however, dismissed the arguments of Scalia et al.; instead, the majority granted the detainees direct access to U.S. district courts to have civilian judges rule on the appropriateness of military captivity. This dangerous holding was based upon the premise that the Guantanamo Naval Base is, although within a sovereign nation, under exclusive U.S. control and thus, "some parts" of the Constitution should apply to the detainees.[11] The ramifications and practical realities of this decision will no doubt result in huge backlogs within our federal court system. Under the Court's reasoning, the overseas base in Cuba is U.S. territory and therefore, the constitutional requirements of habeas corpus rights apply. Although Justice Kennedy went to great lengths to limit his decision to the unique circumstances at Guantanamo and to the al Qaeda fighter,[12] able defense counsel will now undoubtedly analogize the Guantanamo base to other military bases within foreign, sovereign nations as well. The United States maintains military bases under U.S. exclusive control all over the world. The numbers of detainees in both Iraq and Afghanistan alone are estimated in the thousands by most accounts—huge numbers compared to the mere 245 or so remaining at Guantanamo.[13] In my conversations with senior members of the Justice Department in July (less than one month after the decision), they confirmed that the Court's decision has created a massive, resource-intensive effort for the Department of Justice. For example, the department is now forced to "detail" federal lawyers from around the country to handle the 200-plus cases being filed in the Federal District Court of D.C. These numbers are incredible and there is little doubt they will continue to grow. In no time at all, the U.S. civilian court system will unnecessarily be bogged down in litigation over whether the holding in *Boumediene* also does in fact apply to those detainees held in Bagram or Baghdad.

Applying the Supreme Court's analysis in *Boumediene*, it seems difficult to argue that the holding does not apply to those detained in Afghanistan and Iraq. Both countries have U.S. bases that are located in nations that are sovereign, like Cuba, with the U.S. military bases under complete and total U.S. control. It will quickly become apparent to most that the opinion may have ventured too far and has disregarded long-established precedent. The Court also created a dangerous new precedent that disregards military decisions made about whether any particular detainee is appropriately held. This, arguably, has a negative impact on the U.S. fight against international terror. While I have argued that the military commissions are an inappropriate forum for the current war, it is important to stress that the civilian courts will prove equally ineffective as a forum. In *Boumediene*, the narrow majority overreacted to perceived flaws in the current system. They injected their policy preferences into military decision making during an ongoing armed conflict. This overreaction did not help the nation heal the divide over Guantanamo or offer any concrete, helpful resolution to the detainees' continued legal ambiguity. Instead, the decision has deepened the divisions and hardened both sides of the debate. Questions continue to rage, even more since the decision, about whether this is really a war or a law enforcement action, and which paradigm is the correct one to embrace.

The Impacts of Boumediene

The Supreme Court's 5–4 decision in *Boumediene v. Bush* justifiably sent shock waves through the legal community. The majority opinion, authored by Justice Anthony Kennedy, disregarded centuries of precedent and the military deference doctrine and also intruded on what is clearly the province of the political branches. As a result of this case, Guantanamo Bay detainees now formally have more rights than do prisoners of war under the Geneva Conventions. To say the least, citizens, regardless of their political affiliation or view on the status of Guantanamo, should be concerned over the ramifications of this decision. As some conservative scholars asserted, "Judicial modesty, respect for the executive and legislative branches, and pure common sense weren't concerns here either.... [J]udicial micromanagement will now intrude into the conduct of war."[14]

The *Boumediene* holding permits aliens to exercise constitutional rights within U.S. courts of law. This has never been the policy of the United States nor has the court ever granted such rights to those detained outside of U.S. jurisdiction. As discussed earlier, it is the first of the Supreme Court cases since the attacks of 9/11 that declares the military commission process to contain a constitutional violation. *Rasul, Hamdi,* and *Hamdan* all chipped away on the edges of the commissions but had refrained from holding any portions of the military commissions unconstitutional. While many on both sides of the aisle believe that Guantanamo and the military commissions are flawed as a matter of policy (and some of law), and think it is in the best interests of the nation to close Guantanamo, this case actually goes further and will have greater impact than if the commissions themselves were found to violate the Constitution. In reality, the decision has only further confused and complicated the entire military commission process. It has done little other than to ensure any actual trials of the detainees are delayed further. Justice Kennedy went to lengths to limit the decision to only those detained at Guantanamo now,[15] but his decision clearly will be analogized by some to other military bases overseas (e.g., in Afghanistan, Iraq, and other bases in the future) where detainees are held. The practical effect is the flooding of an already overburdened federal court system. These detainees will not only have access to federal district courthouses but will gain the rights of American citizens to challenge their cases within the United States. One can only imagine further unprecedented constitutional challenges, such as applying the Fourth and Fifth Amendments to the detainees, arguing that these provisions of the U.S. Constitution apply to those searched or captured on the field of battle. This is not a stretch, but a frightening, arguably unintended consequence, of the decision.[16] Some have asserted that these concerns are alarmist. Professor Richard Epstein of the University Chicago School of Law (who wrote an amicus brief on behalf of *Boumediene*) wrote a piece for the *New York Times* praising the decision: "It is a rejection of the alarmist view that our fragile geopolitical position requires abandoning our commitment to preventing Star Chamber proceedings that result in arbitrary incarceration."[17] It seems that Epstein's references to the military commissions or military law (detention) as "star chambers" is disingenuous toward the armed forces. Unfortunately, the Court's decision in *Boumediene* as well as op-ed pieces such as those by Epstein and Professor Jack Balkin of Yale Law School reveal a perhaps unintended negative perspective of the military, and one that in many ways is dismissive of military input— even during a time of war.[18]

Boumediene removed the military from the habeas corpus process altogether. Few doubt we are a nation involved in some sort of an armed conflict and that the military is detaining and adjudicating the unlawful combatants accused of war crimes within the military commissions. Under the holding, however, now only civilian federal judges (without any opportunity for the military to formally review, or determine, the status of those they detain), within federal district court, will determine whether the detainee is held appropriately and subsequently whether to issue a writ of habeas corpus.[19] The same military that has captured and detained the alleged al Qaeda fighters will now not have the opportunity to fully review, recommend, and determine the status of the individuals they detain. After *Boumediene*, the decision regarding military detention of enemies is purely in the hands of the civilian courts.

Traditionally, courts refrain from interfering with ongoing military operations or policy decisions and have repeatedly avoided intruding in this arena if at all possible.[20] In *Boumediene*, however, the Court inserted itself into what has traditionally been purely military decision making. Justice John Paul Stevens (for the majority) had written in

Hamdan v. Rumsfeld that the Uniform Code of Military Justice should be applied to these detainees.[21] In *Hamdan,* the Court had also held that the commissions must be approved by Congress and be in compliance with Common Article 3 of the Geneva Conventions.[22] The political branches responded to this prompting by the Court and enacted the Military Commissions Act embracing virtually all the recommendations found within *Hamdan.*[23] Strangely, just two years later, *Boumediene* disregards most of the *Hamdan* edicts. In essence, they now injected new policies to be considered by the political branches. This nibbling away at the edges of the military commissions is burdensome and confusing for policy makers. Additionally, the Court has intruded in what the Founders clearly intended to be decisions best left to the political branches.[24] With so much angst over executive power in the past few years, one hopes reasonable minds will recognize this overreach by the Court. Clearly, Congress and the president are better able to make these military decisions.

Ironically, an unintended consequence of the holding is that it affords greater protections to the alleged unlawful belligerents than those granted prisoners of war under the Geneva Conventions. This confusing result should be shocking to Americans. POWs are supposed to receive the "gold standard" of treatment, but no one ever envisioned that they would have access to the domestic courts of the detaining country to challenge their detention and status.[25] The detainees, of course, are not even signatories to the tradition of the Geneva Conventions. But now the least accountable branch, the judiciary, has determined that someone such as Khalid Sheik Mohammad (the mastermind of 9/11) should be given access to U.S. courts of justice.[26] Change of some sort in the process is clearly necessary. Inaction on such concerns by the political branches should not be the catalyst for the Supreme Court to intervene—particularly when such decisions impact a nation at war.

Rather than debating back and forth, critiquing the commissions and producing no concrete resolutions, policy makers should quickly review the implications of the decision and find mutual ground on how best to proceed. The Supreme Court in *Boumediene* seemed to now view the armed conflict as more of a law enforcement action. This could prove dangerous in law, military operations, and policy. Most serving in the military are not comfortable having the Supreme Court as their new operational commander. The civilian courts are not equipped nor were they ever intended to address the unique aspects of military detention and needs. Since the founding of the country up through today, a separate federal criminal system has been used for military members. This is especially important when applying the law of armed conflict during ongoing combat operations.

The reality is that the political branches must seek a third way—neither within the existing federal courts nor the military commissions but through a specialized hybrid court with civilian oversight as the best means to balance the interests of both national security and human rights interests. *Boumediene*, despite all its faults, might just be the catalyst necessary for the creation of a new system better suited to meet the needs of policy makers and lawyers in this hybrid armed conflict.[27]

The Current (Confusing) State of Affairs

As argued earlier, relying in large part on *Ex Parte Quirin*,[28] it appeared that the military commissions would provide the appropriate venue for handling the prosecution of the detainees. However, seven years later, not one prosecution has been completed; nearly 242 detainees remain at Guantanamo and thousands more are being held in Afghanistan. National and international support for the commissions has steadily eroded, particularly over the past two years. Rather than relying upon the paradigms of the past, the United States must aggressively pursue new ways to meet the needs of twenty-first-century warfare.

As this problem—a virtual crisis—escalates, Congress must entertain a new approach. This is a new war, one that mixes law enforcement and warfare and does not fit neatly in either category. We are engaged in armed conflict and do use our traditional armed forces in various ways, but in this conflict they are supported in great measure (more than ever before) by the efforts of civilian law enforcement entities, such as the FBI and the CIA. In some cases, even local police officers are now involved in training and teaching the foreign militaries as well. The War on al Qaeda requires both armed force as well as a law enforcement response. It truly is a hybrid. In cooperation and concert with the Foreign Intelligence Surveillance Act (hereinafter referred to as FISA), a new security court apparatus needs to be created. The Military Commissions Act[29] enacted in the fall of 2006 has started the process of looking toward specialized antiterrorism courts roughly based on the military tribunals currently employed by the U.S. government. This legislation is the continuation of what I believe to be an evolutionary process dealing with this new threat—one that is new to U.S. policy makers and must be routinely reviewed and updated as necessary. This experience with international terror is relatively new and the political branches must necessarily remain flexible as the United States and the world continue to confront this new threat and make changes as we better understand the enemy and their tactics.

Thus, the MCA was a good start to what will be an ongoing dialogue among policy makers from both major political parties in the United States. *Boumediene* now creates the opportunity for greater dialogue and the possibility for developing real, concrete solutions. Regardless of the incremental steps taken toward achieving the appropriate balance between promoting human rights and the rule of law as well as ensuring the nation's security, the issue of detainees will not go away soon, nor will the War on al Qaeda or the greater "war on terror" end in the foreseeable future. We need to be able to achieve both the reality and appearance of justice for both the short and long term. Creating a federal terrorist security court system will enable us to adequately fight the war, maintain international support, and continue to display our resolve to uphold the rule of law. In order to lay the foundation necessary for a congressionally mandated court system for national security, I will first briefly discuss the background of the law of armed conflict, argue that the United States is in fact "at war" against international terrorism, detail some of the problems uncovered at Guantanamo (and in Bagram, Afghanistan), offer some ideas on how to proceed and fix perceptions both domestically and internationally, and discuss why civilian courts will prove as problematic for the United States as the commissions have been during the past few years. My hope remains that the political branches will act courageously in bipartisan fashion to adopt this new system. We must avoid finger pointing and casting aspersions and find new, fresh ways to "fight" this war. With a new president and a new Congress sworn in in January 2009, the chance for real "change" in our detention of the alleged al Qaeda fighter is at its apex. If the political branches do not act, I remain cynical and see the nation remaining divided on this critical issue in the years to come. As history tells us, a nation divided is a nation unable to ever attain victory. This war remains one where defeat is not an option.[30]

Brief Background on the *Jus in Bello*

As part of public international law, the law of armed conflict regulates the rules that govern actual combat operations, *jus in bello*, versus the rules governing the resort to armed force, *jus ad bellum*. Laws regulating the conduct of hostilities have existed for thousands of years. In fact, the Greeks and Romans incorporated humanitarian concepts in their conduct of hostilities—many of which have become customary components of the law of armed conflict (hereinafter referred to as LOAC).[31] Later, the founder of modern international law, Grotius, provided an analysis of international law that included important foundational principles associated with the conduct of hostilities.[32] Throughout history there has been a conscious recognition of the need to incorporate humanitarian principles into the laws of war. As technology and the ability to inflict harm and damage increased, the LOAC adapted and changed as well. The twentieth century witnessed vast increases in technological capability to inflict damage, and thus the LOAC remained flexible to meet the needs of both policy makers and warriors. The *jus in bello*, in particular, has become increasingly progressive in the past three decades. Since the collapse of the Soviet Union, many nongovernmental organizations and lawyer advocacy groups have been successful in implementing reforms regarding the way warfare is conducted and how militaries should treat one another once captured.[33] The goal of the LOAC has always been to inject human rights into what is essentially inhumane behavior. Policy makers and lawyers often overlook or forget (either willfully or negligently) what an extraordinarily destructive tool war is when used by nations to achieve political objectives.[34] Civilians are normally innocent bystanders, and only engage in combat support as the sovereign permits. In essence, they are nothing more than bystanders to the slaughter. As such, the LOAC seeks to minimize damage to life and property and to reduce the collateral impacts of the catastrophe of warfare on civil society.[35] In addition, the members of the armed forces are not policy makers but merely the "implementers" of the designs of the sovereign. Recognizing this, the LOAC provides protections for the actions warriors take in accordance with the orders of their superiors. Treatment of each others' soldiers, once captured, in like fashion is a critical component of the concept of reciprocity. It has become customary that reciprocity (between legitimate armed forces of nation-states) is necessary to "regulate" the activities of warriors, both in combat and when captured.[36]

In the current War on al Qaeda there is ambiguity as to how best to lawfully respond to the current threat, fulfill our obligations under the *jus in bello*, and uphold the rule of law. Al Qaeda does not respect the laws of war and virtually all of the enemies captured in this conflict are best categorized as "unlawful belligerents." But they are clearly more than international criminals or mafia drug lords. While struggling to appropriately "label" these fighters, policy makers must be mindful to provide the right framework to achieve "victory." Adding to this ambiguity, the war does not fit into the customary laws of war nor does it fit comfortably into any legitimate criminal law regime. Thus, many continue to struggle with whether we are truly at war. This confusion leads to another problem: are captured combatants such as those in Guantanamo Bay and in Bagram, Afghanistan, "warriors" as defined by the Geneva Conventions? These questions continued to plague the Bush administration seven years into the fight with al Qaeda, and these same issues have now been inherited by President Obama.

Are We at War?

Any new system for detention and adjudication of unlawful belligerents in the so-called war on terror must be based upon the premise that we are a nation at war against international terrorists including al Qaeda and other like-minded and loosely associated affiliates. It needs to overtly recognize, however, that this is a unique war, one that mixes law enforcement and warfare. It is the new twenty-first-century warfare. The experiences of traditional nation-state warfare are not preeminent in this international struggle; it is truly an asymmetric war. The enemy does not provide another nation to negotiate with; there is no one to engage in compromise or diplomatic measures short of war; the enemy is not a signatory to treaties such as the Geneva Conventions; and there is no regulatory framework ideally suited to conduct operations, adjudication, or detention of the al Qaeda fighter (other than customary international law). As a result, such armed conflict can seem to more resemble criminal activity than war. But the reality is that the attacks of 9/11 ushered in a new way to wage war and shattered traditional notions of how nations go to war.

The president, Congress, and the United Nations all authorized the use of force in self-defense after the attacks of September 11, 2001 (hereinafter referred to as 9/11).[37] Al Qaeda, on myriad occasions since 1996, has "declared war" on the United States. The level of attack inflicted on New York City and the Pentagon were construed by most, if not all, as an armed attack.[38] The antiterrorist tactics employed over the past two decades, which use a law enforcement model, manifestly failed. The terrorist threats continued to gather throughout the 1990s. The bombings on the World Trade Center in 1993, the attacks on the U.S. embassies in Africa and Bali, and the attack on the USS *Cole* in Yemen were all indicia of a more coordinated and destructive approach by terrorist groups. Despite the fact that al Qaeda has declared war on the United States on numerous occasions since 1996, the country has responded in the past with only increased FBI details and other law enforcement actions. In the fall of 2001, after the attacks on 9/11, the Bush administration sought a change in the U.S. approach. Clearly, the tactics of the enemy had changed and it was necessary to change our response to combat this new wave of terror. The administration made clear that the U.S. response needed to be an armed one. In 2001, al Qaeda had the resources, ability, and will to inflict damage on an enemy commensurate with those possessed by a nation-state. The administration, and many in Congress, understood this to be a new, asymmetric threat that now required military intervention, making it painfully obvious that the law enforcement model would simply not suffice to fight this new, enhanced threat. Still, there are those who continued to advocate a response to al Qaeda by the United States and its allies that employed a law enforcement model.[39] Based on the aggressive acts of violence by these organized terrorist groups, however, it is difficult to describe what has transpired over the past decade as anything less than a declaration of war by organized terrorists who seek nothing less than the destruction of Western civilization. Contrary to some scholars' assertions, the War on al Qaeda is now a three-front conflict—in Afghanistan, Iraq, and the United States.[40]

Scholars continue to debate whether the current armed conflict should be considered a "new war." The enemy, however, is unlike any other in the history of warfare. Al Qaeda does not compare to any former or present enemy, and it follows that our laws (both domestic and international) do not specifically provide for the treatment of such an enemy.[41] But the fact remains that this conflict must be distinguished from the way the United States "combats" the mafia, drug cartels, or other criminals. War involves more than simply monetary interests; it ordinarily involves opposing political objectives.[42] Like nations we have fought throughout the twentieth century including Germany, Korea, and Vietnam, al Qaeda is highly organized, military in nature, and aimed at achieving ideological as well as political objectives.[43] As has been noted, "War is a set of discrete and violent acts undertaken by a nation or entity for political gain."[44] Al Qaeda undertakes its operations not to acquire wealth (as organized crime does) but for military operations and intelligence gathering. They use their resources, both financial and otherwise, to engage in jihad. These actions must necessarily be contrasted against criminal activities and enterprises. Admittedly the line is fine, but al Qaeda has certainly crossed that threshold from engaging in mere criminal activity to waging armed conflict against the United States.

Additionally, international law considers the actions taken by a nation in response to an attack in determining whether the actions being undertaken amount to "war." Certainly the U.S. military invasion of Afghanistan was an armed response to the attacks of 9/11. Additionally, soldiers returning from combat overseas have difficulty viewing their experiences as "law enforcement."[45] It seems inescapably true that the current War on al Qaeda is a war, albeit a new war, which requires new strategy, new tactics, and new policies.

Guantanamo Bay, Cuba

Earlier chapters have argued that the military commissions, ordered by President Bush in 2001,[46] were, at the time, a legitimate and lawful means of adjudicating war crimes committed by alleged illegal combatants. The administration believed that the struggle against international terrorism was a war and determined that the combatants, de jure and de facto, were in fact illegal.[47] The United Nations supported such assertions and defined the attacks on 9/11 as an armed attack and one that permitted an Article 51 response in self-defense.[48] At this time, most Americans were of the opinion that the War on al Qaeda was a new war in the twenty-first century and thus the United States needed both to respond and to adapt in the appropriate way.[49] This was particularly important because the administration anticipated that more attacks could be carried out against U.S. interests and/or within our sovereign territory.[50] It became evident to most policy makers that there was a need to prepare for a generation-long conflict, and the majority supported military commissions as the best available means of detaining, interrogating, and adjudicating alleged terrorists. As discussed in earlier chapters, from both an international law and domestic law perspective, relying on customary international law and the precedents of the Supreme Court,[51] these commissions were lawful and legitimate in handling the new enemy threat.[52] They have long been a recognized tool in warfare for field commanders and the executive branch to use in adjudicating war crimes committed by unlawful combatants. Regardless, seven years later, as a matter more of policy than law, we still have not witnessed a completed prosecution nor have we witnessed a completed adjudication of any detainees at Guantanamo.[53] After the holdings in *Rasul*,[54] *Hamdi*,[55] *Hamdan*,[56] and now *Boumediene*,[57] detainees indeed have access to U.S. courts for resolution of their status and for other judicial proceedings. Although it can be argued that the administration did appropriately react to the attacks (and held the reasonable expectation that multiple attacks were imminent), implementation of the commissions has been a failure and they are clearly not the appropriate forum for use against al Qaeda.

Additionally (relying on the holding in *Eisentrager*)[58], the administration chose Guantanamo Bay as the proper location to hold the detainees and thus, they determined that such access to our federal courts was not foreseeable.[59] This administration's legal analysis is now moot. The detainees, many of whom have been confined and detained for nearly seven years, present the United States with a crisis: how best to handle the existing caseloads and still properly prosecute cases that will inevitably arise in the future. These detentions and the appearance of a lack of process have eroded critical support for the war and diminished U.S. prestige abroad and at home. Although it is a misnomer to call this the "Global War on Terror,"[60] in fact it is a global conflict and one that requires allied support to win. It is essential that the United States remain capable of advancing its interests in all areas internationally without being hampered by the detainee situation.

To achieve this goal, the United States must take several baseline steps in its approach to the War on al Qaeda. The first requires the administration to take responsibility for the mistakes made. They must admit that the detentions at Guantanamo as well as the military commissions have been unsuccessful and have unintentionally raised legitimate questions as to our commitment to the rule of law. Furthermore, the United States needs to find new, fresh, and flexible policies in accordance with the law to both adjudicate the existing cases and to move forward on future cases. Immediate steps must be employed by the United States to begin the process of removing ourselves, with dignity, from the situation in Guantanamo Bay, Cuba, while still advancing legitimate concerns of U.S. national security. President Obama has initiated this process; however, the key remains what to do with the detainees once the detention center is closed in 2010.

Articulating the War on al Qaeda as an Armed Conflict

The Obama administration and the West need to better articulate the struggle against al Qaeda as a war.[61] There needs to be a consistent, persuasive public relations campaign in both the media and academia to convince citizens, both domestically and internationally, that the fight against terror is a "war."[62] The existing confusion over whether this requires a law enforcement or a military response has altered the public perceptions of the conflict. The *Boumediene* case has further confused the issue and created greater ambiguity. There is growing resistance by many to view the threat as one requiring an armed response. To date, the effort at influencing the debate on this issue has been largely unsuccessful. Beyond the fighting in Afghanistan, the war in Iraq, although disputed by some initially, is now a front in the fight against international terror.

The fighting in Iraq is now part of the strategy to better protect the homeland of the United States. If it was not accurate during the initial invasion of Iraq in 2003 as part of Operation Iraqi Freedom (OIF), al Qaeda is now the biggest threat to U.S. forces in the Iraq region.[63] Furthermore, the war in Iraq now needs to be seen as part of the greater Western effort to counter the real threats posed by international terrorism. This requires a more thoughtful agenda, reinforcing the notion that the nation is best protected by an aggressive fight overseas rather than employing the "wait and see" tactics of the past. The "wait and see" attitude, one could assert, was partly responsible for the success of the massive attacks of 9/11 against the World Trade Center and the Pentagon. Some have become complacent once again and have recently been arguing against armed responses overseas. They cite as support that there has not been an attack on U.S. soil since 2001 and therefore the threat of al Qaeda is exaggerated. Simply because there has not been an attack does not mean the enemy has stopped trying. In fact, report after report reveals that al Qaeda remains intent on attacking the United States. We must resist naive impulses and temptations to go backward in time and implement a pre-9/11 mind-set; rather, we must look forward and embrace a "third way."

Al Qaeda and the Jihadists Are Not Warriors

Along these same lines of reasoning, the enemies we face in the War on al Qaeda are not warriors in the historical context or current use of the term. The Geneva Conventions (specifically those dealing with international armed conflict) of 1949, presumptively do not apply to the international terrorist as a matter of law. One of the instrumental reasons for the adoption of the Third Geneva Convention[64] was to provide reciprocity to warriors in combat when captured. Within the context of the current armed conflict, al Qaeda fighters are considered by many to be outside the reach and scope of the Geneva Conventions. They are not lawful belligerents and therefore, once captured, are not prisoners of war. Their ambiguous status does not fit comfortably in existing international and domestic legal constructs. These international terrorists certainly do not provide protections to soldiers of coalition forces or the U.S. armed forces when they capture these soldiers. The United States needs to be conscious of and ready to counter the "lawfare"[65] being employed by the enemy as well as conducting combat operations on the field of battle. A coherent, logical articulation must be formulated in a national security document[66] (much like the National Security Strategy released in March 2006) that lays out the reasons we are engaged in the War on al Qaeda. Such a White House policy document must be tailored specifically to the threat posed by al Qaeda (and like-minded entities) and in contemplation of future wars in the twenty-first century. It is critical that the document intellectually distinguish this threat from the threats of nation-states.

Process

The United States must institute a better process for ascertaining the status of the detainees currently held in Guantanamo and Afghanistan. At a minimum, there does need to be habeas proceedings for the detainees. The United States needs to be able to better articulate who and why alleged fighters are being detained. It now seems clear to most that there should be some form of civilian oversight of the military determinations of the status of those captured and detained. *Boumediene*, as discussed earlier, actually mandates such civilian oversight. The key, of course, is deciding how to do this effectively and determining the best means to provide such civilian oversight over military detentions without further delaying detainee trials and confusing the legal academy.

After the Supreme Court holdings in *Rasul* and *Hamdi*, it became clear that there was a need for some habeas proceeding to occur. The political branches, recognizing that they could not, and should not, afford the same constitutional protections to aliens located outside the boundaries of the United States (as are available to U.S. citizens or even those residing within the United States), responded to the holdings by creating a new system that would balance the detainees' rights under international law (and public opinion) and the military's need to have control and input over the process. The Congress enacted the Detainee

Treatment Act of 2005. This legislation thus created what were known as the Combat Status Review Tribunals (hereinafter referred to as CSRTs). Although not strictly required for the unlawful combatants and consistent with the position that the Third Geneva Convention does not necessarily apply to international terrorists, the CSRTs did not require many resources, did not deviate from our desire to distinguish between lawful combatants and enemy combatants, and were viewed by some as a clear demonstration of "good faith" on the part of the United States. However, they never garnered much support and were routinely criticized by lawyers, academics, and some politicians.

A now widely cited Seton Hall Law School study, conducted by Mark Denbeaux and his students, revealed deep flaws in the CSRT process.[67] Others, such as retired Army officer Lieutenant Colonel Stephen Abraham, who was as an officer involved in the CSRT processes, have declared that these proceedings were, in fact, shams.[68] Although other studies challenged many of Denbeaux's assertions—most notably a study by West Point's Counter-Terrorism Center—the damage was done.[69] Political leaders, such as Senator Chris Dodd of Connecticut, responded by introducing legislation to replace the CSRT process with the traditional means of habeas proceedings in our own domestic courts.[70] Although such legislation was never enacted, in many ways, once again, the administration sat back and did not get ahead of this issue of habeas corpus rights of the detainees.

After *Boumediene*, which declared that the detainees as a matter of constitutional law do indeed have direct access to U.S. courts, a reasonable compromise must be reached by Congress. Any proposed system should strike the appropriate balance necessary to provide habeas proceedings to the detainees without flooding our district courts with petitions. It needs to afford a reasonable compromise providing civilian oversight of the habeas proceeding while still ensuring that deference is given to our military commanders' decisions regarding capture and detention.

Novel Approaches

U.S. policy makers must now initiate fresh policies to act as a catalyst for regaining national consensus and international support for how we detain and try the al Qaeda fighters. Closing Guantanamo and creating a new hybrid court is not enough. Although these two steps are critical, they cannot be done in a vacuum. Other changes must occur in how we are fighting al Qaeda. While domestically changing our adjudication policies toward the detainees, a fresh and pragmatic internationalist approach should be entertained by the new administration as well. Indicative of such actions would be for the United States to lead the call for a convention or commission to review the laws of war as they apply to international terrorists. Such a blue ribbon commission should review the existing Geneva Conventions to determine whether modification might be appropriate for the new threat or if Common Article 3 or Additional Protocol I already provide an adequate legal regime. This idea has been raised by different constituencies in different parts of the country and many have received this idea with enthusiasm. Perhaps such a commission will decide that a new protocol is the best way to "regulate" armed conflict with al Qaeda. While the exact details of such a new international agreement will require very careful analysis and discussion, at a minimum, the following list provides some of the necessary features of a protocol for international terrorism:

1. Geneva Conventions would still apply to those serving in combat operations, openly displaying their uniform and nation, and otherwise observing the laws of war;
2. Limited protections must be afforded to non-military enemy combatants, including the right to a military commission, the opportunity to pray and observe their faith, access to a detailed military defense counsel while imprisoned, access to adequate military facilities, and quarters that are habitable;
3. Torture must be strictly forbidden; however, interrogation should be permissible. Interrogations should be in accord with customary international law and applicable Torture Conventions;
4. Neutral nations, persons, and property shall be forbidden from capture;
5. Use of protected places, such as temples, churches, hospitals, mosques and other areas generally recognized as protected, must be exempt from attack. If used as haven or occupied through perfidy, as in some means supporting the war effort, such actions shall be prohibited and violators shall be tried by military commissions;
6. The use of chemical weapons must be prohibited and in accord with the Chemical Weapons Convention;
7. The principles of necessity, proportionality, and distinction would apply to all activities.[71]

In essence, aware that international terrorists will, as a matter of policy and tactics, violate the existing LOAC with regard to the *jus in bello* as well as the *jus ad bellum*, we must adapt international law to afford some elements of conventional protections to those who fight wars in this fashion. The existing status for "enemy combatants" and international terrorists has left the West open to criticism from both the new Europe and the Muslim world. Cognizant that the threat will remain for some time and conscious that this will be the form of war of the twenty-first century, adapting and changing our paradigms for treatment of prisoners in the global War on al Qaeda will help resolve many of the ambiguities we now face. It is critical for international lawyers not merely to criticize existing policies or actions by the administration with regard to international law obligations but to accept the idea that the rules might have to change and to adapt to the new wars of the twenty-first century rather than remaining trapped in the laws of the past.

Some conservatives have chided me for advocating this idea, reminding me "to be careful what you wish for.... [S]uch a conference would open up a can of worms." I appreciate their concerns, but it is essential to recognize that nations, faced with the realities of twenty-first-century warfare, truly do not have an appropriate international legal regime to regulate their conduct when they are confronted by the asymmetric threat of al Qaeda. Part of what the next administration and the Congress must do is regain our moral position in the world. Demonstrating a commitment to the international rule of law is an important step to shift current perceptions. There needs to be dialogue with our partners on what legal regime should apply to this war. If there is to be such dialogue between nations, I strongly believe it is in the United States' best interests to take the lead in creating such a convention. In short, the benefits of such international meetings will greatly outweigh any possible negative, unintended results. Regardless of the results of these efforts, the United States needs to be seen leading the call to determine what is appropriate and to be the proponent for any reforms that will better promote the rule of law.

Long-Term Solution

The United States should provide firm, distinct, long-term solutions for handling legal issues associated with the War on al Qaeda, solutions that would be in place for the foreseeable future and be palatable to both sides of the domestic debate currently raging. The judicial branch nibbling away at the edges of the Military Commissions Act will not help resolve these differences but rather will continue to create greater ambiguity in how the United States should legally proceed. The Supreme Court's intervention, just within the last two years, has confused lawyer and non-lawyer alike. Judicial intrusion into the effort has complicated the mission for both the commanders in the field and the executive branch during an ongoing war on at least three fronts.

The fact remains, however, that the military commissions have been tarnished irrevocably, either by misfortune, defense delays, procedural issues, or by design. Faith in this otherwise lawful measure has eroded. The best means of accomplishing the goal of "rethinking" the laws of war in this armed conflict is the creation of a federal terrorism court system. The Bush administration admirably adapted in many ways to meet the new threat. This is evidenced by the fact that the United States has not suffered another attack on its soil since 9/11. The one area that is in dire need of overhauling, however, remains the detention and employment of military commissions against illegal combatants. The new administration needs to overtly recognize (with authorization and support from Congress) that there is a need for a new legal system to adjudicate the new war. We also need new laws to evolve over time to meet the requirements of domestic and international laws, treaties, and other entities.[72] The time for real change is now. A federal terrorist court offers just such an opportunity to move the nation forward and regain moral authority beginning in 2009.

Why Not Civilian Courts?

Many of my colleagues have recommended the use of civilian courts as the best means of adjudicating the detainees. They wonder why some scholars are now advocating a new court system; they believe one already exists that can accomplish the task. Indeed, my colleague, Mark Denbeaux of Seton Hall Law School, has emphatically declared that there is no need to seek some third way or different way to try the al Qaeda suspects. He believes that the civilian courts are open and operating, they have performed several prosecutions already, and it seems pointless to look for some "magic bullet" to get us out of this mess.[73] Others assert that using the U.S. justice system, as it exists, is the best way to demonstrate American adherence to the rule of law.[74] Dean Harold Koh of Yale Law School also emphatically argues in support of using the civilian courts as the correct path to proceed, claiming that both the military commissions and a new national terrorist court are unnecessary. In his updated version of his book on the National Security Constitution and in public statements,[75] he strongly suggests that the best way to demonstrate U.S. adherence to the rule of law is through the employment of our own Article III courts for the al Qaeda prosecutions.[76] These learned critics believe al Qaeda members are international criminals and do not see them as anything more. In fact, they believe that calling the al Qaeda fighters "warriors" is mere exaggeration.[77] As much as such advocacy for using standard federal courts is a good "sound bite" for policy makers and some academics, and noble in theory, it is impractical. These critics misunderstand the situation the United States is currently embroiled in. An asymmetric ideologically driven entity has declared a fatwa (war) upon the United States and continues to wage war against this country and its interests in Afghanistan, Iraq, and our homeland. In their patriotic zeal to shut down the military commissions in Guantanamo, these critics are looking at the existing courts—open and operating[78]—as the appropriate venue to prosecute the al Qaeda members. *Boumediene*, perhaps unintentionally, supports this thinking. However, the likelihood of successful prosecutions in our own Article III courts against alleged al Qaeda fighters (particularly those captured during battle) is unlikely. Issues of evidence, court procedures, witnesses, juries, and other concerns will create chaos in our courts and additionally provide valuable propaganda opportunities for al Qaeda. "With traditional crime, we try suspects in part because trial represents the only means at the government's disposal to incapacitate criminals from further damaging society."[79] The confusion in mixing the international terrorist into our traditional U.S. court system is best summed up in that

> criminal trials in the federal system give defendants a bonanza of procedural opportunities to gouge sensitive information from the government and to force the government to choose between the vitality of its prosecution and other crucial interests.... Terrorism trials consume immense resources...offer a defendants a platform from which to command public attention and communicate with confederates.... [T]he mismatch between the manners in which intelligence officers collect information and in which criminal investigators amass evidence can paralyze prosecutors who inherit defendants from intelligence investigations.[80]

As noted earlier, the military commissions have proven unmanageable; so too, will our own Article III courts fail to meet the needs of policy makers. Using the civilian courts would make the legal landscape even more confusing. As former *Washington Post* reporter and now Brookings Institution Legal Fellow Ben Wittes argues, "the desire to conduct a large volume of criminal trials presents strong reason to stick with some form of military tribunal, even as the detention migrates to a civilian agency—presumably the Department of Justice. Trying terrorists in a federal court is tricky business."[81] Andy McCarthy, in his recently published book *Willful Blindness*, echoes these concerns throughout by detailing his experiences and the inherent flaws in trying terrorists within the existing federal court system.[82] Besides which, it cannot be emphasized enough that prisoners of war, in accord with the Geneva Conventions, do not have access to U.S. courts at all. In giving the detainees full access to U.S. courts and constitutional protections, we actually now provide more process to the detainees than we do to prisoners of war in traditional armed conflict. This is certainly not required, or desired, in our fight against international terrorism.

Critics supporting the use of current federal courts to "showcase" the U.S. justice system disregard altogether the previous use of the "law enforcement" approach prior to the attacks of 9/11. Most policy makers in the months following recognized that 9/11 represented a war and that the traditional methods of "prosecuting terrorism" had failed. Memories of this conclusion have vanished as the United States has been blessed with not having another attack on its soil. Perhaps supporters of the civilian system, should reread the bipartisan 9/11 report widely acclaimed by all who have read and studied the document. It clearly cautions policy makers to avoid returning to the pre-9/11 mindset and not to confront terrorism with our courts. Specifically,

> The law enforcement process is concerned with proving the guilt of persons apprehended and charged. Investigators and prosecutors could not present all the evidence of possible involvement of individuals other than those charged, although they continued to pursue such investigations, planning or hoping for later prosecutions. The process was meant, by its nature, to mark for the public the events as finished— case solved, justice done. It was not designed to ask if the events might be harbingers of worse to come. Nor did it allow for aggregating and analyzing facts to see if they could provide clues to terrorist tactics more generally—methods of entry and finance, and mode of operation inside the United States.[83]

There are numerous reasons the Article III courts are inappropriate for trying alleged al Qaeda fighters but I will attempt to explain issue by issue why this is so. Just as the military commissions are ineffective against this hybrid fighter, the civilian courts would prove (once again) equally ineffective and unmanageable. The following provides a list of the primary reasons I believe the civilian system of law is unworkable in the current construct.

Juries

It would be unworkable and unmanageable to obtain unbiased juries when prosecuting al Qaeda in the federal district courts. Imagine an attorney attempting to empanel a jury after an attack on the Sears Tower by al Qaeda. How would you find jury members who have not heard of, or could sit in judgment of, one of the alleged perpetrators of such a horrific act? A more current example would be a civilian trial of Khalid Sheik Mohammad (KSM). KSM was recently arraigned in Guantanamo Bay by military commission. As is well known, he is alleged to have been the mastermind of the attacks of 9/11. Is it reasonable to expect an unbiased "jury of his peers" be empaneled for a man accused of coordinating the worst attack on U.S. soil since the War of 1812? It is ludicrous to imagine someone like KSM's "peers" being brought to the courtroom for jury duty. Such reasoning is simply illogical. An unbiased jury could never be empaneled. Additionally, *voir dire* (jury selection) for the lawyers on both sides would prove difficult beyond comprehension.

Evidentiary Concerns

Marines and soldiers fighting in Afghanistan (or other "battlefields") are fighting a war. We can not possibly ask them to follow the same constitutional procedures required of a police officer in domestic law enforcement operations when raiding an al Qaeda safe house and seizing computers or questioning witnesses. Beyond the constitutional issues associated with the actual seizure of the "computer" (which is likely to provide evidence and information on the alleged al Qaeda member's contacts and communications), the chain of custody would almost certainly be compromised. Able defense counsel would take full advantage of such lapses in constitutional procedure. Our Article III system is devised for police and criminal procedures—not seizures during battle or with "the fog of war." These evidentiary concerns are almost certain to result in acquittals for most, if not all, detainees brought before civilian courts.

Soldiers, in an armed conflict, are not normally accustomed to ensuring that prisoners, or detainees in this context, are afforded the protections of the Fourth or Fifth Amendments. American soldiers can not be expected to perform the same constitutionally mandated procedures while fighting a war that law enforcement agents do in the civilian world. It has been understood for centuries that such an imposition is counterintuitive to a war effort. Captured al Qaeda fighters in Iraq, Afghanistan, Yemen, or anywhere outside the United States are not afforded protection against unreasonable searches or the right not to incriminate themselves during interrogation. These are facts often lost upon those supporting a strictly civilian law enforcement approach to detention and trials of the al Qaeda fighters. Justice Kennedy, however, may actually have opened the door to providing such constitutional protections by holding that the detainees have the constitutional right of habeas corpus. If the detainees are entitled to this protection, why not the other constitutional guarantees of speedy trial, protection against search and seizure, Miranda rights, and so on? Certainly, defense lawyers will attempt to expand the holding. Supporters of greater use of the civilian system miss the point that war is, was, and should necessarily continue to be viewed as distinct from law enforcement activities. Certainly, there is more at stake in war than in traditional police work, and the systems thus require completely different response to supposed "threats." Up until *Boumediene*, the courts agreed with this presumption and did not afford noncitizens living outside the United States constitutional rights.[84] The understood catalyst for interrogation while a nation is at war (throughout history) is to get information to prevent further attacks. In the law enforcement context, the intention of the constitutional protections is to prevent outrageous behavior by law enforcement personnel. Again, in this context, the warrior is not a police officer. Soldiers fighting overseas or in the battlefield can not possibly be burdened by a new requirement to obtain a search warrant. Stopping ongoing operations to obtain warrants from neutral and detached judges back in the United States would be absurd. The normal result when evidence is tainted by improper questioning of a suspect (or obtained as a result of an illegal search) is that such evidence would not be admitted because of the exclusionary rule. Such application of our standard Article III court procedures would be catastrophic to any successful prosecution. Without such evidence being admitted—confessions, laptop computers, weapons, cell phones, letters, e-mails—the prosecution would be set up for failure from the outset and prosecution likely would not even be pursued.

Classified Material

Introduction of classified material, even if in compliance with the Classified Information Protection Act (CIPA),[85] would be problematic in the context of an ongoing armed conflict. One has to look no further than the problems encountered by the prosecution in the "Sheik" case as part of the first World Trade Center bombings in the 1990s. The judge in that case, later attorney general of the United States Michael Mukasey, has on numerous occasions spoken of the problems in this context of trying al Qaeda in a civilian courtroom. His concerns about the presumptive openness of U.S. courts are compelling.[86] Further, the prosecutor in that case, Andy McCarthy, also now a proponent of the national security court,[87] has poignantly written how classified information was almost immediately leaked to Osama Bin Laden himself. This fact was confirmed when U.S. forces captured copies of the witness list and other information while operating in the Afghan theater. Exposing our troops to such lapses in intelligence, during ongoing military operations, is irresponsible at best. The U.S. court system is not suited for handling the sensitive nature of war secrets—particularly while U.S. forces remain in harm's way.

Clearances for Defense Counsel

The time delays associated with obtaining clearances for civilian counsel, in a civilian court setting, would be great. Beyond the time constraints, the many different lawyers needing and requiring clearance could unnecessarily put national security at risk. There is little doubt that lawyers will act professionally and do their utmost to zealously defend their clients. However, the more clearances that are granted to nongovernmental persons for the myriad cases to be tried, the more likely it is that leaks will inevitably occur. The inadvertent disclosure of even the names of nations cooperating with the United States could prove disastrous for maintaining support from our partners in this global conflict.[88] Many governments and their intelligence agencies work with the United States, understanding that such cooperation will not be made public. Disclosure of their cooperation would deter those who might also choose to assist the nation in battling global terrorism. It is predictable that such mistakes, or leaks, will occur. This is particularly so when clearances are temporary in nature and given only for the period of the trial from start to finish. While true that such clearances are now given in some limited terrorist cases already, this occurs only for the one or two terrorist cases prosecuted every few years. The number of cases to be tried now (and in the future) and the national security consequences of such leaks in the current context clearly outweigh any benefit toward giving such mass clearances to the literally hundreds of defense counsels, judges, and witnesses who would need one.

Pro Se *Counsel*

The problems with demanding the right to represent oneself before a U.S. court of law are best demonstrated by the Zacarias Moussaoui case. A French citizen, originally thought to be the twentieth high-jacker in the attacks of 9/11, he refused court-appointed counsel early in his proceedings. Despite contrary assertions by Judge Brinkema,[89] this case has been recognized by many as a primary example of why civilian courts are not the proper venue for trying al Qaeda combatants.[90] As a *pro se* litigant, in open court, Moussaoui used the opportunity to mock the U.S. justice system and make various declarations in support of al Qaeda and their efforts. Additionally, he went to great lengths to lambaste U.S. foreign policy and the existence of Israel as a nation-state. His comments immediately spread through "the street" and were used as propaganda tools against U.S. interests.[91] Again, it can not be overstated that this case was being tried while troops were in harm's way and engaged in ongoing armed conflict. Permitting this sort of "pulpit" for al Qaeda members to spread propaganda through the twenty-four-hour news media is not, and never was, the intent of permitting *pro se* litigation. Further, his antics slowed down the proceedings and, instead of showcasing U.S. justice, made a mockery of it.

Exculpatory Evidence and the Brady Rule

The burden on the prosecution in accord with the "Brady Rule" to provide any exculpatory evidence to the accused can be damaging to the proper adjudication of the detainees. Certainly, some obligation on the prosecution to divulge such information is necessary (as is currently contained within the Military Commissions Act of 2006) and proper, but not the expansive view of such activities expected of our prosecutors in our own domestic court proceedings. Doing so could risk unnecessarily compromising intelligence sources, means, and methods. It does not recognize the unique status of the accused and, once again, is perfectly suited for traditional law enforcement court proceeding but not in the setting of an ongoing armed conflict.

Inconsistencies within the Circuits

There is the strong likelihood that various decisions made in different circuits would depend upon the ideological makeup of each individual court and circuit. The need for consistency in the U.S. adjudications of suspected al Qaeda fighters would be impossible if the cases were heard in different regions and within different district courts. These varying decisions could not, and would not, be helpful in demonstrating that the United States has a united front against the al Qaeda operatives. Changes in venue would be sought by savvy defense lawyers seeking the most lenient districts or regions for their clients. These inevitable (and ethically required) defense tactics and posturing would not be the appropriate way to try cases against the detainees.

Unanimous Votes for Guilty Verdict

Within the civilian court system, unanimous verdicts by juries are required to convict. The MCA now requires, similar to courts-martial, a two-thirds vote to convict and a unanimous verdict only for capital cases. Thus, those who would be tried for conspiracy or other crimes (under a civilian legal regime) would require unanimous votes to be convicted in the traditional federal courts. War crimes prosecutions (if applicable) in a civilian court would then provide protections well beyond what was ever envisioned or expected within the courts-martial system of military justice. This burden would be extremely difficult, particularly with the myriad evidentiary issues discussed earlier. Acquittals in this context will both hinder the war effort and ensure that many of these fighters would immediately go back to the battlefield to fight U.S. forces or plan new attacks on the United States. As Justice Scalia predicted in his vigorous dissent in *Boumediene*, fearing that al Qaeda fighters will merely be freed and head back to the battlefield, warned, "almost surely American lives will be lost."[92] The Department of Defense has published a list demonstrating confirmed accounts of nearly sixty-five fighters who have gone back to the battlefield since being released from detention. Although in a traditional construct, or even in a traditional armed conflict, such numbers of the many who have been released seem small, the nature of the current fight requires only one or two fighters to inflict massive and at some points incomprehensible damage to U.S. forces, U.S. interests, or even infrastructure within the homeland. This is the reality that members of the national security agencies face in fighting the so-called war on terror. Obtaining unanimity of decisions by a jury would prove to be an enormous burden on prosecutors as well as the courts in general.

Protective Details

If the United States employs the civilian, open court system, protection would have to be provided (in most cases, for life) for anyone involved in a trial; security details would have to be assigned to the judges hearing the cases, witnesses, lawyers, and juries. This already occurs in the few cases where national security concerns have been at issue. Different from ordinary, traditional criminal trials, the numbers of cases involved with the fight against international terrorists, and the tremendous threat imposed by the al Qaeda fighters to those involved in such national security cases, would result in an extraordinarily large numbers of persons requiring such details. This would put an enormous burden on the judicial system.

Expertise of Judges

Article III judges, by necessity, are generalists. This niche area of the law requires training and experience in intelligence, military law, national security law, international law, and the law of armed conflict. Ironically, the Supreme Court, throughout the years, has applied the "deference doctrine" to issues impacting military operations.[93] The Court has often referred to the inefficiencies associated with having "nine persons less qualified to make decisions as to the armed forces."[94] Similar to other niche areas of the law like bankruptcy and immigration, it seems that generalists are not best suited to preside over the multitude of cases that would have direct impact on the security of the United States. This is not to say that our federal judges are incapable of performing such tasks. That is not the case at all. On the contrary, the federal bench is filled with brilliant, reasonable, just men and women. However, the decisions being made now in a national security context seem to require strong expertise within this area of the law.[95] Perhaps even more important, since *Boumediene* placed civilian judges in the uncomfortable position of ruling on military detentions, the need for specific, national security judges seems all the more urgent. It is illogical to suggest that a civilian generalist in the law, regardless of how bright or seasoned, is the best person to rule over what are often strictly military decisions. Certainly, the founders could have never intended such a result. They placed such decision making in the hands of the political branches.[96]

Bleed Over

Perhaps the greatest concern to me (as well as many others concerned about the use of U.S. courts) is the potential for "bleed over" from the inevitable relaxations in traditional constitutional expectations when trying international terrorists in civilian courts. Some recognition by the Article III courts of the need for different standards (relaxed evidentiary and procedural rules) required for admitting evidence, prosecution guidelines, and other areas of procedure when prosecuting "war criminals" could begin a "slippery slope" within traditional law enforcement prosecutions. The civilian Article III courts would have to make exceptions in certain areas because these would be "unique" prosecutions—brought against an enemy of the United States that we are engaging in armed conflict and certainly in the context of a national emergency, and especially when the prosecution involves possible future attacks on the United States. Therefore, the potential for using these new, different standards in drug prosecutions or Racketeer Influenced and Corrupt Organizations Act (RICO) prosecutions or others would likely have some advocates claiming that these too are "national crisis" cases that also require similar relaxed rules of evidence and decreased expectations of constitutional protections. In doing so, society, as well as some members of the bench and bar, may seek to employ similar relaxations in these ordinary cases. This seemingly innocent and well-intentioned relaxation of traditional standards would create the unintended consequence of erosion of the constitutional principles Americans hold as part of their citizenship. This, above all other concerns, should be paramount to both policy makers and civil libertarians who seek to employ civilian courts. Ironically, some proponents' zeal to give terrorists their "day in court" would create the potential of weakening our traditional protections held in such high regard by all U.S. citizens. Every effort should be made to ensure that this does not occur. The best means to do so is to keep the terrorist prosecutions out of traditional courts and place them into specialized court systems. This ensures that the civilian system does not become tainted with such necessary relaxations and gives formal recognition that these international terrorists are not the average criminal—nor the average warrior. Thus, although seemingly benign and well intentioned, the use of civilian courts to handle this threat is inappropriate. Those who advocate this use seem interested in returning to a pre-9/11 mentality that many have asserted set the stage for the attacks of that day. The best advice on why not to use civilian courts can be found in the hearings held by the 9/11 Commission and their report; this report details the need to recognize that the acts committed by al Qaeda are not ordinary criminal acts, or even similar to regional or national terrorists acts. Al Qaeda has declared war upon the United States and the West and we should never return to what we know has been unsuccessful.

The stage is set. The military commissions do not work for detaining and trying al Qaeda fighters. The civilian courts are unworkable and unmanageable. The Supreme Court has just rejected the political branch's response to the *Hamdan* decision from just two years ago. After *Boumediene*, the timing is now perfect for a new system to be entertained by President Obama and new Congress. The Obama administration must oversee the transformation, and evolution, of the military commission into something more suitable and permanent for the long war we are embroiled in. The proposed National Security Court System is a great place to start.

SEVEN

༺❦༻

The National Security Court System

A National Security Court System (NSCS) offers the United States a "way out" of the Guantanamo fiasco.[1] The existing military law tribunal system is simply not meeting the needs of the nation or the West as we battle international terror. Similarly, the current federal civilian courts are not the appropriate forum for adjudicating "war crimes" either. The convergence of law enforcement and warfare embodied in the War on al Qaeda presents new dilemmas and confusion for nations determining which scheme or system to employ. The situation is unprecedented. Not only is the war itself novel but the al Qaeda fighters are unique also—neither warrior nor criminal. They commit, or conspire to commit, acts of international terror and other actions on a massive scale, seeking nothing less than the complete destruction of Western civilization. They do not wear uniforms, they do not carry weapons openly, they have no emblems that distinguish them as members of an organized army, and they flout the law of armed conflict (LOAC) as part of their established doctrine.[2] This routinely unlawful belligerency increases the level of threat these international terrorists pose to the world community and makes classification of their status extraordinarily difficult. Regulating their activities and trying the individuals in an appropriate forum has been confusing at best. Policy makers need a "third way" to adjudicate war crimes committed by these illegal combatants that will be supported (at least to some degree) by the international community. James Baker III, former cabinet member of both the Reagan and Bush (41) administrations, has argued that pragmatic idealism should be the foundation of U.S. foreign policy in the twenty-first century.[3] The National Security Court System is a legal system based upon this philosophy.

I had a brief discussion of the Guantanamo issue with Baker, former secretary of state, in which he agreed that the detention center located there must close. He is one of our distinguished statesmen of the twentieth and twenty-first centuries, and his opinion on the detainees left a great impression on me. Similar to the policy makers of today, he too was unsure of how best to proceed after closing Guantanamo. This exchange highlighted for me the difficulties of dealing with the detainees now and in the future. It reaffirmed that we urgently need a new way of handling the al Qaeda fighter once captured. It made me even more supportive of exploring a new way—different from the past, but still embracing the traditional U.S. idealistic values of human rights; at the same time, such a system must demonstrate the necessary limits of our idealism as we seek to protect our homeland.

A specialized terrorist court, such as the national security legal apparatuses already employed in other nations confronting terrorism, is the key to remedying this dilemma. Other nations, such as France, Great Britain, and Turkey, have acknowledged that legal cases against terrorists are extraordinary and need to be handled differently from standard criminal prosecutions or even military tribunals. All struggled with how best to create their distinct systems. If properly constructed, a national security court system in the United States will help this country begin to regain its position of moral authority in world affairs. At the minimum, it will bolster national and international support for the United States that has eroded over the past few years. It would be a fresh start and one that demonstrates the country's recognition that changes in how we fight our "war on terror" are necessary. This new system would provide the appearance of enhanced justice, as well as real justice, to the detainees and resilience to an adjudication process that has been admittedly unsuccessful.

Other Models

When considering the different forms a terrorist court might take, policy makers need not start from scratch. This is particularly important since the Obama administration has established an aggressive one-year deadline to end the military commissions process and to close the Guantanamo Bay detention facility. There are at least three models policy makers can examine to see how parts of each can work within the U.S. constitutional framework. Although several nations use similar courts, the French, British, and Turkish experiences demonstrate some of the positive (as well as negative) attributes of the new courts. The United States can learn from the mistakes made by these nations as well as from their relative successes. One caveat, however, is to remember that some of these courts (Great Britain and Turkey in particular) were designed to hear cases of domestic terrorism instead of addressing the new, broader threat encompassed by international terrorism. For example, England used its system for trying members of the Irish Republican Army, which was in armed revolution against the British government and used terror as a tactic; however, this was not an international armed conflict but an internal armed conflict. Policy makers should keep these distinctions in mind as they review the judicial systems of other countries. Regardless, the efforts of our allies and their attempts at creating terrorism courts must necessarily be thoroughly examined by the U.S. Congress as it explores what to do once the detention facility is closed.

France

"Could Paris teach Washington a thing or two about protecting civil liberties while tracking down terrorists at home?"[4] Well, yes. Contrary to American conventional wisdom, international terrorism has been impacting the larger world for quite some time. France was the first Western country struck by Middle Eastern state-sponsored terrorism. Of note, as Ken Timmerman has written about in the *Washington Times*, the French uncovered a plot in 1994 to have airliners crash into the Eiffel Tower, a foreshadowing of the tragic events of 9/11. They have been victims of attacks since the 1950s (as a result of their war in Algeria) as well as from Palestinian-linked groups in the 1970s. In the mid 1980s, however, the French government and people were still caught completely off guard by a series of terrorist attacks in Paris. Like the United States now, their existing law enforcement personnel and legal systems were unprepared for dealing with this new threat.[5] The attacks prompted legislation in 1986 to create new counterterrorism laws. The French created a centralized magistrate system that wields enormous prosecutorial powers. The system was led by the well-known judge Jean-Louis Bruguiere, who initially handled all terrorism cases. Unlike ordinary French criminal proceedings, terrorist trials in France are overseen by a panel of judges—with no juries involved whatsoever. The magistrate has the powers of both a prosecutor and a judge.[6]

The French counterterrorism "judges" have awesome powers. They oversee any terrorist probes, can file charges, order wiretaps, and issue warrants and subpoenas. Additionally, they can request the assistance of police or intelligence agencies, order the preventive detention of suspects for up to six days without charge, and justify keeping someone incarcerated for several years while investigations are pursued. Interestingly, they also retain an international mandate when a French national is involved in a terrorist act, either as a perpetrator or victim.[7] As a direct result of this legislation passed over twenty years ago, France now has a learned pool of specialized judges and investigators who are experts in prosecuting terrorists. This separate legal system, specifically tailored to terrorism and terrorist cases, has generally been accepted as necessary by the French people, who agreed that it was needed to confront the threat of terrorism. Although any U.S. system would not, and should not, merge the role of prosecutor and judge, the French system does offer some valuable insights into how others have created specialized terrorism courts and the benefits of having judges specialize in this niche area of the law. Harvey Rishikof has noted that the creation of terrorist court judges is "one benefit of the French system that we could readily emulate."[8]

Great Britain

Another system to review is the once infamous, and now defunct, Diplock court system in Great Britain that tried members of the Irish Republican Army. These courts, established by Lord Kenneth Diplock at the height of the "troubles" in Northern Ireland in 1973, permitted one judge, sitting alone, to hear suspected terrorist-related cases.[9] Diplock courts were frequently criticized as being unfair since juries were not a part of the court system. In contrast, even U.S. military courts-martial give the person charged the option of a trial by judge alone or by a jury of "peers." It is interesting that many of the accused actually choose "judge alone" because they often find that the decision of a judge is fairer than one delivered by their peers.

The suggestion for using judges only for terrorism cases was born out of legitimate fear for the safety of jurors and witnesses. Many had been intimidated or threatened. The British government believed there was reluctance by many jurors to convict members of their own community even when the evidence submitted was overwhelming.[10]

The Diplock courts heard, at their height in the 1980s, close to 350 cases per year. The offenses over which the court had jurisdiction were laid out in what was known as the Northern Ireland (Emergency Provisions) Acts. Although the courts were viewed by many as arbitrary and set up to convict, the reality is that nearly 45 percent of the defendants were acquitted.[11] Professor John Jackson of Queens University (Belfast) has pointed out that "the real hostility was focused on many of the unsatisfactory sources of evidence that were presented in trials of the time. In the 1970's they were seen as rubber stamping confessions that were highly dubious.... [I]t wasn't necessarily the Diplock courts themselves that were the problem."[12]

The number of cases heard in the Diplock courts continued to decrease as the peace process progressed. This process took firm root during the 1990s and by 2001, the annual number of cases heard by these special courts had dwindled to an average of 64.[13] The decrease in cases was mostly attributed to the success of the peace process. As a result of the diplomatic efforts of Sinn Fein and the British government, terrorism and the threat from the IRA became nearly negligible. Thus, when the courts were officially closed in the summer of 2007, there was little celebration or even reaction from the civilian populace. The Diplock courts had already become part of the past history of the six counties in Ireland and were essentially no longer relevant to the British or Irish people. The threat of terrorism had diminished, and thus there was little need for the Diplock courts to continue.

Obviously, a Diplock court–type system could not and should not be adopted by the United States. But there are parts of the system we can use, and we can learn from our allies' experience. Using special judges, as in France, and special courts, as in the UK, for terrorism cases are two responses of nations that recognized the need to preserve national security while affording trials and justice for those accused of "national security crimes."

Turkey

Turkey has also used a type of national security court in the past. State Security Courts were employed, under the 1982 Constitution, to try cases involving crimes against the security of the state as well as organized crime.[14] The Turkish security court, from my perspective, is the weakest of the three models and the most prone to abuse. The State

Security Courts (SSC) began to operate in Turkey in May 1984. They replaced military courts that had been in operation during the period immediately preceding the imposition of martial law. Rather than being centrally located or spread widely throughout the country, they operated in only eight (of then 67 and now 81) provinces.[15]

In April 1991, the system began to evolve and progress. The Law to Fight Terrorism[16] entered into force and cases involving national security crimes were now punishable under this law. Under the new trial system, each panel had three judges, one of whom had to be a military officer. Thus, the Turkish government mixed both military officers and civilians to sit in judgment over terrorism cases. The inclusion of a military officer on the judge panels created concern among many. As at least one judge was a member of the armed forces of Turkey, it was widely suspected (both domestically and internationally) that many of the judges were subject to influence and coercion by the military during the trial of these cases. The legitimacy of these special courts as a system of "justice" was consistently questioned. The suspicions and concerns are similar to many raised today about the U.S. military commissions in Guantanamo regarding unlawful command influence. As in the U.S. military system (and virtually all military systems), salary, pension benefits, and promotion to higher rank are all performance based. It is understood by many within military systems that the best way to advance in rank is to not "rock the boat" or take risks. Many within Turkey, and in the human rights community, viewed the military's involvement in these proceedings with great suspicion.

In a number of cases, the European Court of Human Rights found the presence of military judges in the State Security Courts to be a violation of the fair trial principles set out in Article 6 of the European Convention for the Protection of Human Rights and Fundamental Freedoms (ECHR).[17] In June 1999, the Turkish government removed the military participation within the SSC and thereby made the three-judge panels all civilian. As part of a package of reforms to the Constitution passed in June 2004, the State Security Courts were formally abolished. The Turkish government, like the British, decided that such security courts were no longer necessary as the terrorist threat had diminished considerably. The number of threats was small enough to no longer require a "special system."[18]

Again, clear flaws existed within the Turkish security court system. In particular, the mixture of military and civilian judges serving on the panels hearing cases was inappropriate. The Turkish SSCs, however, do provide insights into how such systems worked and why in many respects they were predestined to fail.

All three courts—the French, the British, and the Turkish—offer ideas for policy makers to consider when writing any legislation for a U.S. terrorism court. Of the three mentioned, the French model seems to be the most closely aligned to my proposal, and it has worked exceedingly well for the French people for over twenty years. Of note, the French have not been victims of a major terrorist attack since their system was adopted in the mid 1980s.[19] At a minimum, congressional leaders, key members of the Obama administration, academics, and select members of the bar should meet with various French participants and judges to better understand how the French system has maintained national support and balanced the need for national security with the promotion of basic human rights. Some parts of their system might, in fact, work in the United States.

The United States

Within the United States, the two existing paradigms—the law enforcement model and the military law model—are not suited for the unique nature of the country's current conflict. As argued earlier, using the existing Article III courts is not appropriate for confronting this relatively new threat, international terrorism. The military commissions, while initially employed in 2001 as the best means available for trying the detainees, now appear unworkable, or unmanageable, for dealing with the alleged al Qaeda fighters. I anticipate that historians will study these tribunals for years and debate the reasons that, while acceptable legally, they failed in implementation.[20]

Almost seven years after the attacks of 9/11, it is critical to move forward with the debate on detention. We must refrain from partisanship, constant criticism, calling one another unpatriotic, or labeling people war criminals; it is essential to rise above the bickering and look for real solutions. To date, the advocacy has essentially been divided into two camps: (1) those who view the conflict with al Qaeda as requiring a law enforcement response and thus civilian courts and the due process ordinarily accorded U.S. citizens; and (2) those who view the conflict as an armed conflict, believing the law of war paradigm to be appropriate for handling the detainees. Unfortunately, neither solution is working effectively. It seems as though both sides are jamming "a square peg into a round hole." If we remain on this tack, nothing will ever be resolved and U.S. foreign policy will continue to be hampered by the Guantanamo detainee problem. Advocates on both sides of the debate, rather than attacking each other, should be viewed as thoughtful patriots—with each group earnestly promoting what they believe to be the correct way to handle the detention and trial of the captured al Qaeda fighters. All policy makers, academics, and lawyers are trying to determine the best way to proceed. To say the least, this is an extremely difficult problem to address. This new armed conflict of the twenty-first century has shattered all previous notions of traditional warfare. Thus, neither paradigm fits neatly. In fact, I suggest that both sides (in many respects) are right on many issues and both sides are wrong on an equal number of issues in applying their analyses to the current threat. Components of each paradigm are ideal to implement while others could never be successfully applied in the context of the al Qaeda detainees.

Foundations

The armed conflict we are fighting is truly a mix of law enforcement and warfare, and the al Qaeda fighter is a mix of international criminal and traditional warrior. Viewing the conflict in this fashion—as a hybrid—both of the prevailing paradigms alone is ineffective as a framework for detention and prosecution. Before going into the specifics of my proposed system, we should review and summarize the need for a new court system from four perspectives: (1) the legal perspective, (2) the policy perspective, (3) the perspective of other federal terrorism court proposals offered by U.S. academics and lawyers, (4) and the perspective of my new solution—a specialized security court, a National Security Court System.

Law

As argued throughout this book, the legality of military commissions has been demonstrated as a matter of history, statute, and Supreme Court decision. They have evolved and will continue to evolve in the future. Contrary to some assertions in popular literature and culture, the administration did not make up the idea of using military commissions as the proper venue to try illegal belligerents in time of war.[21] Such commissions have been used throughout history; the most famous early commission was employed by General Washington against Major Andre during the American Revolution.[22] Field commanders and presidents throughout American history have made use of these commissions for handling illegal belligerents, and they have done so with virtually no input from Congress. Generals Washington and Jackson, Presidents Lincoln and Franklin D. Roosevelt all made use of military commissions during periods of armed conflict. In at least two sections, the Uniform Code of Military Justice (enacted by Congress in 1950) provides legislative authority to use such tribunals or commissions. And in *Ex Parte Quirin*, the case most relied upon by the Bush administration, the Supreme Court unanimously upheld the use of commissions. The president's order of November 13, 2001, and the choice of Guantanamo as a location for holding many of the detainees during a period of attack (or at the minimum, armed conflict) was a reasonable, legally supportable decision to make in the atmosphere of the post-9/11 environment. Intelligence agencies were intercepting "chatter" and other information leading to the belief in government and among the American citizenry that imminent attacks were inevitable. As combat was continuing in Afghanistan, the decision makers had to decide on the best way to detain the illegal belligerents (or "enemy combatants") and adjudicate their war crimes. To do so, the president and his staff appropriately relied on the historical use of military commissions during a period of armed conflict by warfare commanders and presidents, the statutory authority embodied in the UCMJ (although ambiguous), and Supreme Court precedent.

The presidential order of November 13, 2001, however, did not long remain in its original form. It began to mature into more appropriate twenty-first-century military law jurisprudence. It was, in fact, modified over the next few years; some of the changes were *sua sponte* (without prompting by the Bush administration) and some were at the prompting of the Congress, academics, and the bar. Just six months after the original order, in the spring of 2002, the Department of Defense made modifications to provide more process to the detainees. DoD issued what is known as Military Order No. 1.[23] Again, in March 2003, when finally promulgating the orders for the military commissions, the DoD further updated the specific orders to ensure that they used a more progressive, justice-oriented process.[24] After several cases came before the Supreme Court (*Hamdi* and *Rasul*), resulting in minor adjustments, the Court in the *Hamdan* case declared the existing military commissions unlawful as constructed. The political branches reacted, and in bipartisan fashion they enacted the Military Commissions Act (MCA) in October 2006—just four months after the decision by the Supreme Court in *Hamdan*. The MCA addressed the two major concerns expressed by the Court: (1) Congress must approve the commissions, and (2) Common Article 3 of the Geneva Conventions must apply. The decision in *Boumediene* declared that the detainees do retain, at the least, the U.S. constitutional right of habeas corpus. However, the commissions currently still exist and operate under the provisions of the MCA—excluding the Detainee Treatment Act process, which has been superseded by the *Boumediene* case. Contrary to many critics' assertions about the lack of process afforded detainees, many of the detainees have greater rights than they would receive in their home countries[25] as well as greater rights than they would receive as prisoners of war under the Geneva Conventions: as POWs, they would never have access to U.S. courts to challenge their detention. Objectively, the detainees are actually provided a laundry list of process rights. Kyndra Rotunda, a former military prosecutor for the Pentagon at the Office of Military Commissions and now on the law faculty of Chapman Law School, has written and argued about how well the detainees are actually treated.[26] Although they may not have been treated as well at the outset of their detention, the military has worked hard to ensure that the detainees are now treated with dignity and respect. Bolstering my conclusions, in February of 2009, a 30-day review by the Obama administration has found that the detention facility itself is in conformity with the provisions of the Geneva Conventions.

Since 2001, the military commissions have morphed, adapted, and changed, with input from the executive branch, the military, the judiciary, and most recently, the Congress. In a new war in a new century, we have watched our republic deal with the detainees in an uncomfortable fashion. The process is evolving before our eyes. I still maintain that the military commissions as currently constructed remain a lawful, authorized means to try those accused of war crimes committed during a period of armed conflict.

Policy

However, aside from the legality of the Military Commissions Act, the policy ramifications of employing military commissions must also be measured. Critics of the commissions and the detention of combatants at Guantanamo have increased dramatically over the past five years. Until 2008, we had not had a single prosecution in the seven years since the order of 2001. Allegations about the harsh treatment of those in the detention center—such as the claim by Amnesty International in 2005 that Guantanamo is the "gulag of our time"—have had a major impact on how the commissions are viewed internationally. Reports that the detainees were tortured—particularly after the Abu Ghraib incident in Iraq—added to concerns by government leaders about Guantanamo both domestically and internationally. Greater focus was placed on the operations at the detention center by nongovernmental organizations, the media, and the U.S. government. Some of these allegations were accurate; others were hyperbolic or exaggerated. Indeed, several of the more inflated ones have been used as propaganda tools by al Qaeda. A noteworthy example of the hyperbole was *Newsweek's* (later retracted) article about soldiers flushing down the toilet copies of the Koran belonging to detainees.[27] This story fueled suspicion about our intentions in our "war on terror" among many within the international community. Regardless of whether the allegations have merit or are exaggerations, the impression gained by most people, both domestically and internationally, is that Guantanamo has been tainted and in many ways is irrevocably flawed as a matter of policy. Other studies by nongovernmental organizations have consistently claimed that detainees experience poor treatment, lawlessness, and even torture.[28] In fact, General Taguba (now retired), who conducted a study on Guantanamo for the Pentagon while on active duty, recently testified before Congress and confirmed that some allegations were in fact true.[29]

Affirming many of these suspicions or criticisms is the glaring fact that not a single trial has been completed at Guantanamo, and some 240 persons still remain at the detention center there; the likelihood of any successful, fair prosecutions diminishes daily. The credibility of the commissions has been severely tarnished. Many question the commitment of the United States to human rights and to our role as a world power. Guantanamo, regardless of blame or fault, has hurt the United States' ability to fight the War on al Qaeda and lead in many other areas of geopolitical concern. Whether the allegations being made are correct or not, the United States has clearly lost the public relations war addressing the circumstances, safety, and treatment of detainees at Guantanamo.

With this policy backdrop and its impact on U.S. foreign policy, many called for Guantanamo to close. And one of President Obama's first actions in office was to announce that the detention center would be closed within one year. In fact, many members of the Bush administration had stated their desire to close the facility—mostly based upon policy concerns.[30] During the presidential campaign, both Senator McCain and Senator Obama support closing the facility.[31] Five former secretaries of state (from both major political parties) called to close the facility.[32] The question still lingers, however, about what to do with these detainees and the inevitable future detainees now that we have decided to close the facility and use a different system. A "third way" must be entertained that is different from the existing law enforcement or law of war paradigms. It seems logical that since we are fighting a hybrid warrior—in a hybrid war—the best way to detain and adjudicate the detainees is through the use of a hybrid court—a mix of our Article III courts and the military commissions. This court would be overseen by the Department of Justice, and the detention, trial, and incarceration would take place on military bases. I believe that this is the right solution if properly constructed by the U.S. Congress. In crafting such a court system, the political branches need always to be mindful to incorporate human rights considerations into legislation creating the system. Obviously, in legislatively enacting such a national security court, the devil will be in the details.

Others in academia and within think tanks have now come to agree this is the way to proceed. Professor Harvey Rishikof, Brookings scholar Ben Wittes, Professor Ken Anderson, columnist Stuart Taylor, national security law expert Andy McCarthy, and others have recognized and now advocate for some specialized court. Even here, some differences emerge. To me, the most noteworthy proponent of some type of specialized court is Professor Neal Katyal of Georgetown Law School— the same law professor who represented *Hamdan* before the Supreme Court in 2006 (and still represented *Hamdan* in his habeas proceedings and during his military commission). His support for the new system is important to show that someone actually litigating the cases before military commissions has come to realize that neither the existing civilian court system nor the military commissions adequately meet the balance between justice and national security.[33]

The major difference between many of the supporters of any new federal terrorist court to be used in the War on al Qaeda is primarily based upon whether to simply try the detainees or to use this new court system for some type of preventive detention. Professor Katyal (now deputy solicitor general), as well as Ben Wittes and others, emphasizes the need for a strong form of preventive detention as part of a new system. I respectfully disagree. To me, it is clear—any new system created must be used to try the detainees. If we simply move the detainees to the United States and still employ some new preventive detention model, all we will do is transfer the same problems experienced in Guantanamo but make the situation even worse by trying these cases in U.S. civilian courts of justice within the continental United States. With a mandate that the detainees be tried, the rule of law is once again placed in a position of primacy, both in appearance and reality. If the court is properly constructed, and I humbly suggest that the proposed model has this potential (and am confident that Congress can legislate its structure in greater detail), the need for preventive detention will be moot. If an accused al Qaeda fighter is found innocent by the national security court, he or she should be set free and returned to his country of origin. That is the price of applying due process to this unique legal conundrum. If found guilty, the detainee will be subject to confinement in special prisons created on military bases. That is the American system of justice—and such ideals promoting the rule of law should be incorporated within a national security court.

Other Proposals for Security Courts

It is worthwhile to review some of the other proposals that advocate the creation of a federal security court. Like reviewing other nations' systems, this helps give policy makers a starting point in how to statutorily create the new court. In many ways, the following four proposals are all similar, but in other ways, there are marked differences in how the court should operate—and all agree that there is a critical need to create a new system. In fact, Katie Paul of *Newsweek* wrote a piece in June 2008 detailing several of the proposals for what to do "after Guantanamo." She discusses Neal Katyal's proposal, Ben Wittes's proposal, Andy McCarthy's proposal, and mine. She captures the essence of the "state of play" by writing, "A small group of national security buffs is seeking to fill the vacuum. They come from both ends of the ideological spectrum and disagree avidly on many of the details. But they are pushing plans they believe will help balance civil liberties and security, and pave the way toward a post-Gitmo system of handling suspects in the war on terror."[34]

One person she did not write about or mention in the article is really the one who initiated the debate and certainly convinced me there needs to be something different from the military commissions: Harvey Rishikof, now a professor of national security at the National War College in Washington, D.C. Professor Rishikof has written about the idea of a federal terrorism court since June 2002. He and I have been discussing the relative merits/demerits of such potential legislative "fixes" since September 2001 while he was dean of Roger Williams University Law School and I was one of his adjuncts teaching military law. He has had the foresight, as you can read in both his June 2002 op-ed piece in the *New York Times*[35] and his 2003 law review article,[36] that the nation needed to create such a court. His proposed court would be a special court with specialized judges and prosecutors; it would permit jury trials and preventive detention, and the trials would be open to the public. In a more recent piece written for the Progressive Policy Institute he notes, "We already have specialized courts in the federal system of particularly complex issues requiring unique knowledge, including bankruptcy, patents, immigrations, tax, copyrights, and international trade. In short, we have ample precedent for a court dedicated to vital, complicated issues requiring the development of substantive and procedural expertise."[37]

Neal Katyal and Jack Goldsmith published a couple of articles in 2007 and 2008 discussing their views on the need for a specialized terrorism court. Katyal, the director of the Georgetown's national security law center, was a former legal advisor to the Clinton administration, served as co-counsel to Al Gore in *Bush v. Gore*, and was lead counsel in *Hamdan v. Rumsfeld* (as detailed in chapter 5, this was a Supreme Court case that found that the Guantanamo detention system violated the U.S. Military Code and the Geneva Conventions). Of note, Katyal is still representing Hamdan now as his client is scheduled to be the first detainee to actually be "tried" by the military commissions. Jack Goldsmith, now a Harvard Law School professor, is a conservative who was once in charge of the Office of Legal Counsel in the Bush Justice Department and resigned after concluding, as he wrote in his book *The Terror Presidency*, that "some of our most important counterterrorism policies rested on severely damaged legal foundations."[38] Their proposal envisions a national security court that would operate independently of the civilian judicial system but would be staffed by federal judges who could specialize in the subject matter and hear arguments from a pool of lawyers armed with security clearances and steeped in counterterrorism laws. First unveiled in a joint 2007 *New York Times* op-ed piece, their plan argues for treating citizens and noncitizens identically.[39] But detainees would not be afforded the same procedural protections given to traditional criminal suspects. They might not be allowed to meet with their lawyers during interrogations, and press and public access to the proceedings would be restricted. I have been on panels with Neal Katyal, and his analysis and thoughts on this issue are learned and cogent, carrying the additional weight of his experience of actually litigating within the military commission process.[40]

Brookings Institution legal fellow Ben Wittes, whom I have had the pleasure of serving with on several panels and with whom I have exchanged thoughts and ideas on this topic quite often through the electronic medium, recently published his book, *Law and the Long War*. To date, his book gives the most detailed examination of and the reasons for a special terrorism court. Wittes advocates a special federal court to replace Guantanamo's military system and to implement a more legally defensible, rigorous process of preventive detention. He argues that regardless of some critics' assertions, the United States already has precedent for using such preventive detention models both in the past and currently—we employ such detention systems in myriad ways. His insights are exceptional, and his objective analysis of the failures of the military commission process and prediction for problems with the civilian system (if employed) make clear that a new system must be entertained. The real key to his proposal for a special court, however, is founded upon the need for preventive detention. Wittes's grasp of the threat is on point. He fears additional attacks and demonstrates a "realism" approach to the threat posed by al Qaeda. He writes in great detail about the need for preventive detention to keep people incarcerated who "might" or are "likely" to engage in acts of international terrorism in the future. He compares the al Qaeda detainee preventive detention with that of potentially violent patients with mental illness being legally committed without being convicted of any crime.[41] By placing such emphasis on preventive detention, this proposal, in essence, would not remove the taint of long-term detention of suspected al Qaeda members at Guantanamo. This is not to say that Wittes's proposed system would not have trials. In fact, that is not the case at all; Wittes's proposed court would also have options for trials. Similar to my proposal, his would be a mix of the laws of war and the civilian system. "The goal…is narrow and practical: a trial regime that gives detainees enough due process to satisfy the commands of the Constitution and garner international tolerance, if not quite admiration, yet at the same time facilitates the maximum number of criminal trials, thereby lessening the burden that any system of preventative detention will have to bear."[42] The trials should "not have roots only in the laws of war. Military commissions have a nasty sound, in large measure because of their long disuse, the rough injustice they have sometimes administered in the past, and the crudeness with which the administration sought to revive them."[43] He notes that the key in creating such courts is that they maintain their constitutionality by ensuring that they limit their jurisdiction only to war crimes and only to unlawful enemy combatants.[44] Lawyers would receive pertinent classified information, but rules for entering evidence would be more relaxed than in civilian court. For example, chain-of-custody requirements would be relaxed so cases wouldn't get thrown out of court over whether detainees were alerted to their right to remain silent under the Fifth Amendment protections. U.S. citizens and residents, however, would still be tried through standard civilian courts.

In an article "Why We Need a National Security Court" written by conservative former federal prosecutor Andrew C. McCarthy and Alykhan Velshi (for a book edited by the American Enterprise Institute [AEI], *Outsourcing American Law*), they write,

> Congress should use its authority under Article I, Section 8, of the Constitution to create a new National Security Court. Such a court could subsume, and expand on the jurisdiction and duties of, the existing federal Foreign Intelligence Surveillance Court. This new tribunal would be responsible for terrorism trials, as well as the review and monitoring of the detention of alien enemy combatants. It would inject judicial participation into the process to promote procedural integrity and international cooperation, but would avoid the perilous prospect of judicial micromanagement of the executive branch's conduct of war on terror.[45]

In their proposal, the prosecution and defense lawyers would be selected from a pool of lawyers at the Justice Department as well as the military's Judge Advocate General's offices. Judges, interestingly, would be chosen by the chief justice of the United States. McCarthy and Velshi's plan requires all "enemy combatants" to be processed within one year of capture. Trials would be a true mix of the two prevailing systems. Of all the proposals I have looked at, the McCarthy/Velshi court is the most similar to those conducted by military commissions. However, there still are clear differences. The trials would be overseen by civilian judges from the U.S. criminal system. Juries would be part of their proposed system—composed of five military officers. Attorney General Michael Mukasey has written in support of this plan. McCarthy and Mukasey have worked together before; Mukasey was the judge on the famous case against the 1993 World Trade Center bombers that McCarthy helped to prosecute.[46]

Different from my colleagues' proposals, the key element in the statutory creation of my proposed new court system is to ensure that the system is adjudicatory in nature. The United States needs to move away from preventive detention models advocated by some scholars.[47] Ben Wittes writes, "Without a strong capacity to lock up the enemy, America merely waits the next attack."[48] True, but I disagree with my friend on this point. The best means for ensuring that we protect the nation as well as avoid human rights abuse or unlawful detention of innocent persons is for Congress to properly construct a system in which a court of law makes decisions regarding guilt or innocence in a trial rather than relying on administrative detentions. We need to try the detainees accused of war crimes.

The terrorist court, like the bankruptcy, patent, and immigration courts (or other specialized courts within U.S. federal jurisprudence), would be used for this niche area of the law and ensure civilian oversight of the process. In this way, we further distinguish the unique nature of the conflict and ensure that military commissions (authorized and appropriate in traditional armed conflict) are not removed from military jurisprudence altogether. These "terrorism courts" finally will create a solution for many of the long-standing Guantanamo Bay detention camp concerns. I remain hopeful (even more so after the *Boumediene* decision) that as policy makers begin to study this idea of a hybrid model, used to try international terrorists, they will see it as the best, most appropriate "way ahead."

Overview of the National Security Court System (NSCS) Proposal

The National Security Court System would also be used in concert with an updated Foreign Surveillance Intelligence Act (hereinafter referred to as FISA). Although President Bush signed a law in the summer of 2008 updating the 1978 law, further updates can be made by Congress as part of this new system. The NSCS could be used as a judicial check, if one is deemed appropriate, for situations like the Terrorist Surveillance Program. Although I feel strongly that Article II of the U.S. Constitution and the Framers explicitly intended for the president to have the inherent authority to carry out the operations of war, some oversight in this new war is now preferable. There are few who question that intelligence gathering is critical to success in the War on al Qaeda. The existing FISA court and statutes were written in the era of the Cold War seeking to place limits on the executive exclusively for domestic surveillance. As the need for enhanced signals and human intelligence has grown (and technology has increased dramatically since the late 1970s), the need to regulate these activities has also increased. These intelligence tools, without question, are critical for combating the asymmetric international terrorist threat posed by al Qaeda. However, they are also prone to potential abuse. The national security courts can fulfill a critical function in providing a "check" on executive decisions relating to surveillance activities. The expert judges appointed to the National Security Court System would additionally have the responsibility to review procedures and issue advisory opinions on the conduct of the executive branch conducting many of the sensitive operations in fighting international terrorism. Such oversight would only be permissible after a request for opinion is requested by a two-thirds majority of both houses of the legislature. Thus, the judges would not be limited to simply sitting in judgment of the alleged al Qaeda members; their duties would be much greater than that. I envision them to be truly "national security judges" in all respects.

The courts themselves would function as a hybrid of both military commissions and Article III federal courts, but they would necessarily (in order to distinguish between the rights of American citizens, POWs, and ordinary criminals) afford decreased expectations of constitutional protections than those provided to American citizens. Article III judges (with specific expertise in law of armed conflict, international human rights law, and intelligence) appointed to such a court would provide learned expertise in the laws of war and intelligence as well as offer protections to our liberty and national security. In this way, we can best provide an independent and more universally legitimate process to adjudicate atrocities committed by our enemies without being exposed to constant criticism by nongovernmental organizations[49] while still meeting the needs of each individual nation-state's often legitimate concerns.

The current legal regime is confusing, and many scholars, practitioners, and policy makers continue to struggle with how best to proceed.[50] As noted earlier, the holdings in both *Hamdan* and *Boumediene* have made the landscape increasingly ambiguous. The MCA was a response to many of the judiciary's concerns, but a glaring lack of consensus remains. The implementation of a National Security Court System will assist in reducing the ambiguity both in the short term and the foreseeable future. Just by closing the Guantanamo detention facility, ending the military commissions process, and moving the detainees out of Cuba and into the continental United States will no doubt prove helpful in changing the prevailing view that the United States has used Guantanamo as a site where alleged reprehensible conduct has occurred. The world has changed, the means employed by international terrorists have changed, Western expectations of privacy have changed,[51] our responses to such international attacks have changed,[52] the military justice system has changed, and now,[53] our means of adjudicating war crimes committed by our new enemy must change. As

I have argued earlier, the enactment of the MCA as a reaction to the holding in *Hamdan* can be viewed as a continuing response to update and better meet the needs of this armed conflict. Even after *Boumediene*, and so many of the numerous legal flaws contained within the opinion, the military commissions are still operating and functioning as of July 2008. The time for the political branches to act and create a new system is better now than ever before.[54]

However, this legislation should not be viewed as the end of the debate over the detention and adjudication of alleged al Qaeda fighters but rather the beginning. Consensus will continue to evolve as we struggle to understand the new threat posed by these asymmetric world stage actors. We need to break away from the existing paradigms, and Congress must intervene to create a new system to adjudicate alleged war criminals in the War on al Qaeda. A logical step in handling hybrid warriors in a hybrid war is to create a hybrid court.

The National Security Court System

The system would be created under the Article I, Section 8, powers of the Congress. In creating the court, the Congress needs to strike the balance between national security, human rights, and due process. The enabling legislation must make clear that this is a unique court system specifically created to meet the needs of the new armed conflicts of the twenty-first century. The courts would coexist with the ordinary federal courts and the military commissions, and the courts-martial system. Congress must clearly state that the intent in creating the system is to meet the growing demands of the struggle to properly detain and adjudicate international terrorists. Taking into account the history of military commissions in wartime as well as the use of federal courts to try terrorist cases throughout the latter half of the twentieth century, the new system offers a delicate mix of the two prevailing systems—in order to achieve justice in the generational war most anticipate. This process has already been evolutionary: both the military commissions and the civilian system have failed to best meet the need of policy makers and those employed to protect the national security. They are not equipped to properly strike the balance of military law, intelligence needs, human rights obligations, and the need for justice—both perceived and actual. Civilian oversight of the system will be critical to its success and will help garner support from the international community. The system must function as one that achieves justice, attains deterrence, satisfies our human rights obligations, ensures civil liberties protections, maintains the support of our international partners, and gains national consensus. This is no easy task. However, it is one our policy makers need to step forward and confront—as soon as possible.

Department of Justice Oversight

The oversight of the National Security Court must be performed by the Department of Justice National Security Division. Civilian oversight remains the critical component to the system's success. In the twenty-first century, perceptions are now critical to the success of any policy in the media-frenzied environment of the United States, and for that matter, most of the world. The al Qaeda fighter does not appear as a "warrior" in his appearance. The accused enters the military courtroom and stands before the tribunal, not in a military uniform but rather an orange prisoner jumpsuit, and he stands before military officers in "dress" uniforms. This sends an unfortunate, and unnecessarily wrong, signal to the world. The twenty-four-hour media coverage then broadcasts photos or artist renderings of senior military officers holding hearings over a "prisoner" who displays none of the trappings of a military member. This image sends the signal to many within the world community that the United States is holding hearings by the military against civilians. As I have often stated in public forums, military members with ribbons, medals, and uniforms do convey a strong sense of authority. In many ways, it can be intimidating. This military versus civilian dynamic also is often compared with human rights violations being committed by military officers against civilians in other parts of the world. Often these similar "trials" by the military over civilians are harshly criticized by our own State Department as violations of human rights and referred to as "kangaroo courts."[55] I do not believe the tribunals are kangaroo courts, but the wrong impression is still being conveyed to millions worldwide. It appears that the Bush administration never seemed to appreciate these growing negative perceptions and how the world has come to view the military commissions.

Along that same line of reasoning, it is critical that the Department of Defense no longer oversee the detention process. Having civilian oversight by Article III judges will send a strong signal of such change. The Department of Justice needs to be the lead agency overseeing the prosecutions within the NSCS. This shift in oversight from the Department of Defense to the Department of Justice will help remove some of the allegations of "unlawful command influence (UCI)" that defense counsel have repeatedly raised.[56] It is true that one of the weaknesses in the military justice system (in general) is the likelihood of interference from superiors before, during, and after the proceedings.[57] This is even more possible in the heated, politically charged environment of military commissions. Prosecuting alleged members of a group who indiscriminately murder civilians is more susceptible to UCI than a simple court-martial. Unlawful command influence pervades virtually all aspects of the military justice system. This "evil" within military justice has been studied by many leading authorities throughout the past century and attempts have been formally made to remove, or at least reduce, the impact of UCI.[58] It is natural, however, for such influence to exist within the hierarchical command structure of the military. If there is an area of military justice, or particularly military commissions, that is problematic, it is the concept of UCI. Ordinarily, a base commander or a regional commander is charged with overseeing the entire process of a court-martial, from start to finish. The commander initiates the charges, controls the resources, works with both defense counsel and prosecutor (known as a trial counsel in military law parlance), and is required to ensure that justice is served. It is human nature, further exacerbated by the unique nature of the military environment, that when the commander initiates charges against one of his or her members of the command, the commander expects a guilty verdict. This normal human tendency is even more influential by factoring in the needs of command to retain respect, authority, deterrence, and good order and discipline within a military unit. I think any reader, civilian or military, understands the ramifications within a military command (on a cutter, ship, or base) when a commanding officer "loses" a case at court-martial and the alleged is acquitted. This is one of the unique aspects of military justice. Ordinarily, and distinct from civilian perspectives on the subject, commanders expect military verdicts to be in their favor. This is not to say there is no "justice" in military justice. That is not the case at all. In discussing this, my intention is to explain why unlawful command influence is so prevalent within the military justice system and how it can be even more egregious within the military commissions process. There are numerous commanding officers who, despite this arguable "flaw" within the system, resist any temptations and do ensure that justice is done. In fact, in the modern military environment, I would suggest that is more than simply the norm.

Yet, how does one capture unlawful command influence in military proceedings? To some, it is an institutional flaw. It can be "actual" or "apparent" in its character. As is generally well known, military justice is completely dependent upon the authority of the commander who convenes the trial and reviews the record of trial after the verdict is rendered. An example of actual command influence is when a commanding officer talks to the military judge or the counsel or even the members of his or her command about the case or what sentence the commander would like to see given or the importance of a conviction in a particular case. But beyond that, even an appearance of UCI can be detrimental to any hope of attaining justice. An example of apparent UCI occurs when members (the jury) see the military judge and the commander interacting socially during the trial. Although no discussion of the case may have taken place, others involved in the proceedings, such as the members (jurors) or the accused individual, can be impacted by such appearances. Since all military promotions are based upon evaluations by the command, the wrong signal can be sent. Thus, commanders have to be extremely careful once proceedings against an accused have been initiated.

Fortunately, there is a remedy for this within military law. Defense counsel can raise their concerns about unlawful command influence during a court-martial. The UCMJ provides Article 37 that states,

> (a) No authority convening a general, special, or summary court martial may, nor any other commanding officer, may censure, reprimand or admonish the court or any member, military judge, or counsel thereof, with respect to the findings or sentence adjudged by the court, or with respect to any other exercises of its or his functions in the conduct of the proceedings...or, by any unauthorized means, influence the action of a courts-martial or any other military tribunal or any member thereof.[59]

This article deals extensively with actions before the trial, during the trial, after the trial, and even later to ensure that defense counsel and others representing the accused are not "punished" in their performance reports as a result of their "zeal."[60] This illegal influence also applies to "other military tribunals," meaning military commissions as well. This potential for abuse is even greater in the attempts to adjudicate war crimes committed by al Qaeda fighters. Their unique status as hybrid warriors only highlights the need for a different, not strictly military, process for their detention and adjudication. Unlawful command influence exists within the ordinary military justice system. It can be even more egregious, as you might expect, when applied to the current military commissions process.

Within the Bush commissions, from the outset, there were allegations of UCI made against former Secretary of Defense Rumsfeld, former DoD General Counsel William J. "Jim" Haynes II, the legal advisor to the commissions (most recently General Hartman, the legal advisor to the convening authority), and even President Bush himself. The defense counsels have referred to comments made to prosecutors, in public statements, in press conferences, in interviews, and sometimes even in private meetings as indications that unlawful command influence has pervaded the commissions, and in many ways has perverted them.[61]

Concerns about UCI have not only been raised by the defense but also by the prosecution team members who have allegedly been pressured as well. Colonel Morris Davis resigned as the chief prosecutor of the commissions because he was allegedly pressured by the Department of Defense general counsel as well as the legal advisor to the commissions to get convictions and to move quickly on the trials before the next elections.[62] In fact, he has now testified on behalf of the defense in one case. While I refrain from commenting on how Colonel Morris conducted himself or on his decision to write an op-ed piece in the *Los Angeles Times* criticizing his chain of command, his situation and concerns nonetheless highlight the problems inherent in using the military system to prosecute these cases against the detainees. Unlawful command influence, whether imagined or not, suggests to those viewing from the outside, both within the United States and around the world, that the administration is employing an unfair process. The Bush administration repeatedly denied these accusations. However, the perception is the reality and many observers now hold this impression of the military commissions. Like Roosevelt in 1942, or any commander today (up and down the chain), the administration and the Pentagon would unquestionably like to see convictions.[63] However, with these trials being viewed under a microscope by nongovernmental organizations and the media, any comment made by senior officers, presidential appointees, or cabinet members are likely to be viewed as "apparent" UCI. Henceforth, no matter what the Bush administration has said or will say in the future, such comments will always be viewed with suspicion. Meritless claims are normally grounded in some legitimate concern that the military is overseeing a process that "appears" unfair. This is viewed internationally as indicative of the flaws inherent when employing military commissions; and the situation begs for a system that can remove this now almost unavoidable "taint."

The shift to civilian Department of Justice oversight is critical in removing both legitimate and illegitimate concerns about unlawful command influence and the "fairness" of this process. The new war necessitates new ways to look at the whole process to determine what agency is better suited to oversee the detention and adjudication of the al Qaeda fighter. It seems clear that civilian oversight is preferable in the War on al Qaeda.

Jurisdiction

The National Security Court System will have jurisdiction over citizens and noncitizens alike. Similar to the Katyal-Goldsmith model, it is important for the system to not distinguish between citizen and noncitizen when handling alleged al Qaeda fighters. If the court system is properly constructed by Congress, the need for any distinction should not be necessary. The NSCS will incorporate sufficient due process to satisfy any constitutional concerns that may be raised. Since preventive detention is not part of the NSCS, the alleged, regardless of citizenship, will be tried in rapid fashion. Any decreased expectation of constitutional protections would likely be *de minimus*.

Ensuring that the NSCS retains jurisdiction over citizen and noncitizen alike removes the unintended inequality that alleged U.S. citizen al Qaeda fighters would have greater rights than those from other nations. For example, two suspected al Qaeda members' communications are intercepted by U.S. intelligence agents. One member is a U.S. citizen and the other a Canadian. The intercept reveals that the two suspects are conspiring to plant explosives in and around the White House and are assisting in coordinating assassinations of key members of the administration staff. Under the existing process, the U.S. citizen would be granted full access to U.S. courts of justice while the Canadian would be subject to the NSCS. This seems unintentionally unfair. Worse yet, envision the ramifications internationally if a Yemeni and a U.S. citizen were to be involved in a situation similar to the one presented above. To avoid such inequity, the jurisdiction should be of both citizen and noncitizen alike.

Similarly, legislation creating the system should be clear that persons subject to the court, regardless of citizenship, are those alleged to have been, or are, members of al Qaeda or affiliated groups that engage or plan to engage in acts of international terrorism. The Congress needs to clarify that "any terrorist" is not subject to this court but simply those who engage in international terrorism. This removes the fear of some that the court would have jurisdiction over any group or entity that engages in terrorism. The limited jurisdiction of the NSCS would serve as a check on any arbitrary use of the court system.

Judges

The National Security Court System has life-tenured Article III judges with law of armed conflict expertise to preside over the trials. The judges will be appointed by the president, with the advice and consent of the Senate—in the same manner that all federal judges are appointed. As with all Article III judges, this ensures that the specialized court is composed of different jurisprudential philosophies depending upon the president in office who does the appointing. These judges, however, will be expected to possess the educational background necessary to determine the legality of intelligence gathering, terrorist surveillance, and other necessary areas in the field of terrorism and national security. Several scholars, advocating against judicial intervention in the war, correctly note that those who are making such decisions now are not necessarily versed in this unique area of the law.[64] As Andy McCarthy has noted, judges hearing cases within the existing federal criminal justice system "tend to elevate individual rights at the expense of public safety (which is to say, at the expense of the public's collective rights). When opportunities for creativity present themselves—which frequently happens thanks to a pervasive elasticity in the rules governing judicial proceedings, over which judges have a degree of supervisory authority—judges are hard wired to err on the side of providing more process."[65] This is completely appropriate for the criminal justice system when the stakes are not nearly as high as within the national security arena. Specific deterrence within a national security context, however, is often essential in protecting the citizenry. Congress, when drafting the legislation for the court, must be specific as to the specificity and importance of the system as well as the limited authority of the court. As McCarthy notes, the legislation needs to "limit the creativity of the court."[66]

There will be nine judges at any given time assigned to the court. As a result of the inordinate amount of resources and problems with empanelling a jury, judge-alone trials would be the only option available to adjudicate the cases against the alleged war criminals. Juries, in many ways unmanageable in the national security context, will not be available to the accused. As argued earlier, empanelling a "jury of peers" for international terrorists is impractical and unlikely. The proceedings will have three-judge panels, and the system envisions two panels available or operating at any given time. In order to convict, a simple majority will be required (2–1); and unanimity of the panel will be necessary for any capital cases brought by the prosecution. The three judges "out of the court rotation" will be used for all habeas appeals that will remain confined within the national security court system apparatus. Additionally, such special judges will be used for FISA warrant applications as well. The duties of the judges would include the following: (1) the judges would have oversight of the trials; (2) single-judge panels, when in rotation, would hear habeas petitions; (3) the judges would have oversight of the detention and any legal issues arising or emerging from such detentions; (4) the three judges not in the trial rotation would handle all issues surrounding FISA applications/warrants and further, serve on the FISA court; (5) the judges would hear any cases/trials determined to be of a national security nature and that deal with issues of the War on al Qaeda or other international terrorist organizations.

Some of my colleagues and friends on the right do not want any civilian judicial involvement in the proceedings at all. They argue that such involvement will limit the effectiveness of the commander in chief during war operations. As mentioned as foundational for this system, whether you agree or disagree about having civilian judges in this process, the nature of this war does seem to necessitate some form of judicial intervention more than has been custom or standard in previous U.S. military war and operations. The strictly military law system (UCMJ courts-martial or the military commissions) or many of the norms expressed in the Geneva Conventions or the ever evolving customary international law do not necessarily apply to the cases against al Qaeda fighters. The key is to balance, and legislatively guide, national security judges to equate justice in this arena as distinct from that of military criminal law or ordinary federal courts. The stakes in the national security courts are much greater than they are in standard federal courts. As it is currently constructed, the existing system allows for judges who have no background in warfare or national security to intervene, hear, and decide cases when they have little or no understanding of the issues because these are beyond the scope of the judges' expertise.[67] The legislation creating the NSCS must be specific and make clear to the judges that this is not an ordinary criminal court and, as such, the judges should refrain from making analogies to the civilian system in deciding their cases. The threat we face demands these enhanced requirements for specialized judges for this specialized court.

Prosecution Team

Prosecutors, assigned by the Department of Justice National Security Division, would represent the government and exercise prosecutorial discretion over whether to proceed in cases. Overall supervision of the NSCS would be conducted by the chief, Criminal Division of the Department of Justice and ultimately the associate attorney general of the United States. The powers of these prosecutors, as in other nations (employing separate systems of justice for detaining and prosecuting terrorists), would be great, but the prosecutors would still operate under the ethical rules standard for all U.S. government attorneys. Different from the French model, their powers would not be unlimited and they would certainly not serve as judges.

The current use of military lawyers as the prosecutors has not achieved its intended objective. The often unspoken reality is that military lawyers do not have the opportunity to try many contested felony cases. The numbers of contested general courts-martial conducted in all five armed services has dropped significantly over the past two decades and thus, actual felony trial experience is not great for many senior JAGs. Their courtroom experiences are often more limited than those of civilian federal prosecutors or federal public defenders. More specifically, the numbers of capital cases conducted by JAGs are few, with most having never been involved in a capital case in their careers.[68] Many are outstanding lawyers who are dedicated, tough litigators. But the fact remains that most do not have the trial experience in major cases that many assistant U.S. attorneys or criminal litigators have. Under the current Military Commissions Act (MCA), these same JAGs are assigned to prosecute arguably the most controversial cases in at least the last fifty years. Are we really wise to follow this course? As superb as these lawyers are in terms of patriotism, knowledge of the law, ethics, and many other areas of the legal practice, the system should be designed to ensure that seasoned litigators prosecute these cases. The best-case scenario envisions civilian litigators with previous military experience (who have actually served as JAGs in the past) being appointed as prosecutors in the NSCS. The right course of action and the best means of achieving justice and maintaining national security are to ensure that both sides are represented by seasoned, polished criminal litigators. Moving to a Department of Justice-sponsored system helps guarantee that civilian practitioners would carry the caseloads. Active duty military JAGs, however, would still be assigned (or what is known as being "detailed" in military parlance) to the court system to provide their expertise (particularly in military matters and the law of armed conflict) to the Department of Justice lawyers in conducting the prosecutions. This has already been, either tacitly or overtly, recognized by the government in many ways. For example, the military commission for Salim Hamdan was prosecuted by "detailed" civilian federal prosecutors, along with JAG officers.

Defense Team

Active duty judge advocates (military lawyers) would serve as government-provided defense counsel. This group would be similar to those provided for the detainees in the military commissions. The judge advocates would be made available by the Department of Homeland Security[69] and the Department of Defense. Initially, a pool of ten judge advocates would serve on defense teams. If desired, the accused may employ, at his expense, civilian counsel as long as they have requisite classified document clearance. In being able to access civilian counsel (as is currently the case), the defense can secure some of the best legal minds and litigators in the country, if desired. The funds to support civilian counsel would be generated by NGOs, advocacy groups, and philanthropists interested in supporting a fair trial. In the spring of 2008, a fund such as this emerged known as the John Adams fund. Its specific intention is to ensure adequate representation for the five high-value detainees held and in June 2008 arraigned at Guantanamo.[70] Also, the government should provide additional funds to the defense team to ensure access to civilian counsel. Affording such opportunities ensures alleged international terrorists with a defense more than capable of handling their cases. Further, this would help satisfy some of the international concern about any perceived lack of adequate representation. The international community often refers to the military commissions as "shams."[71] In part, this is because they strongly believe the "trials" are heavily weighted against the accused. The National Security Court System again would respond to those concerns by ensuring that the top civilian lawyers, throughout the process, could be retained by the accused.

Presumptively Open Trials

The NSCS will conduct open hearings. However, as a result of the sensitive nature of intelligence gathering (means and methods employed) as well as ensuring that such hearings do not become propaganda tools for the enemy,[72] NSCS judges would be permitted to close the proceedings to the public when necessary. Statements, evidence, witness testimony, and other courtroom activity could all be exploited by the enemy for future attacks. Certainly, it is important to maintain the openness of our procedures and to showcase, in the new court, the benefits of the National Security Court System. However, when drafting the proposed legislation, Congress cannot be blind to the potential ramifications of any desire for complete transparency or "openness." Naïveté will be no excuse for facilitating the next attacks on U.S. soil. As Judge Posner has astutely noted, adherence to our constitution is not a suicide pact.[73] This need to ensure that the trials could be closed at times is not to create a "star chamber," or to expand executive power, or to exert the State Secrets Doctrine into areas where it was never intended to be used,[74] but rather to protect the military members and government agents fighting in the ongoing armed conflict against al Qaeda. As mentioned earlier, a frightening example of the potential harm in keeping the courts open occurred when the Southern District of New York tried the "blind sheik" Omar Abdel Rahman for his participation in the 1993 World Trade Center bombing. The prosecution team, in the federal civilian court, complied with ordinary rules of discovery and turned over 200 possible co-conspirators.[75] Within days, this detailed account of whom the U.S. law enforcement entities were pursuing and why they were thought to be affiliated with al Qaeda was produced and shared with the defense team. It was, essentially, a blueprint of U.S. counterterrorism operations. Without question, national security officials throughout the country were concerned. We later found out, within days of being turned over to the defense legal team, the entire list was in bin Laden's hands. He was now able to see who had yet to be discovered as part of the al Qaeda network. Certainly such knowledge impacts the national security of the United States. Further, the information could be studied by al Qaeda to determine important aspects of U.S. counterterrorism activities: who might be "leaking" al Qaeda information; current trends of the CIA and FBI intelligence collection programs; informants' names and addresses; and other critical, sensitive means of gathering intelligence. Congress should be mindful of these considerations when drafting the new legislation. The NSCS statute should offer specific lists and guidelines detailing when judges are permitted to close the trials. Such legislation detailing when the trials can be closed by the judges should include (1) the court's discussion of specifics on the means and methods of intelligence collection, (2) the risk of mentioning nations involved in supporting U.S. efforts at combating terrorism, (3) identification of informants, (4) information that would impact ongoing military operations or covert intelligence operations, (5) other items deemed by the court to be of such a sensitive nature as to overcome the Western legal tradition's time-honored presumption of an open court for trials.

Another legitimate concern of an open court can be the use of the courtroom as a propaganda platform for al Qaeda. In addition to the case in the trials of the perpetrators of the World Trade Center bombings in 1993 and the Moussaoui case,[76] such antics have been employed most recently during the arraignments of the five al Qaeda members suspected of coordinating, plotting, or planning the attacks on 9/11, including Khalid Sheik Mohammad.[77] However, as distasteful and harmful as it may be, this outrageous behavior should generally be permitted within the National Security Court. Open access to the media and the public should remain as much as practicable. The presiding judge, however, shall be granted liberal discretion to limit such use of the court's resources for actions that are deemed, by the judge, as nothing more than propaganda. This diminution of the accused rights is so *de minimus* as to not impact the proceedings or his due process rights but rather to ensure that the courtroom does not become a circus.

It is critical to note, however, that when the National Security Court judge does determine that the court must be closed for security reasons, some outside observers will still be permitted to attend and observe. This is important for both appearance and reality. Such "observers" will include representatives from several appointed NGOs (Amnesty International, Human Rights Watch, Human Rights First), representatives from the United Nations, and select members of the media to ensure fairness of the trial and to witness the procedural protections expected of a nation dedicated to upholding the rule of law. Each observer, however, would have to maintain appropriate security clearance prior to the trial's commencement. At any point during the trial, if the judge believes the conduct of the "observers" during or after the trial goes beyond the authority to "observe," the judge will have the authority to remove such an observer from the trial. The legislation will mandate ten "observers" permitted during closed session: three from NGOs, three from the United Nations, and four from the media. Keeping observers in the courtroom, even during closed sessions, will ensure that there is outside oversight of the process and will also validate the proceedings as being conducted in conformity with our human rights obligations. Within the United States and internationally, such transparency will be critical to support these trials and the National Security Court itself.

Military Bases within the United States

The detention and trials will be conducted on military bases located within the continental United States. This move would ensure the closing of Guantanamo once and for all. To some, the holding in *Boumediene* was officially the beginning of the end of Guantanamo as a detention center in the War on al Qaeda. Even avid supporters of military commissions conceded that the commissions were now doomed. Former Assistant Secretary of Defense for Detainee Affairs, and current Fellow at the Heritage Foundation Cully Stimson, declared, "This signals the end of Gitmo."[78] I strongly agree with my colleague. Important to U.S. foreign policy, the closing of the camp will have major significance to the world. Correctly or incorrectly, over the past seven years the base has come to signify the "alleged" evils of the U.S.-led war on terror. Combined with Abu Ghraib, the public relations damage caused by allegation of human rights abuse at Guantanamo has tainted U.S. efforts there permanently. That, coupled with the realities of new Supreme Court precedence, makes the need for using some facility within the continental U.S. more logical. However, the political realities of using civilian prisons for detention of these prisoners must be measured as well. As much as there has been criticism by many in Congress about Guantanamo, there will be great "pushback" by many of our policy makers against having these alleged terrorists brought back to main street U.S.A. The not-in-my-backyard (NIMBY) syndrome will be in full swing. The American electorate, even with its vast compassion and concern for fairness and justice, remains on high alert for future terrorist attacks. I anticipate that many citizens would not be pleased in having alleged al Qaeda fighters in their local federal prisons. Politically, in most parts of the country, relocating the al Qaeda fighters to cells where they would be mixed in with ordinary criminals will give pause to a number of members of Congress. It is unlikely that many of those running for office will be fighting to bring the detainees into their own districts. However, bringing them into military brigs on protected U.S. military bases should be more palatable to both the policy makers and the electorate. Although some still contend that the best scenario remains sending many of the detainees back to their countries of origin for prosecution, the reality remains that most of these countries will not accept them.

Besides, as leaders in this fight against international terrorism, it is the duty of the United States to take responsibility and try these detainees. Select military bases will be used as detention centers; the military courtrooms located on the base will be used for the actual prosecution. Military bases are ideal. They are secure, there is room to house the detainees, the professional military can oversee the detentions, and this decision captures and reaffirms the notion that these are, although unique, war criminals. Further, the base can provide adequate safety for the civilian judges as they perform their work and will appropriately limit the access of those interested in attending the proceedings. This would keep the detainees held in a location that is secure (similar to the stated rationale for holding the al Qaeda suspects at Guantanamo), but will incur less of the controversy associated with the United States holding citizens of other nations at a remote location. This would, in part, also remove some of the international concerns about the detention center having been previously located in Guantanamo. Under the NSCS, the detainees will now be located on U.S. soil. In using the military bases in this fashion, the thousands of unlawful belligerents held in Afghanistan (and some in Iraq) could be brought to these bases to be detained and tried both now and in the future. Under the NSCS, alleged and convicted U.S. military criminals will be held at the same location as the international terrorist. Locating the alleged al Qaeda fighters within the United States will answer myriad allegations of arbitrary treatment, and even suggestions of torture of the detainees will likely be mitigated. Such steps forward, in and of themselves, will help to reduce some international cynicism of U.S. intentions and actions regarding the detainees. Without question, sections of the brigs would have to be separated for only those convicted by the National Security Court. Doing so would be for the safety of our own armed forces but it would also distinguish the war criminals from ordinary military criminals. Keeping unlawful combatants (or even POWs for that matter) on a military base (although normally such "camps" are overseas) but separated from ordinary military criminals has been the practice in ordinary armed conflict for generations. This proposal merely applies it to the current fight.

Military brigs are the most appropriate place to detain accused terrorists because they are secure and afford the same protection against abuse given to convicted U.S. service members (who are tried, convicted, and sentenced under the UCMJ by courts-martial). Using military brigs is also a subtle reminder that this is a war and that the al Qaeda fighter is a "military detainee." Unquestionably, having the detainees alongside members of the U.S. military will go a long way toward reducing international concerns of torture and unfair tribunals. In doing so, some of the negative images of U.S. soldiers fostered by the events at Abu Ghraib (and the legitimate criticism following) are likely to be mitigated. In addition, keeping the detainees within our nation provides an additional appearance of process and certainly removes much of the taint of having held the detainees in the base at Guantanamo for the past seven years. Locations such as Fort Leavenworth in Kansas, U.S. Naval Consolidated Brig in Charleston, South Carolina, Camp Pendelton in California, or the supermax prison facility in Colorado would seem appropriate as places to detain, try, and imprison persons accused of engaging in international terror. Since *Eisentrager* has been essentially overruled by recent cases,[79] the extraterritoriality needs are no longer applicable and, in essence, are moot. Guantanamo, as a detention facility, must close.[80]

Procedure, Evidence, and Burden of Proof

As in any proposed legislation, many changes are likely to occur during the ordinary legislative process. This is particularly so when Congress begins wrestling with many of the minute details of the NSCS procedure and evidence. It is recommended that the proposed legislation adopt virtually all procedural aspects of the Military Commissions Act of 2006. As detailed and listed in the previous chapter, the rights afforded within the MCA greatly exceed those of most nations and virtually all international tribunals, including the International Criminal Court (ICC) codified in the Rome Statute.[81] There will be five critical areas of distinction: (1) habeas appeals will be permitted but different from what was mandated in *Boumediene*; (2) the death penalty sentencing provisions will be altered; (3) there will be a right of interlocutory appeal at any point in the proceeding allowing the prosecution to challenge any court order regarding evidence, to be available if the judge deviates from the legislatively adopted rules of the new court;[82] (4) the appellate structure will be tailored specifically to the National Security Court System; and (5) statements obtained in violation of the Convention against Torture, the Army Field Manual, or Federal Law will be inadmissible.

The right to determine the status and propriety of detention are at the heart of Western traditions of law. Although it is critical to distinguish war criminals from ordinary criminals, there still must be some form of right for the detainees to challenge their detention. Contrary to many critics' assertions, there was a mechanism in place within the MCA; this was not the traditional habeas proceeding, but it did allow the detainees to challenge their detention. As argued earlier, prior to the *Boumediene* decision, the Detainee Treatment Act (DTA) of 2005 applied a two-level review process—the military review of the detention annually known as the Combatant Status Review Tribunals (CSRTs), and when appropriate, review by the D.C. Circuit (the second highest court in the land). *Boumediene* placed civilian judges with oversight of military detention. Within the civilian law context, this is reasonable. However, during armed conflict such a decision can have major impacts on the security of the United States.[83] It seems to me the Court was legitimately concerned about the process at Guantanamo and, as Justice Souter noted in his thoughtful and impassioned concurrence, the length of time the detainees have been in custody without charges.[84] However, it may have overreacted to these perceived injustices. The Supreme Court has now formally given greater due process rights to the detainees than would be afforded to prisoners of war under the Geneva Conventions.[85] This is simply not the best means to ensure the legality of the detainees' detention. The National Security Court System will ameliorate these suggested weaknesses contained within the Supreme Court's holding. The NSCS ensures a habeas corpus hearing is held before a civilian Article III federal judge but without necessarily granting constitutional rights to noncitizens captured outside the United States. The system, once again, captures the middle ground.

The National Security Judge, an impartial and detached magistrate (not in the trial rotation), would conduct the habeas hearings with military JAGs representing the government as well as the detainees. The strength of this process is that it includes the military's input and can be seen as overt recognition that this is a war requiring military expertise while still retaining civilian oversight of the process. This will respond, to some degree, to the recent concerns about habeas corpus rights for detainees while still remaining faithful to the Supreme Court's ruling in *Boumediene*.

The three-judge panels in the trials will use the "beyond a reasonable doubt" standard and require a two-thirds majority of the judges to convict any alleged detainee. Unanimity of the three judges will be required only for capital cases. The evidentiary standards will also be diminished from standard, civilian prosecutions—or military courts-martial for that matter. The NSCS offers the detainee great process and protections but necessarily a decreased expectation of the process ordinarily afforded U.S. citizens. No detainee should, by virtue of his or her status, have traditional U.S. constitutional rights attach. Specifically, the Fourth and Fifth Amendment rights so precious within our judicial system must necessarily be reduced in significance or removed altogether in the NSCS. To do otherwise would be to ensure acquittals in virtually all cases against the detainees. As some scholars have suggested, such actions would be absurd.[86] However, if al Qaeda suspects are searched or questioned on U.S. territory and are U.S. citizens, such protections would still exist, although at a reduced level. The exclusionary rule (excluding evidence from being considered by a court when constitutional violations have occurred in obtaining it), which is court created and not necessarily envisaged by the Constitution per se, would not be applicable within the National Security Court System. To permit application of the exclusionary rule would undoubtedly wreak havoc on the proper adjudication of the detainees. The NSC permits reasonable accommodations without unintentionally reducing standard constitutional protections afforded citizens of the United States.

A "speedy trial" rule will be part of the NSCS. Distinguishing the system from the military commissions and other proposals for a new security court, rules will be imposed on both the length of time until charged and the time required for commencement of a trial. The NSCS requires all detainees, from point of capture, to be charged within three months. Further, all trials must be initiated within one year from the date of being charged. In this way, the system permits legitimate, lawful interrogation of suspects over a period of time but does not permit indefinite detention. It accounts for the needs of intelligence professionals and also promotes the rule of law.

Appeals

Appeals of decisions made by the National Security Court shall be heard by the D. C. Circuit Court of Appeals and ultimately the Supreme Court. Deference shall be accorded to the holding of the national security court in all cases that come before the D. C. Circuit Court. The cases, obviously, will not be tried *de novo* but will be based upon errors committed in applying the National Security Court legislation.

An alternative appeals process, if properly constructed, could utilize some of the already existing military law appellate courts. The first level of review of national security cases could be the already existing Courts of Appeals of the Armed Forces (CAAF).[87] This limited right of appeal would ensure that the cases were heard by an outside panel of judges well versed in military law and the laws of war and have some background in the procedural nuances of national security law. Appellate counsel would be provided by Air Force, Coast Guard, Navy, Marine Corps, and the Army. However, the CAAF judges are currently Article I judges. These judges are not life tenured, are created out of Article I of the Constitution, serve for specified periods of time (in the case of the CAAF judges, fifteen years), and are not viewed with the same prestige as Article III judges. Thus, if embracing this alternative appeals process, Congress would have to ensure that the CAAF judges are reconstituted as Article III judges (those federal judges who are created out of the judicial branch, or the third article of the Constitution) with life tenure within any proposed legislation. In doing so, this alternative appeals process would make the CAAF the first level of review, the D. C. Circuit as the second level of review, and the Supreme Court the court of last resort after a proper *writ of certiorari* has been issued.

Death Penalty

To make the death penalty acceptable to our international partners, the system envisions modifying the existing federal rules regarding it. Under this system, the death penalty would still be an authorized punishment, but only if the accused is a citizen of a country where such punishment is authorized. For example, if a citizen of Great Britain is detained, life in prison would be the highest level of punishment authorized. Since the death penalty is viewed as a human rights violation within the European Union (EU), it is important in this global conflict to maintain support from our traditional allies.[88] One way of ensuring support would be to recognize the expectations and rights of citizens of other nations. The unique nature of this war demands that we be overtly conscious that the enemy we fight is not from one or two nations as in traditional armed conflict. Many detainees are from nations that are allies of the United States. Every effort should be made not to alienate such allies (and their citizens) from the ongoing, generational struggle. Overt gestures such as the modification of the death penalty standard within the NSCS are not "the solution" but rather one step toward healing wounds incurred in relationships over the past seven years.

Even if deemed applicable in a particular case, the death penalty would be authorized only in those cases deemed sufficiently egregious to warrant it and those that severely impact the national security of the United States. Certain aggravating factors would have to be developed and codified by the Congress to distinguish between what cases are appropriate for life sentence and what could merit capital punishment. Recognizing that this would still cause concern among our European and other international colleagues, this proposal certainly requires further elaboration by the Congress and the White House prior to implementation.

The National Security Court System is fundamentally a balance and an accommodation of many competing legal and policy interests. It is structured upon the foundations of the U.S. understanding of the rule of law; it exceeds the standards of most requirements of international law and embraces human rights by ensuring that the dignity of each alleged detainee is maintained. It is an outgrowth—or an evolution—of the military commissions. It provides the answer for policy makers to get us out of the quicksand we find ourselves in regarding detainees. We have been attempting to force the civilian justice model or the military justice model onto a new entity—the al Qaeda fighter. Neither will work. The proposed system provides a delicate balance between the competing interests of U.S. national security and our human rights obligations to the detainees. The National Security Court System provides a system of justice that will answer the needs of policy makers for years to come. We simply can not remain mired in the ways of the past or the ideals of our generation, but rather must step forward with pragmatic idealism as our guide and promote the rule of law while bringing unlawful combatants to justice.

Conclusion

The Way Ahead

THE MILITARY COMMISSIONS ordered by President Bush in 2001 should have been his easiest policy to implement in the ongoing War with al Qaeda. Instead, the military commissions convened at Guantanamo Bay Naval Station in Cuba have turned into one of the biggest black eyes of the seven years we have been officially at war with international terrorism. Guantanamo Bay, once viewed as a beacon of human rights on the southeastern tip of communist Cuba, has become a lightning rod of criticism both domestically and internationally. Although military commissions have been, and should remain, a part of military law, they are clearly not the right forum for trying the al Qaeda fighters once captured. As this is written, the days of the detention facility at Guantanamo Bay Naval Station are numbered. As highlighted throughout this book, military commissions are permissible as a matter of law, but as a matter of policy, they are inappropriate for trying unlawful belligerents in the current armed conflict. The commissions have been evolving since the first order of November 13, 2001, and have adapted and changed as a result of criticisms from the academic community, the legal community, the Supreme Court, and perhaps most important, the Congress. They must continue to evolve to best balance the needs of justice, deterrence, and our human rights obligations. I have been fortunate to observe this evolution of military justice and remain convinced that the next step in this process of change must be the creation of a special security court apparatus, a National Security Court System (NSCS). I am not brazen enough to assert that this is the definitive answer, but instead I offer this model as a concrete proposal for policy makers to review, study, consider, and hopefully adopt. This is not the end, by any means, of the discussion, but I do hope it is the beginning.

Military commissions have been used throughout American history. They have been a part of military jurisprudence since the founding of the country. The executive branch, or operational commanders in the field of battle, has consistently valued their flexibility and rapidity. Initially, President Bush was hopeful that he could capitalize on the relative speed of these forums. The commissions have also been employed during periods of martial law. Great leaders in U.S. history have used these unique, unspecific, military tribunals to achieve "justice" when deemed necessary. As discussed herein, Washington, Jackson, Lincoln, and Franklin Roosevelt all used them in different forms and for different reasons but nonetheless saw them as necessary in times of emergency or during armed conflict. Prior to 2001, they had not been used since the Second World War. The Bush administration's use of the commissions, as well as their location at Guantanamo Bay, relied heavily upon existing Supreme Court precedent, particularly the *Quirin* case of 1942 as well as the *Eisentrager* case of 1950. At the time, the Bush "war council" considered these commissions lawful as a matter of constitutional law, statute, and precedent.

However, we are in a unique war, different from others in U.S. history. The administration, from the outset, understood this to be the case and conveyed the same to the public. While understandably resistant to returning to the pre-9/11 mentality of combating international terrorism with a law enforcement approach, they consistently tried to apply a law of war approach that never fit comfortably when being applied to the alleged al Qaeda fighters. Military commissions throughout history had been used for their rapidity of procedure and swift justice. They had not, to the best of my research and knowledge, been employed to detain alleged war criminals for the duration of conflicts. Preventive detention was never a reason before to employ by act, ommission, or unintentionally (as in the Bush administration case) military commissions. They previously had always been adjudicatory in nature. Although it is true that prisoners of war can be held until the cessation of hostilities in accordance with the Geneva Conventions, the administration had already declared that the Geneva tradition does not apply to this novel "war criminal." As Vice President Cheney noted, and former Attorney General Gonzales later made clear in a speech to the American Bar Association, the detainees "don't deserve to be treated as a prisoner of war."[1] I believe this to be true. The detainees are alleged unlawful belligerents and *de jure belli*, presumptively the Geneva Conventions do not and can not apply to a nonstate actor who additionally was never a signatory to the Conventions drafted in 1949. In the past, however, the designation as unlawful belligerent (or currently referred to as "enemy combatant") meant that the cases of those so designated would be adjudicated—as was done in the Revolutionary period, throughout the nineteenth century, and in the Second World War. These individuals could be detained and not afforded the gold standard of treatment that a POW receives during traditional armed conflict and capture, but that did not provide legal support to detain without charge—never mind without trial. Preventive detention was never a part of the military commissions process, but that is exactly what has occurred, whether intentionally or not, with the detainees captured in the War on al Qaeda. The glaring reality remains that over the past seven years, Guantanamo has functioned as a detention facility and not as a courtroom.

Although *Quirin* appeared on point to the administration in 2001—particularly with having to make decisions rapidly in the immediate aftermath of the attacks on the World Trade Center and the Pentagon—several factors made the heavy reliance on this case in the end misplaced. First, since *Quirin* was decided in 1942, a virtual revolution in military justice had occurred. Congress and the military itself "liberalized" many of the more arcane aspects of military law. For example, the Military Rules of Evidence are now virtually identical to the Federal Rules of Evidence, and the role of the judge advocate corps has been significantly enhanced. Second, the Roosevelt Order had applied to only a small number of identifiable unlawful belligerents. Bush's Order applied to all al Qaeda fighters; even those captured under an "associational status" were now subject to the order. Most important, in *Quirin*, the unlawful belligerents were tried before the tribunal in just two short months. The detainees, many of whom have been at Guantanamo for over six years, have not been subject to any trials. In fact, many remain detained without being charged with any crime. As such, it is critical that adjudication be the key to any new framework that policy makers embrace in the next administration and Congress.

Regardless of intentions or rationale, Guantanamo Bay is now irrevocably tainted as a detention center. The Bush administration lost the public relations war. As a matter of policy, it must close. Our international partners question its viability, the Democrat-led Congress now views the current policies as unsupportable, many previous supporters of the commissions now question their viability, and the Supreme Court has intervened and held many aspects of the commissions illegal, or in the *Boumediene* case, unconstitutional. Additionally, within his first days in office, President Obama ordered the facility closed within one year.

Congress needs to intervene and generate new legal policies for this generational war. While the military law construct has not met America's needs, we also must refrain from retreating to the policies that embraced a purely law enforcement model. The 9/11 Commission made clear that this new threat of international terror does demand, in fact, a new approach. While some from both political parties in the legislature (for example Congressman Bill Delahunt, D-MA, Senator Lindsay Graham, R-SC, and others) have been working hard to "fix" the Guantanamo problem, such noble efforts have never gained the necessary momentum to create real change. Unfortunately, it often seems that domestic politics has prevented many legislators from seeking new solutions. Many legislators apparently fear being labeled "soft on terror"; they worry about voters' reactions to such changes in U.S. detention policies and further, how any progressive change in our policies might impact their election (or reelection) prospects.

I am not naïve enough to think the proposals contained within this book will answer all of the criticisms of the current policies. On the contrary, I am certain they do not. The political branches must first recognize that we are still dealing with a relatively new threat and must enact laws and procedures appropriate to the captured al Qaeda fighters. As I have said herein and elsewhere (and for that matter to anyone who would listen), we are dealing with a mixture of law enforcement and warfare, and thus, any legal system created must necessarily be a mix of both. The al Qaeda fighter is a hybrid of a warrior and an international criminal; the war itself is a hybrid of traditional armed conflict and law enforcement operations; thus, it logically follows that we need a hybrid court—a mix of our Article III courts and the existing military commissions. Of all options available, and with the benefit of 20/20 hindsight, this is the best construct from which to begin the task of creating a viable, long-term legal solution to the ambiguities so prevalent in the current legal landscape.

We can not afford to go back to the law enforcement approach of September 10 to confront those who declare jihad against the United

States and the West. When drafting legislation for the new system, lawmakers must remain ever mindful that the enemy is engaged in armed conflict against our homeland, interests, and way of life. As Osama bin Laden made clear in October 2001, "If inciting people to do that [9/11] is terrorism, and if killing those who kill our sons is terrorism, then let history be witness that we are terrorists."

To echo this sentiment, as I write this conclusion, al Qaeda fighters simultaneously attacked and killed nine U.S. servicemen at a remote outpost on the border of Pakistan and Afghanistan. No matter how much we would like not to believe it, and some still do not, this is a war. This is not one we asked for but one thrust upon us by Osama bin Laden and his colleagues.

Yet, as I have argued before, this is a different kind of war—a war of the twenty-first century. Traditional techniques and legal systems used before are not working in this conflict. It is vital that we continue to adapt and learn the best methods to employ—strategically, tactically, and most relevant to this book, legally. Different from previous wars, every al Qaeda fighter captured is an unlawful belligerent. Wars throughout American history have been more traditional conflicts in which unlawful belligerency was the minority and handled on a small scale. Most of those captured would be entitled to POW status. In the War on al Qaeda, however, the current enemy embraces unlawful belligerency as part of its tactics and part of its doctrine. In this war, virtually all captured enemies are, in fact, unlawful belligerents. Thus, rather than being the minority in a small sampling of cases, the "war criminals" in this conflict represent by far the majority of those captured.

With no nation to declare war against, and no sovereign to negotiate with or to engage in diplomatic dialogue to achieve peace, the United States must adapt. To the administration's credit, they have done so in many ways. We see the results of the adaptations in the relative success of the "surge" in battling al Qaeda in Iraq, the creation of the Department of Homeland Security, and the merging and collaboration of the various intelligence communities in the creation of the Director of National Intelligence (DNI). Perhaps the best indicator of the success of the Bush policies is the reality that the homeland has not been attacked since 9/11. We now use the Central Intelligence Agency, the Federal Bureau of Investigation, and even local police departments more in this armed conflict than any other in our history. We have been forced, in many ways, to mix law enforcement operations and warfare within the armed forces to properly confront and hopefully to defeat this enemy. Similarly, U.S. policy makers must now mix the existing paradigms of legal constructs and procedures to best detain, interrogate, and adjudicate those captured and determined to be al Qaeda fighters. A mix of civilian and military justice is best suited for this task.

I have spent many hours researching, debating, and discussing these proposals and policies with numerous people and at numerous venues. I have had the good fortune of getting to study these issues over the past two years at both Berkeley Law School and Harvard's Kennedy School. During these ventures, I have been exposed to the human rights concerns expressed in many civil libertarian critiques, to national security supporters' perspectives, and to homeland security experts' viewpoints. Scholars from both institutions have provided me with keen insights into both sides of the debate surrounding Guantanamo Bay—from critical perspectives of the policies employed by the Bush administration to supporters' perspectives. Having the benefit of often opposite views on these issues has helped me ensure that the proposal I have presented in this book is as nonpartisan as possible and is focused on results, not politics. Only a nonpartisan/bipartisan solution for the way ahead will help to resolve the heated debates under way about Guantanamo.

As of the summer of 2008, it is clear to most that the Guantanamo Bay detention center will close and the military commissions will cease to operate by the latest sometime in 2009. Rather than simply discarding the efforts of so many in the Bush administration, Congress, and the Department of Defense, I suggest that readers continue to view this process as one that is evolutionary. The system has slowly evolved since first being adopted in November of 2001 and has continued to respond and adapt to the edicts of Congress, the judiciary, the bar, our international partners, and most important, U.S. citizen concerns about how we properly adjudicate war crimes committed by al Qaeda fighters. As such, the proposed National Security Court System (NSCS) should be viewed as the next step in the process of evolving legal norms and procedures. However, as crucial as creating the new special terrorism court is, it can not be done in isolation. Other changes must take place as well—two in particular.

First, we must change the name of the war we are fighting from the "Global War on Terror" (GWOT) to the "War on al Qaeda." The name, Global War on Terror, creates great confusion as to whom we are fighting, whom we can detain, and the legal construct for any detention or trials that will occur. The GWOT gives the perception of an endless fight against all terrorists and terrorism. While noble in gesture and theory, as a matter of practical application, such a name does more harm than good. To many within the Muslim world, waging a global war on terror sounds as if the United States has the will, authority, and intention of invading or attacking any nation that holds terrorists. Also, such a misnomer unnecessarily confuses those engaged in domestic revolution who use terrorism as a tactic with the al Qaeda (and like-minded affiliates) who are actually engaged in war against the United States. Additionally, it makes cessation of hostilities (a key term in the law of war) virtually impossible. It alludes to never-ending armed conflict. We can never declare victory on "terror" per se. Also, the reality remains that we are not fighting Hamas, Hezbollah, the Red Brigades, the Shining Path, the Irish Republican Army, or other terror groups. Although the United States condemns the tactics of these domestic terrorist groups, we are not engaged in armed conflict with them. We are fighting al Qaeda in Iraq (AQI) and al Qaeda. By calling the conflict what it has been and remains—an armed conflict against al Qaeda (and like-minded international terrorists)—we can hope at the minimum to achieve victory by rendering such nonstate actors irrelevant on the world stage, and at the maximum, to defeat them completely as an entity.

Second, the United States needs to take the lead in clarifying the legal status of the al Qaeda-type fighters within international law. Since they do not appear to fit neatly within any of the existing international agreements or the customary law of war, the international community needs to review the Geneva Conventions for their applicability to the al Qaeda-type international terrorist. As part of this review, world leaders must struggle with the difficult task of determining what and how existing legal treaties and norms apply in the "global war." The end result might be to suggest an additional protocol to the Geneva Conventions. Such a gathering alternatively might recommend that the existing Geneva Conventions (or portions of them) apply. Either way, such a diplomatic undertaking will require years to complete. I remain painfully aware of that reality. But in calling for such meetings, the United States could help the world community better understand and agree upon the rules and standards of conduct that regulate this armed conflict. Additionally, such steps by the U.S. government will mitigate the perception that the United States is indifferent to our allies' concerns. As it stands now, the detainees' status under international law remains mired in ambiguity.

Having suggested these two prerequisites, I hope that the political branches answer the call from many U.S. citizens, scholars, and advocates to create some new system of law and procedure for the captured al Qaeda fighters. The National Security Court System helps to answer many of the criticisms of Guantanamo Bay from advocates of both of the existing paradigms—the law enforcement approach and the law of war approach. It offers a hybrid system that

1. Is overseen by civilians rather than the Department of Defense;
2. Requires that the detention and trials would be held on U.S. soil— military bases located within the continental United States;
3. Is adjudicatory in nature and provides a set period of time in which a person must be tried for crimes alleged;
4. Promotes international human rights by respecting other nations' concerns about the death penalty;
5. Is a separate system from both the existing Article III federal courts and the military justice system;
6. Provides more traditional habeas corpus rights to the detainees;
7. Prohibits indefinite detention of the accused by requiring detainees to be tried within one year of capture;
8. Creates new Article III judges who will oversee the process and who are versed in the law of armed conflict, intelligence law, and national security law;
9. Creates a more efficient and effective appellate process than employed under the military commissions;
10. Prohibits any manner of torture of detainees when being interrogated;
11. Promotes the rule of law while still ensuring that the accused are held accountable for their alleged "war crimes."

Different from other proposals for such a system, my proposal emphasizes trying the detainees.

The preventive detention models offered by several of my colleagues do not offer a workable construct in the current conflict. While permissible in conventional wars, and in some cases within U.S. domestic law, the detention of those captured in this war should be minimized. The NSCS requires trial within one year. During that period, interrogation can occur and valuable intelligence can be obtained. Keeping alleged "war criminals" in preventive detention only fuels hatred of the United States and unnecessarily weakens our standing within the international community. The NSCS is based on trials, not detention.

Boumediene v. Bush was just decided in June 2008. For so many reasons, the Supreme Court's holding is problematic. Beyond the many concerns I mention throughout the book, the most dangerous aspect of the opinion is that, perhaps unintentionally, the Supreme Court seemed to go back to viewing the fight against al Qaeda as requiring more of a law enforcement paradigm. This holding not only disregards the reality of the threat but is also in contradiction to the holdings the same Supreme Court has made over the past five years. Worse yet, it completely disregards the findings of the political branches as well as the 9/11 Commission that cautioned against retreating to the complacency toward international terror embraced in the twentieth century. Although I did not think it possible, this decision has caused even greater divisions among citizens and greater debates among the advocates of both of the existing paradigms. For example, lawyers for Salim Hamdan filed motions in federal district court as well as within the military commissions challenging the constitutionality of the proceedings. The able counsel representing Hamdan (including Katyal) argued that their client should be entitled to a long list of constitutional protections, including the Fourth Amendment, the Fifth Amendment, and the equal protection clause. After all, if *Boumediene* decided the detainees should have at least one constitutional protection (habeas corpus), then logically, why not allow the full constitutional protections of a U.S. citizen? Instead of making the legal situation clearer for the detainees, the Supreme Court has once again made it more confusing and ambiguous.

It now appears that President Obama (and the new Congress) elected in November of 2008 are perfectly situated to make substantive changes in the adjudication process of the detainees. The political branches must be careful not to permit the judicial branch to dictate war policies that are better (and constitutionally mandated) performed by the executive and legislative branches. Again, the NSCS should be viewed as another step in the process of adapting our legal systems to better meet the challenges presented by twenty-first-century warfare.

Continuing Evolution

International terrorism will not go away any time in our near future. It is a disease on the international order that will likely remain for quite some time. While it exists, we must continue to manage it to ensure that it does not further spread and become even more disruptive to the international community. As such at this moment in history, the NSCS provides the right forum to balance national security, human rights, and the rule of law. But it bears repeating—this is an evolutionary process and is merely a point on the continuum of evolving norms of justice and internationalism. For now, the NSCS is a concrete solution that mitigates many of the concerns about Guantanamo Bay and the military commissions.

The United States is now detaining the hundreds of citizens of American allies in the Guantanamo Bay detention center and even more in Bagram, Afghanistan. U.S. policy makers must remain mindful, however, that the war we are fighting impacts many citizens and nations from all over the world. Other suggestions for detaining and trying al Qaeda suspects have come from our allies and human rights organizations.

While embracing the NSCS immediately, the United States should still be amenable and open to other long-term propositions being suggested for the adjudication of the al Qaeda fighters. Some have called for international tribunals, such as those employed in the former Yugoslavia and Rwanda conflicts, as better able to address the reality that the conflict is, in fact, international in scope. Others have asserted that the use of the International Criminal Court (ICC) might be the correct venue in the future. Such proposals are all worthy of consideration. But to me, an ICC of the future, if properly constructed and afforded jurisdiction over international terrorism by consensus, might wind up becoming the most appropriate venue for the adjudication of international terrorists.

The ICC (Rome Statute) was created by treaty in Rome 1998.[2] It was created to provide an international court to try the most egregious of international crimes. It initially was an idea generated after the Nuremburg Trials of the Nazi atrocities committed during the Second World War. Many believed that rather than have ad hoc forums, there should be one court for crimes committed that were best identified as universal. The idea gained momentum after the collapse of the Soviet Union in the early 1990s. Currently, 106 nations have signed the treaty. As of 2009, the United States has not ratified this treaty. Although the United States signed onto the Rome Statute in 2000 at the end of President Bill Clinton's second term, the Bush administration opted out and "unsigned" the statute in 2002. It has never gone before the U.S. Senate for ratification. As the ICC is currently drafted, however, it is not in the U.S. interests to sign on to it. The military establishment generally does not support the statute. Many in the service fear a prosecution regime that has fewer rights than they would have at court-martial. As the armed forces deploys overseas, they would be the U.S. citizens most impacted by participation in the ICC. Additionally, many remain uncomfortable that the prosecutor has virtually unlimited power to initiate charges. These concerns have been heard by many politicians and human rights organizations who have been feverishly attempting to address them.[3] Obviously, it is important to the viability and legitimacy of the ICC to have U.S. participation. As of now, significant diplomatic work remains to be accomplished before the United States would sign on and eventually ratify the treaty.

The International Criminal Court (ICC) is an independent, permanent court that tries persons accused of serious crimes of international concern, namely genocide, crimes against humanity, and war crimes. Currently it does not include international terrorism. As is well known, the international community has been unable to even come to agreement as to the definition of "terrorism." However, participants in the ICC meet frequently to better define the court's authority and jurisdiction. In fact, there is discussion currently on adding an additional crime of "aggression" to the list of crimes the ICC would have jurisdiction over. As the Rome Statute will be renegotiated in 2009, it is in the U.S. interest to participate, if only as an observer, to help define crimes under the jurisdiction of the Court. While observing, U.S. representatives would still be afforded the opportunity to offer suggestions and thoughts on "tightening" up the language within the existing Rome Statute. The United States could, even as an observer, push to have many of our concerns in the 1998 version of the statute answered.

As part of this "observer" status, it is an opportunity for the United States to initiate discussions of a long-term, internationally palatable solution to the legal ambiguities of "terrorism" as well as the prosecution of those, like al Qaeda, who engage in international terrorism. The existing crimes the ICC has jurisdiction over are some of the most egregious crimes the international community faces. This being the case, international terrorism should at least be considered by the parties as a potential crime that would fall under its jurisdiction. Obviously, this would be a long-term project spanning at least two presidential administrations, but while we implement the NSCS domestically, we should continue to search for other, more palatable solutions such as the ICC. The benefit in having the prosecutions occur outside the United States will undoubtedly assist in ensuring that this conflict is viewed as international in character. Further, it removes some of the cynicism that the United States is unilaterally deciding how to treat other nations' citizens—particularly since the other nations impacted are allies and certainly nations we are not at war with. Again, aware that this is a very long-term process, it is worth beginning the discussion now, even while we respond domestically to the immediate needs of trying the numerous unlawful belligerents within the proposed NSCS.

Last Thoughts

The War on al Qaeda has introduced ambiguity as to the appropriate legal regime best suited to comport with the law of armed conflict and satisfy customary legal obligations. Of the many new issues and legal problems confronting policy makers in the West, the most problematic has been the proper handling of al Qaeda fighters once captured. Simply, the adjudication and detention of those accused of engaging in, or conspiring to engage in, international terror against the United States has not worked. The detentions at Guantanamo have led to an erosion of national consensus and international support of our efforts in this armed conflict.

International concern over Guantanamo is severely impacting our ability to lead effectively, and to provide guidance, counsel, and policies in this and other areas of critical concern. Although traditionally, such "war crimes" trials have been a creature of the executive branch, it is now clear that Congress must play a role as well with the detainee prosecutions. Bipartisan efforts that took place to enact the MCA by updating the existing military commissions to better comport with domestic and international law are indicators of the benefits of including all perspectives in determining how best to move forward with the detainee issues. However, these efforts are not sufficient. In order to legitimately deal with the threat of international terror, Congress now, more than ever after being prompted by the Supreme Court in *Boumediene*, must enact legislation to create a hybrid court. Initially, I suggest convening an open, bipartisan study commission to take a long-term view of the best means of adjudicating the al Qaeda fighters once captured. This should begin immediately. In January 2009, President Obama declared his support for such a commission soon after taking office. As Harvey Rishikof and others have called for since 2002, a bipartisan commission of academics, national security experts, lawyers, and human rights advocates could put their collective thoughts and ideas together to create a model legislative proposal for the creation of a National Security Court.[4] Regardless of blame assigned or the reasons the implementation of the military commissions has been unsuccessful, such a blue ribbon commission (chartered by the president) should immediately be convened to address questions as to proper detention, adjudication, intelligence gathering, terrorist surveillance, and other legal issues associated with the threat of international terror.

The National Security Court System, a natural maturation of the military commissions enacted under the MCA, affords an opportunity for U.S. policy makers to respond forcefully and effectively to calls, both domestically and internationally, for a way out of the myriad problems associated with Guantanamo. *Boumediene* has now pushed the policy makers to act. Rather than having no credible solution or merely engaging in attacks against the existing structure, policy makers need to emerge with fresh new ways to look at the proper detention and adjudication of captured al Qaeda fighters. It is time for the United States to regain the initiative and reaffirm our leadership in the humane prosecution of terrorists, a group that wishes to undermine the ideals of democracy. There is no better way to protect those ideals than to remain consistent with them in the prosecution of those who wish to destroy them. President Obama and the Congress need to create a National Security Court System.

Notes

Introduction

1. *Platt Amendment of 1903*, Article VII. To enable the United States to maintain the independence of Cuba, and to protect the people thereof, as well as for its own defense, the Government of Cuba will sell or lease to the United States lands necessary for coaling or naval stations, at certain specified points, to be agreed upon with the President of the United States. Found at The Avalon Project at Yale Law School 20th Century Documents, http://www.yale.edu/lawweb/avalon/diplomacy/cuba/cuba002.htm.

2. Irene Khan, Speech before the International Press Club, AMNESTY INTERNATIONAL REPORT, May 25, 2005; see also Richard Norton-Taylor, *Guantanamo as Gulag*, GUARDIAN, May 26, 2005.

3. ANDY McCARTHY AND ALYKHAN VELSHI, WE NEED A NATIONAL SECURITY COURT (2006).

4. Glenn Sulmasy, *The Legal Landscape after Hamdan: The Creation of Homeland Security Courts*, 13 NEW ENG. J. INT'L & COMP. LAW 1 (2006).

5. *Ex Parte Quirin*, 317 U.S. 1 (1942).

6. *Boumediene v. Bush*, 553 U.S. (2008).

7. THE CONSTITUTION PROJECT, A CRITIQUE OF NATIONAL SECURITY COURTS, June 23, 2008.

8. THE NATIONAL COMMISSION ON TERRORIST ATTACKS UPON THE UNITED STATES (the 9/11 Commission) (2004).

9. THE NATIONAL COMMISSION ON TERRORIST ATTACKS UPON THE UNITED STATES (the 9/11 Commission) (2004).

10. Harvey Rishikof, *Is It Time for a Federal Terrorist Court? Terrorists and Prosecutors: Problems, Paradigms, and Paradoxes*, 8 SUFFOLK J. TRIAL & APP. ADVOC. 1 (2003); BENJAMIN WITTES, LAW AND THE LONG WAR: THE FUTURE OF JUSTICE IN THE WAR ON TERROR (2008); ANDREW C. McCARTHY, WILLFUL BLINDNESS: A MEMOIR OF THE JIHAD (2008); Jack L. Goldsmith & Neal Katyal, *The Terrorist Court*, N. Y. TIMES, July 11, 2007, at A14.

11. Glenn Sulmasy, *A New Look for the War on al Qaeda*, SAN FRAN. CHRON., Sept. 11, 2007.

12. *Rasul v. Bush*, 542 U.S. 466 (2004).

13. *Hamdi v. Rumsfeld*, 124 S.Ct. at 2639 (plurality opinion).

14. *Hamdan v. Rumsfeld*, 548 U.S. 557 (2006).

15. *Boumediene v. Bush*, 553 U.S. (2008).

16. *Jus in bello* is the law of armed conflict. Distinct from the *jus ad bellum*, the *jus in bello* deals with the legality of ongoing military operations.

Chapter 1

1. Michael Lacy, *Military Commissions: A Historical Survey*, 2002 ARMY LAW 42 (March 2002); see also Glenn Sulmasy, *The Military Commissions Act of 2006*, 33 OK. C. L. REV. 2 (Summer 2008). Sulmasy offers an in-depth view of this topic directly as it relates to the MCA.

2. THE FEDERALIST No. 70 (Alexander Hamilton).

3. *See* John D. Hutson, Testimony before the Committee on the Armed Services (July 12, 2006); see also Neal K. Katyal & Laurence H. Tribe, *Waging War, Deciding Guilt: Trying the Military Tribunals*, 111 YALE L.J. 1259 (April 2002).

4. *Uniform Code of Military Justice*, 10 U.S.C. §§ 801–950 (2006).

5. *See* WILLIAM WINTHROP, MILITARY LAW AND PRECEDENTS (rev. 2d ed. 1920).

6. Lacy, *supra* note 1; see also David Glazier, *Precedents Lost: The Neglected History of the Military Commission*, 46 VA. J. INT'L L. 5 (Fall 2005).

7. *See* FREDERICK LEDERER, MILITARY LAW, CASE AND MATERIALS (2003).

8. W. GENEROUS, SWORDS AND SCALES (1973).

9. F. GILLIGAN & F. LEDERER, COURT MARTIAL PROCEDURE, §§ 1–43—1–47 (2 ed. 1999).

10. *Ibid*.

11. *Ibid*.

12. *See* Edmund M. Morgan, *The Background of the Uniform Code of Military Justice*, 28 MIL. L. REV. 17 (1965).

13. *Military Justice Act of 1968*, Public Law 90–632, 82 *Stat*. 1335.

14. The current version of the Manual for Courts-Martial was updated in 2008. It includes minor changes, for example, the U.S. Coast Guard now operates under the Department of Homeland Security instead of the Department of Transportation.

15. *Uniform Code of Military Justice, supra*, The Punitive Articles 77–134.

16. *Ibid*.

17. *Uniform Code of Military Justice, supra*, Article 15.

18. Manual for Courts-Martial (MCM) (2008).

19. MCM, Part I-III.

20. Summary Courts-martial have been viewed by some as an unnecessary tool for the commander in the modern era.

21. Gordan D. Henderson, *"Courts-Martial and the Constitution: The Original Understanding,"* 71 HARV LAW REV 293 (1957).

22. *Uniform Code of Military Justice, supra*, Article 21; *see also* John Yoo & Julian Ku, *Hamdan v. Rumsfeld: The Functional Case for Foreign Affairs Deference to the Executive Branch*, 23 CONSTITUTIONAL COMMENTARY 179 (2006).

23. *Uniform Code of Military Justice, supra*, Article 36; *see also* John Yoo & Julian Ku, *supra* note 22.

24. *Supra* note 1.

25. There are different types of military commissions and these have been known by different names throughout history. Normally referred to as military tribunals, they have been known as panel of officers, war courts, and since the mid-nineteenth century, military commissions.

26. *Madsen v. Kinsella*, 343 U.S. 341 (1952) (providing a list of the specific uses for commissions). It appears the Court was being thorough (and helpful) in ensuring that it was clear to the litigants the different types and the one that was at issue in this particular case.

27. Lacy, *supra* note 1; see also Sulmasy, *supra* note 1.

28. *Id.*

29. H.W. KOCH, THE RISE OF MODERN WARFARE 30 (1981).

30. *See* David Glazier, *Precedents Lost: The Neglected History of the Military Commissions*, 46 VA. J. INT'L L. 5 (Fall 2005).

31. *The First British Mutiny Act* (1689), reprinted in WILLIAM WINTHROP, MILITARY LAW AND PRECEDENTS app. VI at 929 (2d ed. 1920).

32. Glazier, *supra* note 30.

33. *Id.*

34. SAUL K. PANDOVER, THE WASHINGTON PAPERS (1955).

35. *See generally* Brian Haagensen II, *Federal Courts versus Military Commissions: The Comedy of No Comity*, 32 OHIO N.U. L. REV. 395, 400 (2006).

36. PANDOVER, *supra* note 34, at 367; *see also* Louis Fisher, *Military Commissions: Problems of Authority and Practice*, 24 B. U. INT'L L. J. 15 (Spring 2006).

37. JOHN YOO, THE POWERS OF WAR AND PEACE, 31–32 (2005).

38. HAROLD KOH, THE NATIONAL SECURITY CONSTITUTION (2d ed. 2008); Fisher, *supra* note 36.

39. Fisher, *supra* note 36.

40. *Id.*

41. JACK N. RAKOVE, THE BEGINNINGS OF NATIONAL POLITICS, 383 (1979).

42. Michael D. Ramsey, *The Textual Basis of the President's Foreign Affairs Power*, 30 HARV J. L. & PUB. POL'Y 141 (Fall 2006); JACK N. RAKOVE, ORIGINAL MEANINGS: POLITICS AND IDEAS IN THE MAKING OF THE CONSTITUTION (1996).

43. *Id.*, Rakove, *supra* note 41–42.

44. Rakove, *supra* note 41–42.

45. *Id.* at 41.

46. *Id.*

47. THE FEDERALIST No. 74 (Alexander Hamilton).

48. RAKOVE, *supra* note 45; *see also* BERNARD BAILYN, THE IDEOLOGICAL ORIGINS OF THE AMERICAN REVOLUTION (1992).

49. Ramsey, *supra* note 42, at 143.

50. Yoo, *supra* note 37.

51. *Id.* at 39.

52. *Id.* at 40–41.

Chapter 2

1. 3 THE PAPERS OF ANDREW JACKSON 205 (Harold D. Moser, ed., 1991).

2. ROBERT V. REMINI, ANDREW JACKSON AND THE COURSE OF THE AMERICAN EMPIRE (1767–1821) at 310 (1977).

3. LOUIS FISHER, MILITARY TRIBUNALS AND PRESIDENTIAL POWER, 25 (2005).

4. *Id.*

5. *Id.*

6. *Id.*

7. CONG. GLOBE, 27th Cong., 2d Sess. 304 (1842).

8. David Glazier, *Precedents Lost: The Neglected History of the Military Commission*, 46 VA. J. INT'L L. 5 (2005).

9. 1 AMERICAN STATE PAPERS: MILITARY AFFAIRS, Vol. V at 721, 731 (trial of Ambrister, et. al. by military commission on April 27, 1818) (1832).

10. This was an issue in the Major Andre affair as well. Andre had asked Washington not to hang him due to his social status and that he was not actually a "spy" per se. As is well known, Andre was convicted by military tribunal and hanged after being sentenced to death. Washington, clearly, was not satisfied by the pleas of Andre.

11. FISHER, *supra* note 3.

12. David Glazier, Note, *Kangaroo Court or Competent Tribunal? Judging the 21st Century Military Commission*, 89 VA. L. REV. 2005, 2027, 2046 (2003).

13. David Glazier, *Ignorance is Not Bliss: The Law of Occupation and the U. S. Invasion of Iraq*, 58 Rutgers L. Rev. 121 (2008) (discussing the comparisons between previous U.S. actions during periods of military occupation as compared to the twenty-first-century version); Carol Chomsky, The U.S.–Dakota War Trials: A Study in Military Injustice, 43 STAN. L. REV. 13 (1990) (discussing the use of military commissions against Indian tribes and noting the great latitude offered Commanders in the field during the nineteenth century. Also notes that many of the crimes prosecuted under General Order No. 20 were not listed as offenses where the commissions actually had jurisdiction); General Winfield Scott, General Orders (G.O.) No. 20 in ORDERS AND SPECIAL ORDERS, HEADQUARTERS OF THE ARMY, WAR WITH MEXICO, 1847–48, Vol. 41 (actual date of the order Feb., 19, 1847).

14. 1 AMERICAN STATE PAPERS: MILITARY AFFAIRS at 735 (the military commission trial of April, 1818) (1832).

15. JOHN YOO, WAR BY OTHER MEANS (2006).

16. FISHER, *supra* note 3 at 41–45.

17. *A Compilation of the Messages and Papers of the Presidents* 324–330 (James D. Richardson ed., 1897).

18. 10 Op. Att'y Gen. 74, 81 (1861).

19. 12 Stat. 326 (1861).

20. MARK E. NEELY, JR., THE FATE OF LIBERTY: ABRAHAM LINCOLN AND CIVIL LIBERTIES, 168–177 (1991).

21. General Order 100, Instructions for Government Armies in the United States in the Field (April 23, 1863). This Order is better known as the Lieber Code.

22. *See* David B. Rivkin & Lee Casey, *The Use of Military Commissions in the War on Terror*, 24 B.U. INT'L L. J. 123 (2006).

23. *See* Harold Hongju Koh, *The Case against Military Commissions*, 96 AMERICAN JOURNL. OF INT'L LAW 337 (2002).

24. Michael Kent Curtis, *Lincoln, Vallandigham, and Anti-War Speech in the Civil War*, 7 WM. MARY BILL RTS. J. 105, 119 (1998).

25. *Ex parte Vallandigham*, 68 U.S. (1 Wall) 243, 246 (1864).

26. *Id.* at 243, 244.

27. *Id.* at 266.

28. *Ex parte Milligan*, 71 U.S. (4 Wall.) 2 (1866).

29. Numerous examples exist for those who believe the United States should pursue a pre-9/11 response to fighting the al Qaeda threat. *See generally* Koh, *supra* note 23.

30. *Milligan* at 6–7.

31. *Milligan, supra* note 28.

32. Kenneth Roth, *The Law of War in the War on Terror*, FOREIGN AFFAIRS (Jan./Feb. 2004).

33. *Milligan, supra* note 28.

34. For a greater discussion on the issue of "associational status" within the current context, *see* Robert M. Chesney & Jack L. Goldsmith, *Terrorism and the Convergence of Criminal and Military Detention Models*, 60 Stan. L. Rev. 1079, 1081 (2008).

35. Carol L. Chomsky, *The United States-Dakota War Trials: A Study in Military Injustice*, 43 Stan. L. Rev. 13, 21–22 (1990).

36. *Id.* at 22–24.

37. *Supra* note 3 at 52.

38. *Supra* note 3 at 54; *supra* note 34 at 52–53.

Chapter 3

1. *In re Yamashita*, 327 U.S. 1 (1946).

2. *Ex parte Quirin*, 317 U.S. 1 (1942).

3. Eugene Rachlis, They Came to Kill: The Story of Eight Nazi Saboteurs in America (1961); Louis Fisher, Nazi Saboteurs on Trial (2d ed. 2005); Michael Dobbs, Saboteurs: The Nazi Raid on America (2008).

4. Frankfurter Papers "Observations of *Ex parte Quirin*," signed "F.B.W.," at 1; *see* Fisher, Military Tribunals and Presidential Power, 212–124 (2005).

5. Fisher, *supra* note 3 at 14–18.

6. *Id.* at 1–5.

7. Louis Fisher, *Military Commissions: Problems of Authority and Practice*, 24 B.U. Int'l L.J. 15 (2006); Fisher, *supra* notes 3, 4.

8. Fisher, *supra* note 3 at 1–21.

9. Fisher, *supra* note 4 at 92.

10. Lewis Wood, *Lone Coast Guardsman Put FBI on Trail of Saboteurs*, N.Y. Times, July 16, 1942, at 1, 38.

11. Fisher, *supra* note 4 at 95.

12. Diary of Henry L. Stimson, July 1, 1942, at 136 (available at Yale University Library, New Haven, Conn.); see also Louis Fisher, *Detention and Trial of Suspected Terrorists: Stretching Presidential Power*, 2 J. Nat'l Security & Pol'y (2006); for some accounts of press stories, *see FBI's Master Stroke*, Wash. Post, June 29, 1942, at 6; Will Lissner, *Invaders Confess*, N.Y. Times, June 28, 1942, at 1, 30; *Nazi Saboteurs Face Stern Army Justice*, N.Y. Times, July 5, 1942, at 6E.

13. *Supra* note 4 at 94–96.

14. *Id.*

15. Dobbs, Saboteurs (where Dobbs discusses and cites the memo from Roosevelt to Biddle), June 30, 1942.

16. *Supra* note 12, as cited in Military Tribunals and Presidential Power.

17. Francis Biddle, In Brief Authority, 330 (1st ed. 1962).

18. Proclamation 2561, Denying Certain Enemies Access to the Courts of the United States, 7 Fed. Reg. 5101 (July 7, 1942).

19. Biddle, *supra* note 17 at 331.

20. Fisher, *supra* note 3 at 42–45.

21. *Supra* note 3, at 106.

22. *Supra* note 15.

23. Military Trial at 14 as cited in Louis Fisher, *supra* note 4 at 102.

24. *Supra* note 3, at 64–66.

25. *Supra* note 3, at 107.

26. Gerhard Casper & Kathleen M. Sullivan (eds.), Landmark Briefs and Arguments of the Supreme Court of the United States: Constitutional Law at 297 (2005).

27. *Id.* at 409.

28. Supra note 26 (Landmark Briefs) at 411.

29. *Supra* note 3, at 121–126.

30. Military Trial *supra* note 23 at 2785.

31. *In re Yamashita*, 327 U.S. at 11 (1946).

Chapter 4

1. Elisabeth Bumiller, *Bush: A Second Pearl Harbor,* N.Y. Times, Dec. 8, 2001.

2. *Responding to Anthrax Attacks,* N.Y. Times, Oct. 16, 2001.

3. President Bush, White House Press Release, Oct. 23, 2001.

4. David Frum, The Right Man: The Surprise Presidency of George W. Bush (2003).

5. Louis Fisher, Nazi Saboteurs on Trial, 137 (2d ed. 2005).

6. Tim Golden, *After Terror, a Secret Rewriting of Military Law,* N.Y. Times, Oct. 24, 2004.

7. *Id.*

8. *Id.*

9. *Id.*

10. *Id.*

11. Elizabeth Bumiller & Stephen Lee Meyers, *Senior Administration Officials Defend Military Tribunals for Terrorist Suspects,* N.Y. Times, Nov. 15, 2001, at B6.

12. John C. Yoo, War by Other Means (2006).

13. *See* Jane Perelez, David E. Sanger, & Thom Shanker, *Detention Challenged: The Advisers,* N.Y. Times, Sept. 23, 2001.

14. *Authorization for the Use of Military Force* (AUMF), Pub. L. No. 107–40, 115 Stat. 224 (2001) (authorizing use of force against those responsible for the Sept. 11 terrorist attacks); see also, S. C. Res. 1369, U. N. SCOR, 56th Sess., 4370 mtg. U.N. Doc. S/RES/1368 (2001) (security council resolution authorizing the use of force).

15. Yoo, *supra* note 12.

16. Glenn M. Sulmasy, *The Law of Armed Conflict in the Global War on Terror: International Lawyers Fighting the Last War,* Notre Dame J.L. Ethics & Pub. Pol'y (2005).

17. *See* Ruth Wedgwood, *The Case for Military Tribunals,* Wall St. J., Dec. 3, 2001, at A18; George Lardner, Jr., *Democrats Blast Order on Tribunals,* Wash. Post, Nov. 29, 2001; Douglas Kmieck, *Military Tribunals Are Necessary in Times of War,* Wall St. J., Nov. 15, 2001, at 26.

18. Foreign Affairs, Jan./Feb. 2002.

19. Golden, *supra* note 6 (quoting former White House lawyer Brad Berenson).

20. Jeanne Cummings, *Gonzales Rewrites Laws of War,* Wall St. J., Nov. 26, 2002.

21. This is a new term within military law jurisprudence introduced by the Bush administration. DoD General Counsel William J. "Jim" Haynes II defined an enemy combatant as "an individual who, under the laws of war, may be detained for the duration of an armed conflict." Memo from General Counsel William Haynes to ASIL—CFR Roundtable, Dec. 12, 2002.

22. *See* AUMF, supra note 14; *See also* Louis Fisher, The Politics of Executive Privilege (2004); John C. Yoo, The Powers of War and Peace (2005).

23. For a great review of this unique status of some detainees as well as a discussion on "convergence," *see* Robert Chesney & Jack Goldsmith, *Terrorism and the Convergence of Criminal and Military Detention Models,* Stan L. Rev. (2008).

24. Uniform Code of Military Justice (UCMJ), 64 Stat. 109, 10 USC, ch. 247.

25. David Addington, Testimony before the House Committee on Foreign Affairs, Subcommittee on the Constitution and Civil Rights (June 2008).

26. Neal K. Katyal &Laurence H. Tribe, *Waging War, Deciding Guilt: Trying the Military Tribunals*, 111 YALE L. J. 1259, 1309 (2002).

27. Ken Roth, *The Law of War in the War on Terror*, FOREIGN AFFAIRS, Jan./Feb. 2004; Geoffrey Stone, PERILOUS TIMES: CIVIL LIBERTIES IN WARTIME (2004); *Endrunning the Bill of Rights*, WASH. POST, November 16, 2001, at A46.

28. Human Rights Watch Briefing Paper on U.S. Military Commission, June 2003.

29. JOHN C. YOO, WAR BY OTHER MEANS (2006).

30. *Id.*

31. *Id.*

32. Steven Lee Meyers & Neil A. Lewis, *Assurances Offered about Military Courts*, N.Y. TIMES, Nov. 16, 2001, at A10; Robin Toner & Neil A Lewis, *Justice Department and Senate Clash over Bush Actions*, N.Y. TIMES, Nov. 29, 2001, at A1.

33. Thomas L. Friedman, *A Travesty of Justice*, N.Y. TIMES, Nov. 16, 2001.

34. William Safire, *Seizing Dictatorial Powers*, N.Y. TIMES, Nov. 16, 2001, at A31.

35. LOUIS FISHER, NAZI SABOTEURS ON TRIAL, 138 (2d ed. 2005); at 138 Barr is quoted as saying, "they are not consulting us at all."

36. Friedman, *supra* note 33.

37. Katyal & Tribe, *supra* note 26.

38. *Military Order of November 13, 2001*, Detention, Treatment, and Trial of Certain non-Citizens in the War against Terrorism, 66 Fed. Reg. 57, 833 (Nov. 16, 2001).

39. George Lardner, Jr. & Peter Slevin, *Military May Try Terrorism Cases, Bush Cites Emergency*, WASH. POST, Nov. 14, 2001, at A1.

40. *Supra* note 38, Sections 1 and 2.

41. *See generally* LOUIS FISHER, MILITARY TRIBUNALS AND PRESIDENTIAL POWER, 253–260 (2005).

42. RICHARD CLARKE, AGAINST ALL ENEMIES: INSIDE AMERICA'S WAR ON TERROR (2004).

43. *See generally* THE NATIONAL COMMISSION ON TERRORIST ATTACKS UPON THE UNITED STATES (the 9/11 Commission) (2004).

44. Testimony of John Ashcroft, *Department of Justice Oversight: Preserving Our Freedoms While Defending against Terrorism*, hearings before the Senate Committee on the Judiciary, 107th Cong. 1st Sess. 21 (2001). (Ashcroft was quoted as saying, "your tactics only aid terrorists" and critics were labeled as those "who scare peace loving people with phantoms of lost liberty.").

45. *Id.*; Robin Toner & Neil A. Lewis, *White House Push on Security Steps Bypasses Congress*, N.Y. TIMES, Nov. 15, 2001, at A1.

46. For example, on the left, *see* Jordan J. Paust, *Antiterrorism Military Commissions: Courting Illegality*, 23 MICH. J. INT'L L. 1 (2001); from the right, *see* Ruth Wedgwood, *The Case for Military Trials*, WALL ST. J., Dec. 3, 2001, at 18.

47. Newt Gingrich, *Dear Senator Obama...*, NEWSWEEK, May 19, 2008, at 28. (Gingrich writes in an open letter to Senator Obama suggestions on how to move his campaign forward and discusses the weaknesses of several earlier candidates/presidents.)

48. Department of Defense, Military Commission Order No. 1, Subject: Procedures for Trials by Military Commissions of Certain Non-United States Citizens in the War against Terrorism (Mar. 21, 2002) (superseded).

49. George Lardner, Jr., *Legal Scholars Criticize Wording of Bush Order*, WASH. POST, Dec. 3, 2001, at A10; Harold Hongju Koh, *The Case against Military Commissions*, 96 AM. J. INT'L L. 337 (2002).

50. Barton Gelman & Jo Becker, *Pushing the Envelope on Presidential Power*, WASH. POST, June 25, 2007.

51. *Supra* note 44, Senators Kennedy and Leahy express displeasure with their belief the White House was not acting in conformity with the constitutionally mandated separation of powers.

52. John Mintz, *Lists Created of Captives to Be Tried by Military Tribunals*, WASH. POST, May 3, 2003, at A17; Neil A. Lewis, *Six Detainees Soon May Face Military Trials*, N.Y. TIMES, July 4, 2003, at A1; John Mintz, *First Trial by Tribunal Imminent Official Says*, WASH. POST, Oct. 31, 2003, at A10.

53. Glenn Sulmasy, John Yoo, & Martin Flaherty, *Debate, Hamdan and the Military Commissions Act*, 155U. PA. L REV. Penumbra 146 (2007).

54. *See Rasul v. Bush*, 542 U.S. 466 (2004); *Hamdi v. Rumsfeld*, 542 U.S. 507 (2004).

55. *See, e.g.*, David Glazier, *Kangaroo Court or Competent Tribunal? Judging the 21st Century Military Commission*, 89 VA. L. REV. 2005 (2003); William Safire, *Kangaroo Courts*, N.Y. TIMES, Nov. 16, 2001, at A19.

56. *Hamdi v. Rumsfeld*, 542 U.S. 507 (2004). Justice O'Connor, writing for the plurality, still referred to the conflict as an armed conflict.

57. Sam Dillon & Donald G. McNeil Jr., *Spain Sets Hurdle for Extraditions*, N.Y. TIMES, Nov. 24, 2001, at A1; T. R. Reid, *Europeans Reluctant to Send Terror Suspects to U.S.*, WASH. POST, Nov. 29, 2001, at A23.

58. White House Press Release, President George W. Bush (June 22, 2004) (while holding a press conference in the Oval Office with the Hungarian president, Bush was adamant that "we do not torture" and that he never ordered torture); Richard B. Schmitt & Richard Serrano, *Files Show Bush Team Torn on POW Rules*, L.A. TIMES, June 23, 2004.

59. Bob Hebert, *Promoting Torture's Promoter*, N.Y. TIMES, Jan. 7, 2005.

60. Geneva Convention Relative to the Treatment of Prisoners of War of August 12, 1949, 6 U.S.T. 3316, 74 U.N.T.S. 135 (the Third Geneva Convention).

61. JORDAN J. PAUST, BEYOND THE LAW: THE BUSH ADMINISTRATION'S UNLAWFUL RESPONSES IN THE "WAR" ON TERROR (2007).

62. David B. Rivkin & Lee A. Casey, *Supreme Court Rulings in a Time of War* NATIONAL REVIEW, May 17, 2004.

63. *Johnson v. Eisentrager* 339 U.S. 763 (1950).

64. YOO, WAR BY OTHER MEANS (2006).

65. KAREN J. GREENBERG, THE TORTURE DEBATE IN AMERICA (2005).

66. Associated Press, *Rumsfeld: U.S. Interrogation Techniques Don't Violate Geneva Conventions*, May 12, 2004.

67. SEYMOUR HERSH, CHAIN OF COMMAND: THE ROAD FROM 9/11 TO ABU GHRAIB (2004).

68. Edward Spannaus, *War Crimes Prosecutions: What White House Fears*, EXEC. INTEL. REV. (EIR), June 11, 2004.

69. Michel Isikoff, *Gitmo: Southcom Shutdown*, NEWSWEEK, May 9, 2005.

70. Irene Kahn, Speech, Annual Report of Amnesty International, May 25, 2005; *see also* Richard Norton-Taylor, *Gitmo Is the Gulag of Our Time, says Amnesty*, GUARDIAN (London), May 26, 2005.

71. Joseph Curl, *Gitmo Called Death Camp*, WASH. TIMES, June 16, 2005.

Chapter 5

1. *Hamdan v. Rumsfeld*, 548 U.S. 557, 126 S.Ct. 2749 (2006).

2. *Id.*

3. *Id.*

4. *Id.*

5. The Geneva Convention Relative to the Treatment of Prisoners of War (Third Geneva Convention), Aug. 12, 1949, 6 U.S.T. 3316, 75 U.N.T.S. 134.

6. As oft repeated by the president, attorney general, vice president, and other members of the administration who have testified on this matter, the Bush administration has said, as a matter of law and policy, the Geneva Conventions do not apply to the detainees. *See* Tim Golden, *After Terror, a Secret Rewriting of Military Law*, N.Y. TIMES, Oct. 24, 2004 (Patrick Philbin memo discussed).

7. *Hamdan v. Rumsfeld*, 415 F.3d 33 (D.C. Cir. 2005).

8. Editorial, *A Travesty of Justice*, N.Y. TIMES, Nov. 16, 2001.

9. *Hamdan v. Rumsfeld*, 548 U.S. 557, 126 S.Ct. 2749, 2759 (2006) (Stevens, J., for majority).

10. *Id.* at 2778.

11. *Id.* at 2799 (Breyer, J., concurring).

12. *Id.* at 2759 (Stevens, J., for majority).

13. It seems that Congress has kept the military commissions purposefully vague as the members have had numerous opportunities to detail these unique procedures but they have not, even as late as the 2008 MCM.

14. MANUAL FOR COURTS-MARTIAL, UNITED STATES, pt. I, ¶ (2)(b)(2) (2006) [hereinafter MCM].

15. MCM, *supra* note 15, pt. (g) (2006).

16. *Uniform Code of Military Justice* (UCMJ), art. 21, 10 U.S.C. § 821 (2006).

17. *See Hamdan v. Rumsfeld*, 548 U.S. 557, 126 S.Ct. 2749, 2759 (2006) (Stevens, J., for majority).

18. *Id.*

19. *Id.*

20. *Id.*

21. *Id.*

22. UCMJ, art. 36, 10 U.S.C. § 836 (2006).

23. *Hamdan*, 126 S.Ct. at 2759 (2006) (Stevens, J., for majority).

24. *Id.*

25. *Id.*

26. *Id.*

27. Article 3 Common to the Geneva Conventions.

28. The Geneva Convention Relative to the Treatment of Prisoners of War (Third Geneva Convention), art. 3, Aug. 12, 1949, 6 U.S.T. 3316, 75 U.N.T.S. 134.

29. *Hamdan v. Rumsfeld*, 415 F.3d 33, 41 (D.C. Cir. 2005).

30. *See Hamdan*, 126 S.Ct. at 2759 (Stevens, J. for majority).

31. *Id.*

32. *Supra* note 27.

33. *Hamdan*, 126 S.Ct. at 2810 (Scalia, J., dissenting).

34. *Id.*

35. *Hamdan*, 126 S.Ct. at 2849 (Alito, J., dissenting).

36. *Stenberg v. Carhart*, 530 U.S. 914 (2000).

37. *Hamdan*, 126 S.Ct. at 2823 (Thomas, J., dissenting).

38. *Dames & Moore v. Reagan*, 453 U.S. 654, 678 (1981).

39. *Id.*

40. *Hamdi v Rumsfeld*, 542 U.S. 507, 579 (2004) (Thomas, J., dissenting).

41. *Hamdan*, 126 S.Ct. at 2823 (Thomas, J., dissenting).

42. *Id.*

43. *Id.*

44. *Madsen v. Kinsella*, 343 U.S. 341, 346 (1952).

45. Different from the decisions in *Rasul* and *Hamdi*, the administration could not claim there was some victory contained within this decision. *See* BENJAMIN WITTES, WAR AND THE LONG WAR (2008).

46. *See*, for example, Angie C. Marek, *How to Try a Fanatic*, U.S. NEWS AND WORLD REP., Sept. 18, 2006; Michael Isikoff, et al., *The Gitmo Fallout*, NEWSWEEK, July 17, 2006.

47. *See* David Scheffer, *What to Do about America's Military Commissions*, CHI. TRIB., July 9, 2006.

48. *Standards of Military Commissions and Tribunals*, Hearing Before the House Armed Services Comm., 109th Cong. (July 12, 2006) (Congressman Rob Simmons questioned the judge advocate generals of the various armed forces as to what their thoughts were on the idea of "new laws for the new war").

49. Charles Babington & Jonathan Weisman, *Senate Approves Detainee Bill Backed by Bush*, WASH. POST, Sept. 29, 2006, at A1; see also editorial, *A Dangerous New Order*, N.Y. TIMES, Oct. 19, 2006.

50. Glenn Sulmasy, *Balancing the Needs of Law and War*, PROVIDENCE J., July 11, 2007.

51. Jennifer K. Elsea, *Selected Procedural Safeguards in Federal, Military and International Courts*, CRS Report for Congress, September 18, 2006.

52. WILLIAM WINTHROP, MILITARY LAW AND PRECEDENTS, 48–49 (2d ed. 1920).

53. *UCMJ*, art. 18, 10 U.S.C. § 818.

54. Military juries, known as members, are presumed to be an all-officer panel. If an enlisted person seeks other enlisted personnel on his panel, however, he or she can request this and have at least one-third of the members be of the enlisted ranks. Nonetheless, this would not be a jury of peers as one would expect from the Constitution.

55. Rules for Court Martial (RCM) are the rules required in the conduct of military trials.

56. *See* F. GILLIGAN & F. LEDERER, COURT MARTIAL PROCEDURE, §§ 1–43—1–47 (2d ed. 1999).

57. Ironically, although still not nearly as rights-oriented as the civilian process, the Rules of Evidence are roughly the same in both the FRE and the MRE, so many of the same concerns would have emerged about the Fifth Amendment and the Fourth Amendment.

58. *Military Commissions Act of 2006*, Public Law 109–366, sec. 7(a), 120 *Stat.* 2600, 2636 (to be codified at 28 U.S.C. § 2241(e)(1)).

59. *See Hamdan v. Rumsfeld*, 548 U.S. 557, 126 S.Ct. 2749 (2006).

60. WINTHROP supra note 53, at 784.

61. *Id.*

62. U.S. CONST., art. II.

63. *See supra* note 52, Elsea, CRS Report for Congress, September 18, 2006.

64. *Supra* note 58.

65. *See* Craig Whitlock, *French Push Limits in Fight on Terrorism*, WASH. POST, Nov. 2, 2004, at A1.

66. *Military Commissions Act of 2006*, Public Law 109–366, sec. 7(a), 120 *Stat.* 2600, 2636 (to be codified at 28 U.S.C. § 2241(e)(1)).

67. *See* Michael C. Dorf, *The Orwellian Military Commissions Act of 2006*, 5 J. INT'L CRIM. JUST. 10 (March 2007).

68. This bill was reintroduced in the new Congress as *The Effective Terrorist Prosecution Act. See The Effective Terrorist Prosecution Act of 2006*, S.4060, Nov. 16, 2006.

69. Editorial, *Rushing Off a Cliff*, N.Y. TIMES, Sept. 26, 2006.

70. Lou Fisher, *Military Commissions: Problems of Authority and Practice*, 24 B. U. INT'L L. J. 15 (2006).

71. Glenn Sulmasy, *Government Secrecy in Time of Armed Conflict*, 57 AM U. L. REV. 5 (2008).

72. THE FEDERALIST No. 70 (Alexander Hamilton).

73. *Hamdan, supra* note 30.

74. *See Standards of Military Commissions and Tribunals*, Hearing before the House Armed Services Comm., 109th Cong. (July 12, 2006).

75. Andrew C. McCarthy, et al. *The Military Commissions Act of 2006: Striking the Right Balance*, White Paper, The Federalist Society, available at http://www.fed-soc. org/doclib/20070326_MCA2006StrikingtheRightBalance.pdf.

76. ANDREW C. MCCARTHY, WILLFUL BLINDNESS: MEMOIR OF THE JIHAD (2008).

77. *Id.*

78. David Rivkin & Lee Casey, *Question Time: The Interrogation of Terrorists by an Idealistic Country*, NAT'L REV., Oct. 9, 2006.

79. McCarthy, et al., *supra* note 76.

80. *See generally The Rome Statute for the International Criminal Court*, July 17, 1998, U.N. Doc. A/Conf.183/9.

81. The MRE and FRE are identical in most respects.

82. *See* Trevor Morrison, *Hamdi's Habeas Puzzle; Suspension as Authorization?* 91 CORNELL L. REV. 411 (2006).

83. *Boumediene v. Bush*, 553U.S., 128 S. Ct. 2229 (2008).

84. Hearings before the House Foreign Affairs Committee, Subcommittee for International Organizations and Human Rights, *City on the Hill or Prison on the Bay? The Mistakes of Guantanamo and the Decline of America's Image, Part II*, 110th Cong. (May 20, 2008) (testimony of Lt. Col. Stephen Abrams, Ret.).

85. The Geneva Convention Relative to the Treatment of Prisoners of War (Third Geneva Convention), art. 5, Aug. 12, 1949, 6 U.S.T. 3316, 75 U.N.T.S. 134 (which provides a procedure for determining the status of combatants captured on the field of battle).

86. *The Detainee Treatment Act of 2005*, Public Law 109–148, § 1001, 119 *Stat.* 2680, 2739 (2005) (as included in the Defense Appropriation Act of 2006).

87. *Ex Parte Milligan*, 71 U.S. (4 Wall) 2, 121 (1866).

88. *See* WILLIAM WINTHROP, MILITARY LAW AND PRECEDENTS, 831, 836 (2 ed. 1920) for his discussion on the three types of commissions and the four preconditions for jurisdiction over a case such as that of Hamdan, an unlawful belligerent.

89. *Ex parte Quirin*, 317 U.S. 1 (1942).

90. *Rasul v. Bush*, 542 U.S. 466 (2004).

91. *Ex parte Milligan*, 71 U.S. (4 Wall.) 2, 121 (1866).

92. *In re Yamashita*, 327 U.S. 1 (1946).

93. Matt Apuzzo, *Growing Pains for Terror Appeals Court*, WASH. POST, Aug. 22, 2007.

94. *Habeas Corpus Restoration Act of 2007:* Hearing before the Senate Comm. on the Judiciary, 110th Cong. 110–90 (September 25, 2006) (statement by David B. Rivkin).

95. President George W. Bush, Press Conference of the President: The Rose Garden, On the *Military Commissions Act* (Sept. 15, 2006).

96. John C. Yoo, *The Supreme Court Goes to War*, WALL ST. J., June 17, 2008.

97. The Geneva Convention Relative to the Treatment of Prisoners of War, Aug. 12, 1949, 6 U.S.T. 3316, 75 U.N.T.S. 134.

98. *See generally* EU Memorandum on the Death Penalty (Feb. 25 2000), available at http://www.eurunion.org/legislat/DeathPenalty/eumemorandum.htm (last accessed July 29, 2008).

99. The Geneva Convention against Torture and Other Cruel, Inhuman or Degrading Treatment or Punishment, Dec. 10, 1984, S. TREATY DOC. NO O. 100–20, 1465 U.N.T.S. 85 (entered into force June 26, 1987).

100. S. Amendment 1977 to H.R. 2863 *Relating to Persons under the Detention, Custody, or Control of the United States Government* § 1031(a)(1), 109th Cong. (2005).

101. William Glaberson & Eric Lichtblau, *Military Trial Begins for Gitmo Detainee*, N.Y. TIMES, July 22, 2008.

102. Jeremy Waldron, *Torture and Positive Law: Jurisprudence for the White House*, 105 COLUM. L. REV. 6 (2005).

103. KYNDRA ROTUNDA, HONOR BOUND (2008).

104. *Id.*

105. *See* NAT HENTOFF, THE WAR ON THE BILL OF RIGHTS AND THE GATHERING RESISTANCE (2003); *see also* Martin Flaherty, *Hamdan and the Military Commissions Act, a President, Not a Caesar*, 155 U. PA. L. REV. PENNUMBRA 146 (2007).

106. *Hamdan* at 2823 (Thomas, J., dissenting).

107. Article 3 Common to the Geneva Conventions.

108. *See* Glenn Sulmasy & John Yoo, *Hamdan and the Military Commissions Act, The Military Commissions Act: A Bipartisan Congress Checks the Judiciary*, 155 U. PA. L. REV. PENNUMBRA 146 (2007).

109. John Huston, Speech before the Eminent Jurists Panel, International Commission of Jurists (Sept. 6, 2006).

110. McCarthy, et al., White Paper.

111. *See* Eric Posner & Adrian Vermuele, *Should Coercive Interrogation Be Legal?* 104 MICH. L. REV. 671 (Feb. 2006).

112. McCarthy, et al., White Paper.

113. This is not an issue to be taken lightly by any policy makers. This is not only applicable and cause for concern for the troops or CIA in the field, but for decision makers in Washington as well. For example, the Center for Constitutional Rights filed a lawsuit in Germany against senior cabinet officials including Donald Rumsfeld and George Tenet alleging that they support torture and are "war criminals" subject to prosecution under Germany's universal jurisdiction authority. On April 27, 2007, the German prosecutor declined to pursue the case.

114. U.S. CONST, art. II.

115. *Boumediene v. Bush*, 553U.S., 128 S. Ct. 2229 (2008).

116. Peter Spiegel, *Gates Is Pushing to Move Terror Trials from Guantanamo*, L.A. TIMES, March 30, 2007.

Chapter 6

1. The Bush administration made numerous changes over seven years in their approaches to combating terrorism and al Qaeda. For example, they created the Department of Homeland Security and the director of National Intelligence and employed the "surge" military tactics in Iraq.

2. Glenn Sulmasy, *The Legal Landscape after Hamdan: Homeland Security Courts*, 13 NEW ENG. INT'L & COMP. L. ANN. 1 (2006).

3. Curtis A. Bradley & Jack L. Goldsmith, *The Constitutional Validity of Military Commissions*, 5 GREEN BAG 2D 249 (2002); *see also* Jack L. Goldsmith & Cass R. Sunstein, *Military Tribunals and Legal Culture: What a Difference Sixty Years Can Make*, 19 CONST. COMMENT. 261 (2002).

4. *Hamdan v. Rumsfeld*, 548 U.S. 557 (2006).

5. *Boumediene v. Bush*, 553U.S., 128 S. Ct. 2229 (2008).

6. *SCOTUS Gitmo Ruling*, WASH. POST, June 17, 2008. Washington Post-ABC News Poll found that 61 percent of Americans disagreed with the decision of the Court in *Boumediene* to grant habeas corpus rights to detainees in Gitmo.

7. Boumediene, 553 U.S., 128 S. Ct. 2229 (2008).

8. *Id.* (majority opinion).

9. *Id.* (Scalia, J., dissenting).

10. *Id.*

11. Glenn Sulmasy, *Two Takes: The Supreme Court Made a Mistake in Boumediene*, U.S. NEWS AND WORLD REP., June 19, 2008.

12. *Supra* note 7.

13. *See* Eric Lichtblau, *Administration Calls for Congress to Act on Detainees*, WALL ST. J., July 22, 2008 (stating that there are around 275 detainees at Guantanamo).

14. John Yoo, *The Supreme Court Goes to War*, WALL ST. J., June 17, 2008.

15. *Supra* note 7.

16. *See* Editorial, "President Kennedy," WALL STREET JOURNAL, June 13, 2008, at A14.

17. Richard Epstein, *How to Complicate Habeas Corpus*, N.Y. TIMES, June 21, 2008.

18. *See also* Jack Balkin, *Two Takes*, U.S. NEWS AND WORLD REP., June 19, 2008.

19. *Boumediene v. Bush*, 553 U.S., 128 S. Ct. 2229 (2008).

20. *See Rostker v. Goldberg*, 453 U.S. 57 (1981); *see also Goldman v. Weinberger*, 475 U.S. 503 (1986).

21. *Hamdan v. Rumsfeld*, 548 U.S. 557 (2006) (majority opinion).

22. *Id.*; Geneva Convention Relative to the Treatment of Prisoners of War of August 12, 1949, 6 U.S.T. 3316, 74 U.N.T.S. 135 (the Third Geneva Convention).

23. *Military Commissions Act of 2006*, Public Law 109–366, § 950v(a)(2)(C), 120 *Stat.* 2600.

24. THE FEDERALIST No. 70 (Alexander Hamilton).

25. The Third Geneva Convention Relative to the Treatment of Prisoners.

26. Deb Reichman, *White House Says Ruling Could Free Detainees in U.S.*, A.P., July 4, 2008.

27. Sulmasy, *supra* note 11.

28. *Ex parte Quirin*, 317 U.S. 1 (1942).

29. *Supra* note 28.

30. *See* Jeff Zeleny & Nicholas Kulish, "Obama in Berlin, Calls for Renewal of Ties with Allies," WASH. POST, July 25, 2008; Senator John McCain has repeatedly asserted, "I would rather lose a campaign than lose a war." Thus, both 2008 presidential candidates took the threat of international terrorism seriously and understood the risks involved.

31. *See generally* 2 COLEMAN PHILLIPSON, THE INTERNATIONAL LAW AND CUSTOM OF ANCIENT GREECE AND ROME, 166–380 (1911).

32. HUGO GROTIUS, DE JURE BELLI AC PACIS, LIBRI TRES (1625).

33. International Humanitarian Law and the nongovernmental organizations, such as Amnesty International, Human Rights Watch, and the ICRC, and academic think tanks such as the Carr Center for Human Rights Policy at Harvard Kennedy School have played significant leadership roles in the late twentieth century and early twenty-first century in bringing the laws of war into the policy arena and political culture. *See generally* Colm Campbell, *Peace and Laws of War: The Role of International Humanitarian Law in the Post-Conflict Environment*, 839 INT'L REV. OF THE RED CROSS 627 (2000); *see also* Dinah Pokempner, *Terrorism and Human Rights: The Legal Framework*, 19–29

TERRORISM AND INTERNATIONAL LAW (2002); *See also* Samantha Power, *Our War on Terror,* N.Y. TIMES, July 29 2007.

34. *See* ADAM ROBERTS & RICHARD GUELFF, DOCUMENTS ON THE LAWS OF WAR, 3–17 (1999).

35. *See generally* YORAM DINSTEIN, WAR, AGGRESSION AND SELF DEFENCE (3d ed. 2001).

36. *See* Margaret Stock, *Detainees in the Hands of America: New Rules for a New Kind of War,* TERRORISM AND INTERNATIONAL LAW—CHALLENGES AND RESPONSES, Int'l Inst. for Humanitarian Law (2003); *see generally* Geneva Convention III Relative to the Treatment of Prisoners of War, Oct. 21, 1950, 6 UST. 3316, 75 U.N.T.S. 105.

37. *Authorization for the Use of Military Force* (AUMF), Public Law 107–40, 115 *Stat.* 224 (20010; S. C. Res. 1368, U.N. Doc S/RES/1368 (2001).

38. *Id.*

39. *See* Kenneth Roth, *The Law of War in the War on Terror,* FOREIGN AFFAIRS, Jan./ Feb. 2004, at 2; *see also* Bruce Ackerman, *This Is Not a War,* 113 YALE L.J. 1871, 1873 (2004).

40. *See* Andrew Tulley, *Bush Presses Iraq, Afghanistan as Fronts in Terror War,* RADIO FREE PRESS, July 11, 2005 (beyond these fronts, the war has also progressed in Indonesia, the U.K., Russia, and Spain).

41. Geneva Convention on the Treatment of Prisoners of War, Oct. 21, 1950, 6 U.S.T. 3316, 75 U.N.T.S. 105 (this international armed conflict is distinct from internal armed conflict where Article 3 Common to the Geneva Conventions would apply. This conflict is global in nature and impacts many nations and cultures. The clear intent of Common Article 3 is to govern noninternational armed conflicts, for example. Similar to Additional Protocol II, it is intended for civil war and wars of national liberation such as in Colombia, arguably Palestine and Israel, the Irish "troubles," and similar conflicts. This distinction is critical from both a legal and a policy perspective.

42. JOHN YOO, WAR BY OTHER MEANS (2006).

43. *Id.* at 9.

44. *Id.*

45. *See* Meredith May, *Tearful Easter Reunions as Troops Return Home,* SAN FRAN. CHRON., Apr. 12, 2004, at A1; *see also* Lynn Neary, *Troops Rotation, Coming Home,* NPR, Feb. 11, 2004 (U.S. forces returning from both Afghanistan and Iraq consistently discuss the warfare they have been exposed to while deployed overseas).

46. Military Order of November 13, 2001, *Detention, Treatment and Trial of Certain Non-Citizens in the War against Terrorism,* 66 F.R.57833 (Nov. 16, 2001).

47. *Id.*; 150 CONG. REC. S2701-01 (2004).

48. *See generally* DINSTEIN, *supra* note 35.

49. Donald H. Rumsfeld, *A New Kind of War,* N.Y. TIMES, Sept. 27, 2001.

50. Yoo, *supra* note 42.

51. *Ex parte Quirin,* 317 U.S. 1 (1942); *Johnson v. Eisentrager,* 339 U.S. 763 (1950).

52. *Id.*

53. There has not been a successful prosecution as of July 2008, although one military commission (*Hamdan*) has just started and should be complete at the time of publication. *See generally* Scott Shane & William Glaberson, *Rulings Clear Military Trial of Detainee,* N.Y. TIMES, July 18, 2008.

54. *Rasul v. Bush,* 542 U.S. 466 (2004).

55. *Hamdi v. Rumsfeld,* 542 U.S. 507 (2004).

56. *Hamdan v. Rumsfeld,* 548 U.S. 557 (2006).

57. *Boumediene v. Bush,* 553 U.S., 128 S. Ct. 2229 (2008).

58. *Johnson v. Eisentrager*, 339 U.S. 763 (1950).

59. The administration anticipated and relied on existing precedents to make many of these decisions regarding the detainees. When reviewing these decisions, it is important to view the actions of the administration through the lens of the period in 2001–2002 when most believed an attack similar to or more catastrophic than 9/11 was inevitable.

60. Glenn Sulmasy, *War on al Qaeda*, SAN FRAN. CHRON., Feb. 20, 2007.

61. *See* Jeff Zeleny & Nicholas Kulish, *Obama Speaks to Germany on European Ties*, N.Y. TIMES, July 25, 2008 (quoting Senator Obama as saying in regard to terrorism, "No one nation, no matter how large or powerful, can defeat such challenges alone. None of us can deny these threats, or escape responsibility in meeting them"); *but see* Michael Cooper & Larry Rohter, *McCain, Iraq War and the Threat of 'al Qaeda,'* N.Y. TIMES, April 19, 2008 (quoting Senator McCain as saying, "Al Qaeda in Iraq would proclaim victory and increase its efforts to provoke sectarian tensions, pushing for a full-scale civil war that could descend into genocide and destabilize the Middle East").

62. Glenn Sulmasy, *The Legal Landscape after Hamdan, Homeland Security Courts*, 13 NEW ENG. INT'L & COMP. L. ANN. 1 (2006).

63. General David Petraeus, Testimony before the Senate Armed Services Committee, April 8, 2008.

64. Geneva Convention Relative to the Treatment of Prisoners of War of August 12, 1949, 6 U.S.T. 3316, 74 U.N.T.S. 135 (the Third Geneva Convention). Although there exists a right to detain such individuals during armed conflict in both the Geneva tradition as well as in customary international law, the captured al Qaeda fighter's status does not fit neatly within the current constructs. Since his election, President Obama, relying upon the AUMF as well as international law, has asserted the right to "detain" actual al Qaeda fighters, but it still can be asserted that this unique fighter was never intended to be included within existing legal instruments.

65. *See* General Charles Dunlap, "The Rise of Lawfare and the Global War on Terror," Carr Center for Human Rights Policy, Harvard Kennedy School, Harvard University (Mar. 20, 2006); *see also* General Charles Dunlap, *Lawfare Today: A Perspective*, 33 YALE J. INT'L L. 146 (Jan. 2008).

66. *See generally* The National Security Strategy of the United States (2002). The U.S. needs to have such a document specifically dedicated to the plans, laws, and strategy to defeat al Qaeda.

67. Mark Denbeaux et al., *No-Hearing Hearings, CSRT: The Modern Habeas Corpus? An Analysis of the Proceedings of the Government's Combatant Status Review Tribunals at Guantánamo* (Seton Hall Public Law Research Paper No. 951245, 2006), available at http://ssrn.com/abstract=951245.

68. Stephen Abraham, Testimony before the House Committee on Foreign Affairs, Subcommittee on Human Rights (May 2008).

69. Combating Terrorism Center, *An Assessment of 516 Combatant Status Review Tribunal (CSRT) Unclassified Summaries* (2007) (arguing that the Denbeaux & Denbeaux study has methodological flaws).

70. *A Bill to Restore Habeas Corpus for Those Detained by the United States*, S. 185, 110th Cong. (2007).

71. Glenn Sulmasy, *The Laws of War in the Global War on Terror: International Lawyers Fighting the Last War*, NOTRE DAME J.L. ETHICS & PUB. POL'Y (2005).

72. The enactment of the USA PATRIOT ACT as well as enactment of the recent Protect America Act (PAA) and domestic laws are examples of the government responding to the new threat. Other nations have also responded with new policies and laws aimed at ensuring that governments evolve to better meet the new threats posed by al Qaeda.

73. Professor Mark Denbeaux, Testimony before the House Foreign Affairs Committee, Subcommittee on Human Rights, May 24, 2008.

74. Congressman William Delahunt, Statement of the Chairman, House Foreign Affairs Committee, Subcommittee on Human Rights, May 24, 2008; *see also* Kenneth Roth, *The Law of War in the War on Terror,* Foreign Affairs, Jan./Feb. 2004.

75. Harold Koh, Keynote Address at the Conference entitled, "The National Security Constitution," St. John's Law School (January 29, 2008).

76. Id.

77. Harold Hongju Koh, *The Case against Military Commissions,* 96 Am. J. Int'l L. 337 (2002).

78. *Ex parte Milligan,* 71 U.S. (4 Wall.) 2 (1866).

79. Benjamin Wittes, Law and the Long War (2008) at 169.

80. *Id.* at 171–172.

81. *Id.* at 178.

82. Andrew C. McCarthy, Willful Blindness (2008).

83. National Commission on Terrorist Attacks upon the United States, *The 9/11 Commission Report: Final Report of the National Commission on Terrorist Attacks Upon the United States,* p. 79.

84. *Johnson v. Eisentrager,* 339 U.S. 763 (1950).

85. *Classified Information Procedures Act* (CIPA), S. Rep 96–823, Public Law 96–456 (June 18, 1980).

86. Michael B. Mukasey, *Jose Padilla Makes Bad Law: Terror Trials Hurt the Nation Even When They Lead to Convictions,* Wall St. J., August 22, 2007.

87. *See* Andrew C. McCarthy, Willful Blindness: Memoir of the Jihad (2008); *see also* McCarthy & Velshi, The Case for a National Security Court (2007).

88. *Id.*

89. Judge Brinkema delivered a keynote address at a conference sponsored by the American University's Washington School of Law, "Terrorists and Detainees: Do We Need a National Security Court." She strongly defended the federal judiciary in trying terrorists and used her example of being the judge for the Moussaoui case as the key example. *See also* Associated Press, *Moussaoui Judge Says Prosecutor's Pursuit of Death Penalty Made More Evidence Public,* Int'l Herald Trib., February 2, 2008.

90. John Yoo, War by Other Means (2006).

91. *Moussaoui Scorns 9/11 Victims,* Al Jazeera, April 14, 2006.

92. *Boumediene v. Bush,* 553 U.S., 128 S. Ct. 2229, 2293 (2008) (Scalia, J. dissenting).

93. For an excellent although critical history of the deference doctrine, *see* Stephen B. Lichtman, *The Justice and the Generals: A Critical Examination of the U.S. Supreme Court's Tradition of Deference to the Military, 1918–2004,* 65 MD. L. Rev. 907 (2006); *but see* John F. O'Connor, *Statistics and the Military Deference Doctrine: A Response to Professor Lichtman,* 66 MD. L. Rev. 668 (2007).

94. *See Rostker v. Goldberg,* 453 U.S. 57 (1981).

95. William Glaberson, *Evidence Faulted in Detainee Case,* N.Y. Times, July 1, 2008.

96. The Federalist No. 70, 74 (Alexander Hamilton).

Chapter 7

1. Glenn M. Sulmasy, *The Legal Landscape after Hamdan,* 13 New Eng. Int'l & Comp. L. 1 (2006), *see also* Glenn Sulmasy, *Redeeming Gitmo,* National Review Online, July 29, 2005, available at http://www.nationalreview.com/comment/sulmasy200507280838.asp.

2. The al Qaeda Training Manual is available at http://au.af.mil/au/awc/awcgate/ terrorism/alqaida_manual/; *see also* Kanan Makiya & Hassan Mneimneh, *Manual for a Raid*, N.Y. TIMES REVIEW OF BOOKS, January 17, 2002, at 18, 20.

3. James A. Baker III, *The Big Ten: The Case for Pragmatic Idealism*, THE NATIONAL INTEREST, Aug. 29, 2007.

4. Marc Perelman, *How the French Fight Terror*, FOREIGN POLICY, January 2006.

5. *Id.*, Craig Whitlock, *French Push Limits in Fight on Terrorism*, WASH. POST, Nov. 2, 2004.

6. Harvey Rishikof, *A Federal Terrorism Court*, POLICY REPORT OF THE PROGRESSIVE POLICY INSTITUTE, Nov. 2007.

7. Perelman, *supra* note 4; *see also* Jeremy Shapiro & Benedicte Suzan, *The French Experience of Counter-Terrorism*, 45 SURVIVAL 67–98 (Spring 2003).

8. Rishikof, *supra* note 6.

9. CHRISTOPHER SMITH, HUMAN RIGHTS IN NORTHERN IRELAND (1999).

10. Graham Greig, *No More Sitting as Both Judge and Jury in NI*, SCOTTISH LAW REPORTER, Aug. 14, 2007.

11. *Id.*

12. *Id.*

13. *Id.*

14. *See generally* Hootan Shambuyati, *A Tale of Two Mayors: Courts and Politics in Iran and Turkey*, INT'L JOURNAL OF MID. EAST STUDIES (2204).

15. *Id.*

16. *Anti-Terror Law*, Act No. 3713: Law to Fight Terrorism (published in the Official Gazette Apr. 12, 1991).

17. ECHR, Case of *Incal v. Turkey*, June 9, 1998.

18. AMNESTY INT'L, *Turkey: The Entrenched Culture of Impunity Must End*, July 5, 2007.

19. *See generally* Whitlock *supra* note 5; *see also*, Perelman, *supra* note 4.

20. JOHN YOO, WAR BY OTHER MEANS (2006).

21. PHILLIPE SANDS, TORTURE TEAM: RUMSFELD'S MEMO AND THE BETRAYAL OF AMERICAN VALUES (2008).

22. *Boumediene v. Bush*, 553 U.S., 128 S. Ct. 2229 (2008).

23. Military Commission Order No. 1.

24. Military Commission Order No. 2–9.

25. KYNDRA ROTUNDA, HONOR BOUND: INSIDE THE GUANTANAMO TRIALS (2008).

26. *Id.*

27. Howard Kurtz, *Newsweek Apologizes*, WASH. POST, May 16, 2005, at A1.

28. Deborah Pearlstein, *Advantage, Rule of Law*, AMERICAN PROSPECT, June 30, 2006.

29. Seymour M. Hersh, *The General's Report*, THE NEW YORKER, June 25, 2007; Scott Shane, *Bipartisan Group to Speak Out on Detainees*, N.Y. TIMES, June 25, 2008.

30. For example, as of this writing, Attorney General Mukasey, Secretary of State Rice and Secretary of Defense Gates have all in different venues called for the close of Gitmo and, in some case, to end the military commission process.

31. *See, e.g.*, Elizabeth White, *Obama Says Gitmo Facility Should Close*, WASH. POST, June 24, 2007 (quoting Senator Obama as saying "While we're at it we're going to close Guantanamo"); Phillip Sherwell, *Straight-talking McCain vows to fix world's view of the 'ugly American,'* THE TELEGRAPH (UK), March 19, 2007 (quoting Senator McCain as saying that "I would immediately close Guantanamo Bay, move all the prisoners to Fort Leavenworth (an army base in Kansas) and truly expedite the judicial proceedings in their cases."

32. Editorial, *Shut Jail, ex-Diplomats Say*, L.A. TIMES, March 28, 2008.

33. Jack L. Goldsmith & Neal K. Katyal, *The Terrorists' Court*, N.Y. TIMES, July 11, 2007.

34. Katie Paul, *The Road from Gitmo*, NEWSWEEK, June 27, 2008, available at http://www.newsweek.com/id/143485.

35. Harvey Rishikof, *A New Court for Terrorism*, N.Y. TIMES, June 8, 2007.

36. Harvey Rishikof, *Is It Time for a Federal Terrorist Court?* 7 SUFFOLK J. TRIAL & APP. ADVOC. (2003).

37. Rishikof, *supra* note 6.

38. JACK L. GOLDSMITH, THE TERROR PRESIDENCY (2007).

39. *Supra* note 33.

40. Chicago Federalist Society Panel, *The War on Terrorism and Specialized Counts*, May 12, 2008. Moderated by Judge Frank Easterbrook; panelists included Katyal, Sulmasy, and Rivkin.

41. BENJAMIN WITTES, LAW AND THE LONG WAR (2008).

42. *Id.* at 174.

43. *Id.* at 176.

44. *Id.* at 177.

45. Andrew C. McCarthy & Alykhan Velshi, *We Need a National Security Court* (2006), available at http://www.defenddemocracy.org/usr_doc/NationalSecurity-Court.doc (unpublished submission for AEI).

46. *Id.; see also* Paul, *supra* note 35.

47. Katyal, *supra* note 33; Wittes, *supra* note 42.

48. Wittes, *supra* note 42.

49. Human Rights Watch, United States: *Guantanamo Two Years On—US Detentions Undermine the Rule of Law*, January 9, 2004, available online at http://www.hrw.org/english/docs/2004/01/09/usdom6917.htm (last visited 14 June 2005); see., *Guantanamo and Beyond: The Continuing Pursuit of Unchecked Executive Power* at 139 AMNEST. INT'L. (2005), available at http://web.amnesty.org/library/pdf/AMR510632005ENGLISH/$File/AMR5106305.pdf.

50. *Supra* note 5.

51. *See Uniting and Strengthening America by Providing Appropriate Tools Required to Intercept and Obstruct Terrorism Act of 2001* (USA Patriot Act), Public Law 107–56, 115 Stat. 272 (2001) (codified in scattered sections in numerous titles of U.S.C.); *see also* James Risen & Eric Lichtblau, Bush Lets U.S. Spy on Callers without Courts, N.Y. TIMES, Dec. 16, 2005, at A1 (discussing The Terrorist Surveillance Program [TSP]); *see also* Press Release, Press Briefing by Attorney General Gonzales and General Michael Hayden, Principal Deputy Director for National Intelligence (Dec. 19, 2005), http://www.whitehouse.gov/news/releases/2005/12/20051219–1.html.

52. Max Boot, *The Surge Is Working*, L.A. TIMES, September 8, 2007.

53. Jack L. Goldsmith & Cass R. Sunstein, *Military Tribunals and Legal Culture: What a Difference Sixty Years Make*, 19 CONST. COMMENT. 261 (2002).

54. The attorney general delivered a speech in July 2008 at the American Enterprise Institute, when he called on the legislative branch to act in response to the holding in *Boumediene*. Although not calling for the enactment of a national security court, he nonetheless was pushing Congress to engage and react in quick fashion to the holding to better ensure that his department (Department of Justice) can meet the growing demands.

55. *See* Human Rights Watch, *Fact Sheet: Past U.S. Criticism of Military Tribunals*, at http://www.hrw.org/press/2001/11/tribunals1128.htm (November 28, 2001) (on file with Virginia Law Review Association).

56. Ross Tuttle, *Unlawful Influence at Gitmo*, THE NATION, March 28, 2008.

57. It is a well-known and often repeated saying within the military and particularly with judge advocates that "Unlawful command influence is the mortal enemy of military justice."

58. National Institute for Military Justice, the Army JAG School, the Navy JAG School, and others have spent much time studying and working on the issue of unlawful command influence. Gene Fidell, former Coast Guard judge advocate and president of the Institute for Military Justice, has been a particular leader in this area of the law.

59. U.C.M.J., art. 37, 8 U.S.C. 837.

60. *Id.* at 837(b).

61. *Supra* notes 56, 57.

62. Morris D. Davis, *AWOL Military Justice*, L.A. TIMES, December 10, 2007.

63. *See* LOUIS FISHER, NAZI SABOTEURS ON TRIAL (2d ed., 2005).

64. John Yoo, *Courts at War*, 91 CORNELL L. REV. 573 (2005).

65. McCarthy & Velshi, *supra* note 46.

66. *Id.*

67. *Rostker v. Goldberg*, 453 U.S. 57 (1981).

68. *See generally* Annual Report of the Code Committee on Military Justice for the Period of October 1, 2006–September 30, 2007, APPENDIX—U.S. ARMY MILITARY JUSTICE STATISTICS (available at http://www.armfor.uscourts.gov/annual/FY07AnnualReport.pdf).

69. The U.S. Coast Guard is one of the five armed services and its lawyers are judge advocates; it is the only service not within Department of Defense but has been in the Department of Homeland Security since March 2003.

70. The John Adams Project is a fund/program created and jointly run by the ACLU and the National Association of Defense Lawyers (NACDL). It was formally launched on April 3, 2008. It is intended to assist the detainees in Guantanamo Bay by providing funds and support for defense counsel representing the accused.

71. Cynthia Benham, *Amnesty Atttacks Hicks Trial as Sham Justice*, SPRING MORNING HERALD, Feb. 15, 2005.

72. JOHN C. YOO, WAR BY OTHER MEANS (2006).

73. RICHARD A. POSNER, NOT A SUICIDE PACT: THE CONSTITUTION IN A TIME OF NATIONAL EMERGENCY (2006).

74. Louis Fisher, *State Your Secrets*, LEGAL TIMES, June 26, 2006.

75. ANDREW C. MCCARTHY, WILLFUL BLINDNESS (2008); McCarty & Velshi, *supra* note 46.

76. Yoo, *supra* note 72.

77. Michael Isikoff & Mark Hosenball, *Disorder in the Court*, NEWSWEEK, June 5, 2008.

78. Michael Abramowitz, *Critics Study Possible Limits to Habeas Corpus Ruling*, WASH. POST, June 14, 2008, at A05.

79. *Rasul v Bush*, 542 U.S. 466 (2004); *Hamdi v Rumsfeld*, 542 U.S. 507 (2004).

80. *Boumediene v. Bush*, 553 U.S., 128 S. Ct. 2229 (2008).

81. *See generally* Rome Statute of the International Criminal Court, United Nations Diplomatic Conference of Plenipotentiaries on the Establishment of the International Criminal Court, 10th Session, U.N. Doc. A/Conf. 183/9 (1998) available at http://www.un.org/icc.

82. McCarthy & Velshi, *supra* note 45.

83. *Boumediene v. Bush*, 553 U.S., 128 S. Ct. 2229 (2008). (Thomas, J. dissenting).

84. *Id.* (Souter, J. concurring).

85. Geneva Convention Relative to the Treatment of Prisoners of War, Aug. 12, 1949, 6 U.S.T. 3316, 75 U.N.T.S. 135, entered into force Oct. 21, 1950.

86. Ruth Wedgwood, *The Case for Military Tribunals*, WALL STREET J., Dec. 3, 2001, at A18; *see also* Ruth Wedgwood, *Al Qaeda, Terrorism, and Military Commissions*, 96 AM. J. INT'L. L. REV., 329–337 (2002).

87. The Court of Appeals of the Armed Forces, as of now, are Article I judges who are the second layer of review for military appeals. They are an all-civilian panel that provides the necessary "check" from problems inherent within the military system as discussed herein.

88. The European Union is strongly opposed to the death penalty and has become increasingly alarmed at the number of cases occurring in America. *See* the Universal Declaration of Human Rights (the right to life).

Conclusion

1. Elizabeth Bumiller & Stephen Lee Myers, *Senior Administration Officials Defend Military Tribunals for Terrorist Suspects*, N. Y. TIMES, Nov. 15, 2001, at B6.

2. *Rome Statute of the International Criminal Court*, United Nations Diplomatic Conference of Plenipotentiaries on the Establishment of the International Criminal Court, 10th Session, U.N. Doc. A/Conf. 183/9 (1998) available at http://www.un.org/icc (last accessed July 27, 2008).

3. *See* Richard John Galvin, *The ICC Prosecutor, Collateral Damage, and NGOs: Evaluating the Risk of a Politicized Prosecution*, 13 U. MIAMI INT'L & COMP. L. REV. 1 (Fall 2005); Sonja Starr, *Extraordinary Crimes at Ordinary Times: International Justice beyond Crisis Situations*, 101 NW. U. L. REV. 1257 (Spring 2007); *see also* Victoria K. Holt & Elisabeth Dallas, Henry L. Stimson Center, *On Trial: The US Military and the International Criminal Court* (2006), available at http://www.stimson.org/fopo/pdf/US_Military_and_the_ICC_FINAL_website.pdf (last accessed July 27, 2008).

4. Harvey Rishikof, *A Federal Terrorism Court: The Answer to the Legal Quagmire on Terrorism, Detainees and International Norms*, Progressive Policy Institute Report, available at http://www.ppionline.org/documents/TerrorismCourt111407.pdf.

Index

Abu Ghraib prison, 88–92, 167,
   187, 189
Addington, David, 69, 70, 74, 77
Afghanistan, war in, 71, 76, 139, 141, 188
   detainees in, 130, 131, 134, 135, 137,
      142, 150, 188, 203
   and Iraq war, 89
"Aggression," as a crime, 204
Alito, Justice, 101–2, 129
al Qaeda. *See also* Detainees; War on al
      Qaeda
   "association" or "affiliation" with, 42,
      73, 79, 82, 196
   and the civilian courts, 41–42, 104–5,
      110, 146–56, 185–86
   classified evidence and, 71, 109,
      110–12, 151–52, 171, 184
   courts-martial and, 104–5
   evidence rules and the trials of, 149–50
   fighter as hybrid criminal and warrior,
      6, 157, 164, 197
   goals of, 72
   international adjudication of, 203
   in Iraq, 89, 141, 200, 221n 61
   and the laws of war, 116–17, 136,
      144–45, 157, 195
   status of, 98, 116–17, 128, 198, 200
   sympathy for, 86, 90
   torture claims of, 118, 167
   tried and held in the U.S., 187–89
   U.S. citizens as members of, 180, 191
   war on U.S. declared by, 71,
      137–38, 147

Ambrister, Robert Christy, 34–35
American Bar Association, 82, 196
Amnesty International, 86, 91, 166–67, 186
Anderson, Professor Ken, 168
Andersonville Prison, 43–44
Andre, Major John, 14, 26, 53, 164,
      210n 10
Ansell, General Samuel T., 16–17, 18
Anti-Terror Law, Act No. 3713, in
      Turkey, 162
Arbuthnot, Alexander, 34–35
Arnold, Benedict, 14
Article 32 hearing, 21
Articles for the Government of the Navy
      (AGN), 17
Articles of Confederation, 27
Articles of War, 17–18, 23, 35, 54, 55
   British, 15, 24–25
Ashcroft, Attorney General John, 69, 70,
      80, 213n 44
"Associational status," with al Qaeda, 42,
      73, 79, 82, 196
Asymmetric war, 11, 128, 137, 138,
      173–74
Attorney General, legal opinions of the,
      37, 43, 44
Authorization for the Use of Military
      Force (AUMF), 71, 75, 81, 95

Bagram prison, 90, 130, 135, 137, 203
Baker, James III, 158
Balkin, Jack, 132
Barr, Bob, 75

Barr, William, 69
"Battlefield justice," 19
Belligerents, unlawful or illegal. *See*
    Unlawful belligerents
Berenson, Brad, 69
"Beyond a reasonable doubt"
    standard, 190
Biddle, Attorney General Francis, 52,
    53, 55, 56, 63
Bin Laden, Osama, 94, 151, 185, 198
Blackstone, William, 6, 28–29
Borch, Colonel Fred, 83
Boumediene, Lakhdar, 129
Boumediene v. Bush, 7–8, 12, 88, 114, 116
    civilian oversight mandated by,
        142–43, 147, 154–55, 190
    Guantanamo and, 187
    habeas corpus in, 129–30, 166, 189, 190
    Hamdan v. Rumsfeld overruled in, 128
    as incentive for a security court
        system, 205, 206, 224n 54
    and the law enforcement paradigm,
        201–2
    legal confusion resulting from,
        130–31, 141, 174
"Brady Rule," 152–53
Breyer, Justice Stephen, 96
Brinkema, Judge, 152, 222n 89
Bruguiere, Jean-Louis, 159–60
Burnside, General Ambrose, 39
Bush, President George W.
    administration of, 3–4, 79
    counterterrorism policy of, 138, 170
    credibility after Abu Ghraib, 90–92
    detention policies of, 85–86
    Ex Parte Quirin decision and, 63, 64,
        65, 69, 81–82, 165, 195
    Geneva Conventions and, 122–24,
        195–96, 214n 6
    and *Hamdan v. Rumsfeld* decision, 103–5
    International Criminal Court and,
        203–4
    military commissions and, 14, 38,
        47–48, 65–66, 75–77, 79–82, 176,
        179, 194–97
    Military Order of November 13,
        2001, 70–74, 77–81, 127, 196
    and Roosevelt's use of military
        commissions, 47, 48, 63, 64, 69–70,
        71–74, 77–80, 81
    subsequent attacks anticipated by,
        67–69, 72, 139, 140

on torture, 86, 90, 167, 214n 58
    unlawful command influence and, 179
Bush Order. *See* Military Order of
    November 13, 2001
Bush v. Gore, 170
Bybee, Jay, 70
Byrnes, Justice, 59

Castro, President Fidel, 1, 2, 3
Center for Constitutional Rights,
    218n 113
Central Intelligence Agency, 5, 8, 134,
    185, 198
    interrogation programs of, 123–25
Cheney, Vice President, 70, 195–96
Chesney, Professor Bobby, 10
Circuit Court(s) of Appeals, U.S., 153.
    See also D.C. Circuit Court of
    Appeals
Civil War, 17–18, 37–40
Classified information. *See* Evidence,
    classified infromation as
Classified Information Protection Act
    (CIPA), 151
Colepaugh, William, 63
Combatants, enemy or illegal. *See*
    Enemy combatants
Combatant Status Review Tribunal
    (CSRT), 114, 115, 129, 143, 190
Command influence. *See* Unlawful
    command influence (UCI)
Congress, U.S., 11, 185, 194. *See also*
    Continental Congress
    on anti-terrorist tactics, 138
    Boumediene v. Bush and, 205, 206
    hearings on Guantanamo Bay, 128
    and military commissions, 33–34, 35,
        37–38, 75, 92, 95, 96, 102
    Military Commissions Act debate of,
        111–12, 116–17, 119–20, 123–24
    new security court system proposals
        and, 175, 192, 205
    war authorization powers of, 72, 75,
        76, 80–81, 137
Conspiracy, crime of, 94, 96, 98
Constitution, U.S., 6, 129, 130, 185, 192
    British influence on, 26–29
    Fourth and Fifth Amendments of,
        11–12, 105, 132, 150–51, 172, 191,
        202, 216n57
    free speech and, 32, 39, 40
    habeas corpus rights under, 166

military commissions and, 131
  and proposed security court, 174, 175
  Suspension Clause of the, 113
Continental Congress, 26, 27
Court of Appeals of the Armed Forces
  (CAAF), 19, 191–92, 226n 87
Court of Military Commission
  Review, 115
Courts, civilian
  and the "Brady Rule," 152–53
  evidence rules of, 149–51, 190
  ideological inconsistencies in, 153
  and international terrorism, 163
  and the proposed security court, 175
  protective details provided in, 154
  tainted by terrorist cases, 155–56
Courts, terrorism, 158–60. *See also*
  National security court system
Court(s)-martial, 15, 16, 80, 183, 190
  George Washington's uses of, 25–26
  in *Hamdan v. Rumsfeld*, 98–100
  jury trials in, 160
  military commissions and, 98–100,
    102, 103, 104–7, 109
  and the proposed security courts,
    175, 190
  rules for, 20–21, 73
  types of, 20–21
  and unlawful command influence,
    177–78
Craddock, General, 25
Cramer, Major General Myron C., 52,
  53, 70
Crowder, General Enoch, 16, 23
Cullen, Coast Guardsman John C., 48,
  49–50

Dakota Indians, 44–45
Dames & Moore v. Regan, 102
Dasch, George John, 49–50
Davis, Colonel Morris, 179
D.C. Circuit Court of Appeals, 95, 115,
  153, 190
  Hamdan in, 95
  security court appeals to be heard by,
    113, 191–92
Death penalty, 51, 60, 117, 192–93,
  226n 88
Defense, U.S. Department of, 63, 153, 184
  modifications to military commissions
    made by, 81–83, 92, 165
  Office of Military Commissions, 166

and proposed security court, 176, 201
Defense counsel, clearances of, 151–52
Delahunt, Congressman Bill, 197
Denbeaux, Mark, 143, 146
Detainees, 6–7, 107, 174, 176. *See also*
  Enemy combatants; Unlawful
  belligerents
  allies' citizens among the, 203
  and civilian courts, 129–30, 139–40,
    146–56
  Constitution and, 11–12, 129, 130,
    131
  detention on military bases in the
    U.S., 174, 187–89
  and the Geneva Conventions, 10, 11,
    86–88, 100–101, 102, 121, 195–96,
    214n 6
  habeas corpus and, 60–61, 129–30,
    132, 142, 150
  and *Hamdan*, 104–5
  and the laws of war, 106, 107
  long-term, uncharged imprisonment
    of, 82, 86, 88, 91, 93, 110, 118, 190,
    196
  of many nations, 73, 82, 86, 88,
    192, 203
  Obama administration review of
    facilities of, 166
  prisoner of war status and, 87, 116,
    120–21, 128, 195–96, 198
  returned to the battlefield, 153–54
  rights of, 11–12, 107–9, 113, 114–15,
    119, 131–32, 142, 150, 166, 189–91
Detainee Treatment Act (DTA), 96,
  113–14, 115–16, 118, 129
  Boumediene decision and, 166
  and civilian oversight, 142–43
  habeas corpus review in, 190
Detention, preventative. *See* Preventive
  detention
Diplock, Lord Kenneth, 160
Diplock court system, 160–61
Director of National Intelligence (DNI),
  198
Discovery, rules of, 185
District Court(s), U.S., 143
  D.C. caseload, 130, 143
  detainees and, 129, 132, 149
  Hamdan in the, 94–95
  military commissions and rules of, 23,
    98–100
  prosecuting al Qaeda in, 149

Dodd, Senator Christopher, 108, 143
Dovall, Colonel Cassius, 55–56, 58
Due process
    courts-martial and, 105
    and the Military Commissions Act,
        107, 111–13, 116, 119
    in military law, 19, 21, 36, 65,
        73, 105
    for prisoners of war, 190
    and the proposed security court, 5, 7,
        171, 175, 180, 189–91
    for unlawful belligerents, 119, 133
Durbin, Senator Dick, 91

Eisentrager case, 87, 189, 195
"Enemy combatant," 82
Enemy combatants, 82, 86–87, 125,
        143. See also Belligerents, unlawful
        or illegal
    defining or identifying, 115, 129,
        212n 21
    Geneva Conventions and, 102
    in Hamdan v. Rumsfeld, 122
    monitoring detention of, 172
    protections for, 144
    status and treatment, 145, 146, 196
Epstein, Richard, 132
European Convention for the Protection
        of Human Rights … (ECHR)
    fair trial principles of, 162
European Union (EU), 192, 226n 88
Evidence
    classified information as, 109, 110–12,
        151, 171
    coerced, 118
    exculpatory, 152–53
    Federal Rules of, 21, 112, 149–50,
        196, 216n 57
    hearsay, 109, 112–13
    Military Rules of, 21, 73, 105, 112,
        196, 216m 57
    in proposed security courts, 171–72
Exclusionary rule, 105, 150–51, 191
Executive power, Founders' intentions
        regarding, 26–29
Ex post facto clause, 60

Fair trial principles (ECHR), 162
Federal Bureau of Investigation, 8, 50,
        134, 138, 185, 198
Federalist Papers, 6, 102
    Federalist # 74, 28

Federal Rules of Evidence (FRE), 21, 73,
        105, 149–50, 196, 216n 57
Federative power, 27–28
Feingold, Senator, 83
Fidell, Gene, 225n 58
First Amendment. See Free speech,
        right of
Fisher, Dr. Louis, 27, 43, 45, 49, 52, 63,
        64, 82
Flaherty, Professor Martin, 84
Flanigan, Timothy, 69, 70
"Fog of war," 34, 80, 149
Foreign Intelligence Surveillance Act
        (FISA), 5, 128, 134
    under the proposed security court,
        182
    updates proposed to, 173–74
Foreign Intelligence Surveillance
        Court, 172
Foreign prosecution, of U.S.
        interrogators, 124–25, 218n 113
Fort Belvoir, 189
Fort Leavenworth, Kansas, 189
Fourth and Fifth Amendments. See under
        Constitution, U.S.
France, terrorism courts, 158, 159–60,
        183
Frankfurter, Justice, 59
Free speech, right of, 32, 39, 40
French and Indian Wars, 25

Gates, Secretary of Defense Robert, 7,
        125–26, 223n 30
General courts-martial (GCM), 21
Geneva Convention(s), 10, 11, 87–88,
        89, 116
    Article 5 Tribunals of the,
        94–95, 113
    CIA interrogation programs and,
        123–25
    Common Article 3 of the, 96,
        100–103, 109, 120–25, 133, 144,
        220n 41
    and international terrorists, 141–42
    POWs denied access to civilian courts
        under, 148, 166, 182, 190
    updating review needed for,
        144–45, 200
Germany, universal jurisdiction
        authority in, 218n 113
Gimpel, Erich, 63
Gingrich, Newt, 213n 47

Ginsberg, Justice, 96
GITMO. *See* Guantanamo Bay, U.S.
Naval Station
Glazier, David, 38, 119
Goldsmith, Jack, 10, 170, 180
Gonzales, White House Counsel
Alberto, 69, 70, 196
Graham, Senator Lindsay, 197
Grant, General Ulysses, 43
Great Britain, terrorist courts in, 158,
160–61
Grotius, 136
Guantanamo Bay, 5, 93, 139–40, 173.
See also Detainees
Abu Ghraib and, 90–92
Bush administration detention
rationale, 87
closing of, 7, 12, 13, 140, 159, 167–68,
187, 196–97
Congressional hearings on, 128
detainee living conditionas at, 119
and the Geneva Conventions, 166
and *Hamdan v. Rumsfeld*, 101
Military Commissions Act and trials
at, 107
perceptions and criticisms of, 1–2,
3–4, 13, 90–92, 166–67, 194, 205
as a political issue, 86–92
treatment reports on, 166–67
U.S. control of, 129–30
Guilty verdicts, unanimous votes
on, 153–54
Guirora, Amos, 10
Gustavus Adolphus (king of Sweden), 24

Habeas corpus rights, 7–8, 31, 43
appeals in the proposed security court,
182, 189–90
in *Boumediene v. Bush*, 129–30, 202
Congress and, 37
under the Constitutions, 166
of detainees, 60–61, 129–30, 132,
142–43, 150
in *Ex Parte Vallandigham*, 40
in *Hamdan v. Rumsfeld*, 94, 168, 175
under the Military Commissions Act,
109, 113, 115, 129, 189–90
Roosevelt's denial to sabateurs of, 55
suspended by Lincoln, 37
in *Yamashita*, 65
Hall, Judge, 31–34
Hamas, 200

Hamdan, Salim Ahmed, 10, 94, 118,
127, 184
Hamdan v. Rumsfeld, 10, 27, 59, 94–103,
125, 168
and *Boumediene v. Bush*, 110, 128, 156
constitutional issues in, 202
legal confusion resulting from,
110, 174
majority opinions in, 96–101,
132–33
military commission declared unlawful
in, 165
minority opinions in, 101–3, 120
Hamdi v. Rumsfeld, 12, 85–86, 93,
125, 142
Hamilton, Alexander, 18
Hartman, General, 179
Haupt, Herbert, 50, 52
Haynes, William "Jim," 70, 83, 179,
212n 21
Hezbollah, 200
Hicks, David, 127
Hirota, Minister, 65
Hitler, Adolph, 48–49
Holt, Judge Advocate General, 43
Homeland Security, Department of,
8, 68, 184, 198
Homma, General, 65
Honor Bound (Rotunda), 119
Horton, Scott, 85
Human Rights First, 85, 186
Human Rights Watch, 72, 74, 85, 91,
186, 219n 33
Hussein, Saddam, 89

Indian tribunals, 44–45
International Convention against
Torture, 117
International Criminal Court (ICC),
189, 203–5
International law. *See also* Geneva
Convention(s); Law of armed
conflict
al Qaeda's status within, 200
Military Commissions Act and,
116–18, 205
proposed security court and, 193, 200
Supreme Court and detainee rights
under, 142
and 21st. century warfare, 145, 182
and U.S. domestic law, 123–25,
218n 113

International tribunals, 203
Interrogation programs. *See under* Central Intelligence Agency
Iraq, war in, 41, 89–90, 92
al Qaeda in, 141, 147, 150, 200
detainees in, 130, 131–32, 188
the "surge" in, 198
Irish Republican Army, 159, 160–61, 200

Jackson, General Andrew, military commissions used by, 6, 30–35, 165, 195
Jackson, Professor John, 161
JAG. *See* Judge Advocate General's (JAG) Corps
John Adams Project, 184, 225n 70
Johnson, President Andrew, 42–43
Johnson v. Eisentrager. See Eisentrager case
Judge Advocate General's (JAG) Corps, 15, 62, 84
capital trial experience in, 183
role in proposed security court from, 172, 183–84
Judges
and command influence, 178
expertise of, 154–55
French counterterrorism, 160
of the proposed security court, 172, 174, 181–82
Juries and jury trials, 21, 105, 120, 149, 216n 54
command influence on, 178
in courts-martial, 160
Diplock courts and, 160–61
in proposed security court, 170, 181–82
unanimous verdicts and, 153–54
voir dire in, 149
Jus ad bellum, 135, 145
Jus in bello, 135–37, 144–45, 208n 16
Justice, military. *See* Military justice system, U.S.
Justice, U.S. Department of, 8, 64
roles in proposed security court of, 168, 172, 176–77, 179–80, 183

Kahn, Irene, 91
Karpinski, Colonel, 89
Katyal, Professor Neal, 10, 76, 82, 169, 202
legal career and experience, 170
security court supported by, 168

Kennedy, Justice Anthony, 96, 114, 150
majority opinion in *Boumediene* by, 129, 130, 131
Kennedy, Senator Ted, 83
Kerling, Edward John, 49, 50, 56
Koh, Harold, 27, 82, 146–47
Korean War, 73

Law and the Long War (Wittes), 171
Law enforcement model, 5, 139, 150, 195, 197
Boumediene decision as return to, 201–2
failure of, 7, 9, 137–38, 148
versus law of war approach, 5, 110, 163–64, 198
Law of armed conflict, 135–37, 144–45, 157, 205
Law of war, 60, 98, 106, 107. *See also* Law of armed conflict
al Qaeda fighters and, 116–17, 136
Law of war model, 5, 7–8, 9, 110, 195, 197
Law to Fight Terrorism (Turkey), 162
Leahy, Senator Patrick, 83
Lederer, Professor Fred, 18
Legislative supremacy, 27
Liability, civil, 115
Lincoln, President Abraham, 6, 30, 37–38, 165, 195
assassination conspiracy, 42–43
and the Indian tribunals, 44–45
Litzau, Colonel Bill, 83
Locke, John, 27–28
Lockerbie, Scotland, 69
Louallier, Louis, 31–34

MacArthur, General, 64
Madison, James, 28
Madsen v. Kinsella, 103, 209n 26
Manual for Courts-Martial (MCM), 19–24, 97, 105
Martial law, military commissions under, 31–34, 36
McCain, Senator John
on Guantanamo closure, 167
McCain Amendment authored by, 117–18
McCarthy, Andy, 10, 148, 151, 168, 169
on judges and individual rights, 181
security court proposal of, 172
Meese, Edwin III, 83–84

Mexican War, 35–36
Military bases, U.S., as detention / trial
    sites, 187–89, 201
Military commissions, 3–4, 13, 69,
    109–10, 171. *See also* Military
    Commissions Act of 2006
  appellate body created for, 115
  Attorney General opinions on, 37,
    43, 44
  and the civilian courts, 98–100,
    113–14
  during the Civil War, 37–46
  courts-martial and, 102, 103, 104–7
  criticism of Bush administration use
    of, 13, 69–70, 93–94
  against the Dakota Indians, 44–45
  and deterrence in WWII, 51, 52,
    61–63
  evolution of, 164–66
  and *Ex Parte Quirin*, 50–63
  Founders' understanding of, 6, 24,
    25–29
  and the Geneva Conventions, 94,
    100–101, 102–3
  against Lincoln's assasination
    conspirators, 42–43
  during the Mexican War, 35–36
  and the Military Commissions Act,
    109–10
  and military necessity, 98
  names for, 208n 25
  1945 Military Commission, 63–64
  preventitive detention and, 195, 196
  and the proposed security court
    system, 134, 175, 189
  rapid adjudication and, 5, 54, 61,
    63, 83–84
  during the Seminole Wars of 1818,
    34–35
  during the Spanish-American
    War, 47
  Supreme Court and, 38–40, 59–62,
    65, 93, 95–103, 114, 139–40, 165
  in the Uniform Code of Military
    Justice, 6–7, 23–24, 97–100,
    119–20
  and unlawful command influence, 58,
    162, 177–80
  and U.S. citizens, 40–42
  uses of, 24, 209n 26
  during the War of 1812, 30–34
  world opinion and, 3–4, 93

Military Commissions Act of 2006, 6,
    107–10, 133, 165–66
  and the "Brady Rule," 152–53
  Congressional debate on, 111–12,
    119–20, 123–24
  and the Geneva Conventions, 122–24
  and habeas corpus, 109, 113, 115,
    129, 189–90
  and *Hamdan v. Rumsfeld*, 174–75
  hearsay evidence under, 112–13
  judicial review under, 113–16
  and proposed security courts, 134, 189
  rights of accused under, 107–9
  Supreme Court and, 145–46
  and the Uniform Code of Military
    Justice, 119–20
"Military deference doctrine," 5–6,
    103, 115
  and the proposed security court, 143
  Supreme Court and, 131, 154–55
Military Justice Act of 1968, 19
Military justice system, 14, 15–20
  British models for, 15, 24–27
  and civilian court mix, 199
  Founders' understanding of, 24–29
  liberalization of, 17–20, 73–74,
    105, 196
  occupation forces use of, 36
  rapid adjudication in, 54, 61, 63,
    81, 83–84
  unlawful command influence in the,
    162, 176–80
Military necessity, 98
Military Order of November 13, 2001,
    70–74, 77–80, 127, 165
  criticism of, 74–77, 80–81
  scope of, 196
Military Rules of Evidence (MRE), 21,
    74, 105, 112, 196, 216n 57
Military tribunals. *See* Military
    commission(s)
Miller, General Geoffrey, 89
Milligan, Ex Parte, 38, 40–46, 114–15
  and *Ex Parte Quirin*, 59, 60–61
Mohammad, Khalid Sheik, 133,
    149, 186
Montesquieu, 6, 28–29
Morgan, Professor Edmund, 18
Morris, Judge, 58
Moussaoui, Zacarias, 152, 186, 222n 89
Mukasey, Attorney General Michael,
    151, 223n 30

Murphy, Justice, 59
Mutiny Acts (1689), 25

National security court system, 4–5, 8,
    9–13, 54, 175–76
  adjudicatory nature of, 10, 172, 201
  appeals of decisions by, 191–92, 201
  civilian oversight, 182
  commission to study a, 205–6
  constitutional protections under, 174
  criticisms of Guantanamo and, 201
  death penalty and the, 192–93
  defense team of, 184
  due process under, 5, 7, 171, 180,
    189–91
  evidentiary standards of, 190
  and foreign models, 158–60, 191
  versus French model, 183
  habeas corpus under, 182,
    189–90, 201
  as a hybrid court, 4–5, 8, 134, 143,
    167, 175
  judges of the, 172, 174, 181–82,
    190, 201
  juries under the, 170, 172, 181–82
  jurisdiction of, 180–81
  Military Commissions Act procedures
    in, 189
  other proposals for, 169–73
  outside observers to monitor, 186–87
  preventive detention in, 168–69, 170
  proposals for, 10, 169–73
  prosecution team of, 183–84
  and surveillance activities, 173–74
  trial procedures under, 184–87, 201
  U.S. military bases as detention/ trial
    sites, 187–89, 201
National Security Strategy, 142
Nature and Purpose of Military Law, 20
Nazi attrocities, 91, 203
Nazi saboteur case. *See Quirin, Ex Parte*
Neutral nations, 144
New Orleans, martial law in, 31–32
9/11 attacks, 3, 137
  Commission report on, 9, 80, 148,
    156, 197
  subsequent attacks anticipated, 67–69,
    72, 77, 139, 140
  United Nations on, 139
  "wait and see" attitude and, 141
1945 Military Commission, 63–64
Nonjudicial Punishment (NJP), 22–24

Northern Ireland, 160–61
Northern Ireland(Emergency
    Provisions)Acts, 161
Not-in-my-backyard (NIMBY)
    syndrome, 187
Nuremburg Trials, 203

Obama, President Barack,
    administration of, 7, 126, 137, 202
  commission to study security court,
    205–6
  detention facilities reviewed by, 166
  Guantanamo closure plans of, 158–59,
    167, 197
  Newt Gingrich open letter to, 213n 47
  on terrorism, 221n 61
  and the War on al Qaeda, 140–41
Operation Iraqi Freedom (OIF), 89, 141
Order of American Knights, 41
Outsourcing American Law, 172

Pan Am Flight 103, bombing of, 69
Patriot Act, 39, 75, 221n 72
Pearlstein, Deb, 85
Platt Amendment of 1903, 1, 207n 1
Posner, Judge, 185
POWs. *See* Prisoner(s) of war
Pretrial agreement (PTA), 127
Preventive detention, 10, 118–19, 128.
    See Detention, Preventive
  versus adjudication, 168–69, 195
  and military commissions, 195, 196
  in proposed security court, 168–69,
    171, 172–73, 201
Prisoner(s) of war, 116–17, 120–21,
    128, 198
  access to civilian courts, 148, 166
  detainees and, 70, 87, 116, 133,
    195–96
  due process rights, 190
Pro Se Counsel, 152
Protect America Act (PAA), 221n 72
"Protected places," exempt from
    attack, 144
Punitive Articles. *See under* Uniform
    Code of Military Justice (UCMJ)

Quirin, Ex Parte, 6, 47–50, 54
  Bush administration reliance on, 63,
    64, 65–66, 81–82, 165, 195, 196
  charges in, 56–58
  and *Ex Parte Milligan,* 53, 56

lessons learned from, 64
and the Military Order of November
    13, 2001, 71–74
use of military commissions and,
    50–63, 114, 115, 165

Racketeer Influenced and Corrupt
    Organizations Act (RICO), 155
Rahman, Omar Abdel, 185
Rakove, Jack, 27
Rasul v. Bush, 12, 85, 93, 142
    Eisentrager case and, 87
Red Brigades, 200
Red Cross, International Committee of
    the, 84
Rice, Secretary Condoleeza, 7, 80, 126,
    223n 30
Ridge, Governor Tom, 68
Rishikof, Professor Harvey, 10,
    160, 168
    security court proposed by, 169–70,
    205
Rivkin, David, 38
Roberts, Chief Justice, 59, 95, 129
Robertson, Judge, 94–95
Rome Statute, 189, 203, 204
Roosevelt, President Franklin,
    administration of, 6, 179, 195
    and Bush's use of military commisions,
    47, 48, 63, 64, 69–70, 71–74,
    77–79, 81
    U.S. courts denied to enemy by,
    54–55, 58, 60, 62
    use of military commissions by, 50–51,
    52, 53–55, 62–64, 165, 196
Roth, Kenneth, 72, 85
Rotunda, Kyndra, 119, 166
Royall, Colonel Kenneth, 55–56, 58
Rules for Courts-Martial, 20–21, 105
Rumsfeld, Secretary of Defense Donald,
    89, 179, 218n 113

Scalia, Justice Antonin, 101–2, 129, 153
Scott, General Winfield, 30, 35–36
Seminole Wars of 1818, 34–35
Seton Hall Law school study, 142
Seward, Secretary of State, 43
Shining Path, 200
Sibley, Colonel H., 44, 45
Sioux tribe. *See* Dakota Indians
Stirz, Captain Harry, 43–44
Souter, Justice, 96, 190

Soviet Union, collapse of, 203
Special courts-martial (SPCM), 21
Speed, Attorney General James, 43
"Speedy trial" rule, 191
State Secrets Doctrine, 185
State Security Courts, in Turkey,
    161–63
Stevens, Justice, 88, 96–101, 132–33
Stimson, Cully, 187
Stimson, Secretary of War Henry L.,
    52–53, 59
Stone, Chief Justice, 58–59, 65
Summary courts-martial (SCM), 21
Sundell, Lieutenant Commander
    Phil, 84
Sunstein, Cass, 82
Supreme Court, U.S., 11–12, 37–38,
    133, 146
    appeals from proposed security court
    heard by, 191–92
    and the Bush detention policies, 85
    on declarations of war, 76
    on detainees' habeas corpus rights,
    129–30, 190
    judicial conflicts of interest and,
    59, 95
    and the law of war, 58–59
    and military commissions, 38–40,
    59–60, 61–62, 65, 93, 95–103, 114,
    139–40, 165
    military deference doctrine and,
    154–55
    procedures in *Ex Parte Quirin*, 58–62
Swift, Lieutenant Commander Charlie,
    84, 94

Taliban regime, 3, 86
Taylor, Stuart, 10, 168
Tenet, George, 218n 113
Terrorism, international, 202
    experience abroad, 158–63
    and the International Criminal
    Court, 204
    as jurisdiction of the proposed security
    court, 180
    and review of the Geneva
    Conventions, 144–45, 200
    and war in Iraq, 141
Terrorist Surveillance Program (TSP),
    39, 128, 173
Terror Presidency, The (Goldsmith), 170
Thirty Years War, 24

Thomas, Justice Clarence, 102–3, 120, 129
Thompson, Deputy Attorney General Larry, 70
Timmerman, Ken, 159
Torture, 4, 88–89, 109
    and Abu Ghraib, 88–92, 123–25, 167, 187, 189
    and the proposed security court, 189, 201
    Torture Conventions and, 117–19, 144, 189
Tribe, Laurence, 76
Tribunals. See International tribunals; Military commission(s)
Truman, President, 63
Turkey, national security courts in, 158, 161–63

Uniform Code of Military Justice (UCMJ), 15, 19, 73
    Article 36 of, 23–24, 98–100
    Hamdan v. Rumsfeld majority's reliance on, 94, 96–100
    and military commissions, 23–24, 83, 94, 95, 120, 165
    the Punitive Articles in, 22
    unlawful command influence in, 178
United Nations, 137, 139, 186–87
United States
    Al Qaeda's declaration of war on, 137–38, 147
    civil liability immunity of, 115
    detention and trial sites within the, 174, 187–89
    International Criminal Court and, 203–5
    moral authority of, 4, 145, 158
    and the rule of law, 145, 147, 169, 201
    terrorist attacks since 1993 against, 137–38
    trials and countereterrorism operations of, 185
Universal jurisdiction authority, in Germany, 218n 113
Unlawful belligerents, 14, 15, 23, 27, 52. See also Enemy combatants
    al Qaeda as, 136, 198
    due process rights of, 119, 133
    held in Afghanistan, 188
    and the laws of war, 136

military commissions and, 6, 14, 27, 34, 45, 65, 106
    Nazi saboteurs as, 49, 52
    prisoner of war status and, 70, 133, 195–96, 198
Unlawful command influence (UCI), 58, 162, 176–80, 225n 57
USA Patriot Act. See Patriot Act
U.S. Circuit Court of Appeals. See Circuit Court(s) of Appeals, U.S.
U.S. District Courts. See District Court(s), U.S.

Vallandigham, Ex Parte, 38–40
Velshi, Alykhan, 172
Verdicts, unanimous, 153–54
Vietnam War, 73
Voir dire, 149

Waldron, Jeremy, 118
War and warfare
    Asymmetric, 3, 11, 128, 137, 138, 173–74
    evolution of, 61
    and international law, 137–39, 145
    and law enforcement, 5, 137, 138, 198, 201
War Crimes Act, 115, 124
War of 1812, 30–35
"War on al Qaeda," 10–11, 71, 74, 95, 127–28. See also "War on Terror, Global"
    versus "Global War on Terror," 99–200, 140
    lawful conduct of, 136–37
    National Security Strategy and, 142
    new strategy required for, 139
    as three front war, 138
    warfare versus law enforcement responses to, 157, 163–64
"War on Terror, Global." See also "War on al Qaeda"
    law enforcement vs. law of war approach in, 5, 7–8, 9–10, 74–75
    as unique hybrid war, 4
    versus "War on al Qaeda," 10–11, 140, 199–200
    war status of, 137
Washington, General George, 6, 164, 165, 195
    military commissions used by, 14–15, 24, 25–26, 27

Wedgewood, Ruth, 72
"Why We Need a National Security
    Court System"(McCarthy &
    Velshi), 172
Willful Blindness (McCarthy), 148
Winthrop, Colonel William, 15–16,
    105, 106
Wiretapping, domestic, 39. *See also*
    Terrorist Surveillance Program
    (TSP)

Wittes, Benjamin, 10, 148, 168
    security court proposals of, 170–72,
        172–73
World Trade Center Bombing (1993),
    185–86
World War II, military law after, 18–19

Yamashita, General, 65
Yamashita, In re, 47, 115
Yoo, Professor John, 70, 71